1989

· *Women on the Color Line* ·

· *Women on the Color Line* ·

EVOLVING STEREOTYPES AND THE

WRITINGS OF GEORGE WASHINGTON CABLE,

GRACE KING, KATE CHOPIN

ANNA SHANNON ELFENBEIN

UNIVERSITY PRESS OF VIRGINIA

CHARLOTTESVILLE

THE UNIVERSITY PRESS OF VIRGINIA

Copyright © 1989 by the Rector and Visitors

of the University of Virginia

First published 1989

Printed in the United States of America

LIBRARY OF CONGRESS

Library of Congress Cataloging-in-Publication Data

Elfenbein, Anna Shannon, 1946–

  Women on the color line : evolving stereotypes and the writings of

George Washington Cable, Grace King, Kate Chopin / Anna Shannon Elfenbein.

  p. cm.

  Bibliography: p.

  Includes index.

  ISBN 0-8139-1169-9

  1. American fiction—Louisiana—History and criticism. 2. American fiction—White

authors—History and criticism. 3. Afro-American women in literature. 4. Cable, George

Washington, 1844–1925—Characters—Women. 5. King, Grace Elizabeth, 1852–1932—

Characters—Women. 6. Chopin, Kate, 1851–1904—Characters—Women. 7. Women in

literature. 8. Stereotype (Psychology) in literature. 9. Mulattoes in literature. 10. Local color

in literature. 11. Louisiana in literature. 12. Creoles in literature. I. Title.

PS266.L8E44 1988

813'.4'09352042—dc19   87-37192

                                                                                                                          CIP

CONTENTS

PREFACE

It is now more than a decade since Elaine Showalter, reviewing contemporary feminist criticism, celebrated its discovery of "another plot, hitherto submerged in the anonymity of the background," in literary works we revered and thought we knew.[1] Showalter's voice joined other voices, which were urging us to read these works "first of all as a clue to how we live, how we have been living, how we have been led to imagine ourselves, how our language has trapped as well as liberated us; and how we can begin to see—and therefore live—afresh."[2] The scholarly revision of the American literary canon, already under way at the time of Showalter's review essay, continues to enhance our understanding of the complicated relationship between life and art. Today, because of the resisting readings of Judith Fetterley and other feminist critics, what had been perceived as dead spaces in traditional works begin to yield meaning, allowing us to see and to appreciate these works afresh.[3] As a result of revisionary scholarship, we are able to identify, in literature long ignored, suppressed, misinterpreted, or vilified, an unresolved dialectic concerning gender, race, and class. In works such as Rebecca Harding Davis's *Life in the Iron Mills*, Charlotte Perkins Gilman's *The Yellow Wall Paper*, Kate Chopin's *The Awakening*, Jean Toomer's *Cane*, Zora Neale Hurston's *Their Eyes Were Watching God*, Olive Tilford Dargan's *Call Home the Heart*, and Agnes Smedley's *Daughter of Earth*, to name but a few, this dialectic intensifies our awareness of the dynamics of social change and of the ways in which literary works mirror the largely unconscious forces contending for expression in the culture and the artists that produce such works.[4]

The revisionary project now under way has itself mirrored social change. Product of the civil rights movement and consciousness-raising groups of the 1960s, its initial impulse originated in the recognition of common oppression; but initially, awareness of common grievance focused discussion primarily on the analogy between sexual and racial discrimination. The history of the last twenty years, however, has taught us the intractability of the ideology served by sexism, racism, and classism, forcing us to recognize the many guises of oppression that perpetuate our social order. As a result, we are beginning to reexamine literary works rediscovered in the 1960s and 1970s, in order to reevaluate the achievement of authors who struggled as we are struggling to comprehend the patriarchal world we inherit.

The three authors treated in the pages that follow—George Washington Cable, Grace Elizabeth King, and Kate O'Flaherty Chopin—have benefited from the recuperative work of feminist critics. But their fiction requires new readings in the light of our present concern with the many guises of oppression, for all three were acutely aware of the plight of those barred by gender, race, or class from determining their own destinies. And all three conflated sexism, racism, and classism, locating multiple meanings in racial marginality and subverting the traditional literary categories that have segregated "dark" women and "white" women. Writing their stories of the color line after the Civil War, at a time when Southern patriarchy was shaken and social distinctions based on gender, race, and class were at issue, they attempted to comprehend the dissolution of their world through fiction that returns repeatedly, almost compulsively, to the antebellum stereotype of the "tragic octoroon."

The stereotype inherited by Cable, King, and Chopin has had a long history; as a "sunkissed embodiment of ardency" in American white male fantasy, it antedates American literature and lives on in sexual myths about black people.[5] Today, the beautiful enchantress trapped on the color line between antagonistic races must be familiar to anyone who has escaped for an evening into any turgid plantation "bodice-ripper" such as Kyle Onstott's *Mandingo, Drum, Master of Falconhurst;* Lance Horner's *Mustee, Mistress of Falconhurst, Heir to Falconhurst;* Pete Gentry's *Rafe;* Raymond Giles's *Rebels of Sabrehill, Slaves of Sabrehill;* Richard Tresillian's *The Bondmaster;* Parley J. Cooper's *Dark Desires;* or Frank Yerby's *The Girl from Storyville.* In the portraits of seductive or ravished dark women in these novels and others of their ilk, sexism has replaced racism as the primary determinant of the character of the female commodity. It is, therefore, perhaps as easy as it is expedient for a black writer like Frank Yerby to join his white confreres in pandering to popular taste. It is not so easy to explain the predominantly female readership of these soft-core versions of the sado-masochistic bondage pornography purchased by males.[6]

Although black authors have tended to offer perspectives on interracial sex different from the perspectives of white authors, a fact James Kinney underlines in *Amalgamation! Race, Sex, and Rhetoric in the Nineteenth-Century American Novel* (Westport, Conn.: Greenwood Press, 1985), the pornographic image of the black woman in manacles continues to seduce black men as well as white men, displaying in its most extreme version the sexualization of powerlessness latent in the stereotype of the "tragic octoroon" and in many stories of miscegenation. In "Coming Apart" (1980), Alice Walker condemns the enslavement of men and the debasement of women by pornographic images of this kind, portraying the conflict between a black husband and wife who must deal with his addiction to "girly" magazines and her discovery that she cannot live with the image of black women chained, bruised, and cringing that he finds arousing.[7]

Such hard-core images directed at males also testify to the tenacity of this transhistorical stereotype of liminal femininity, a stereotype that cries out for psychoanalytic, archetypal, or Marxian analysis. For such stereotypes—whether they are realized in literature, art, cinema, or pornography—map social ideology into individual and group subjectivity by binding the reader or the viewer to an image that "inscribes and orients desire."[8] This is also clearly true for other arts that embody ideology. However, those analytical strategies deployed to study such mapping and to illuminate the recesses of the individual, collective, or political unconscious must inevitably slight analysis of the transformations the stereotype has undergone in the works of authors who challenged the prevailing ideology. George Washington Cable, Grace Elizabeth King, and Kate O'Flaherty Chopin, white Southerners who had supported the Confederacy, were three such authors.

Their fiction, licensed by the national demand for "local color," spoke to issues of increasing concern to all Americans by joining the issues of gender, race, and class during a period of intense racial paranoia, 1870–1900, a time of "latent and massive social antagonism against miscegenation . . . among both blacks and whites."[9] In *The Crucible of Race: Black-White Relations in the American South since Emancipation,* Joel Williamson notes that the 1850 census was the first to have a designation of "mulatto" for those whose mixed ancestry was visible and that "by the end of the Civil War whites had invented the term 'miscegenation' to cover the whole phenomenon of mixing black and white, and it was a term that carried dire implications."[10]

By employing fictions of the color line as vehicles for their realism, Cable, King, and Chopin transgressed literary taboo within a culture that demanded genteel hypocrisy to mask the "dire implications" of miscegenation. Their fiction, which catalyzed what Warner Berthoff calls "a New

Orleans renaissance in the '70s, '80s, and '90s,"[11] made important contributions to American realism during this period. Their best works, *The Grandissimes* (Cable, 1880), *Monsieur Motte* (King, 1888), and *The Awakening*
(Chopin, 1899), disclose a complex social reality admitting no easy answers
to sexual, racial, or political questions. In many of their other works as well,
the conjunction of gender, race, and class reveals the social processes that
reconstitute our oppressive political order in each new generation.

Through a contextual and intertextual examination of the evolving image of a woman character, banished or stigmatized by other white American authors of the period because of her presumed "ardency," this study
establishes Cable, King, and Chopin's refusal to accede to stereotype. Although they began by replicating this stereotype, sanctioned by cultural
familiarity and use, their realistic portraits of women maligned by the
stereotype justify the claims of their fiction on our hearts and minds. Today,
when women of color observe their almost total erasure from American
history and literature—noting as Adele Logan Alexander does that "white
women are glimpsed in passing, black men are a footnote, but women of
color are practically invisible"[12]—the portraits drawn by Cable, King, and
Chopin must be seen as notable exceptions.

Not surprisingly, considering the apparent need to filter our perceptions
of these women, we have failed to perceive the full significance of these
indelible portraits. We have not recognized fully the violation of literary
expectation these portraits represent. For to raise such violation to consciousness might commit us to social change. This study reexamines these
portraits to establish the basis for a new and more comprehensive appreciation of the attempts of Cable, King, and Chopin to represent accurately the
society they knew and to show, as Cable wrote, that "the whole community
is sinned against in every act or attitude of oppression, however gross or
however refined."[13]

King's and Chopin's variations on Cable's observation deepen its reso-
nance. Their works also allow us to see afresh the human costs of those
inequalities that characterize our world. The pages that follow attempt to
document both the approaches and the achievements of these authors. For
although their artistic choices were limited, they seized a stereotype and
redefined its terms, freeing themselves from many of the constraints imposed by their literary tradition. As a result, women trapped on the color
line in their fiction have greater depth and more dimension than the heroines admired by genteel critics and readers. Although the life stories of
these characters are usually no happier than those of their "tragic" predecessors in abolition fiction, these characters more often than their predecessors are survivors who live and breathe within the fictions that embody them. The vitality of these women characters and of the world they

inhabit compels us to read Cable, King, and Chopin again to learn what they knew about the multiple personal and political guises of sexism, racism, and classism, those symbiotic servants of the oppressive and pervasive ideology that still determines our chances for personal freedom and fulfillment.

ACKNOWLEDGMENTS

My work has been facilitated by institutional support of various kinds: an NEH summer stipend made it possible for me to give fuller consideration to the cultural contexts that gave rise to stories of the color line in American literature; a School of Criticism and Theory fellowship provided me the leisure to think in a concentrated way about the politics inherent in various critical methodologies; and an NEH summer seminar on "Race and Slavery in American Literature" formed a coda to this study of women on the color line. The following libraries have assisted me immeasurably: the University of Nebraska Library; the University of North Carolina Library; the Library of Congress; Northwestern University Library; the University of California-Berkeley Library.

Although I am fortunate to have had institutional support for my research, I was mainly sustained, not by universities, libraries, and grants, but by colleagues and friends who believed in me and my project. Without them this study might have taken a different shape, or I might have given it up altogether. In particular, I wish to thank Linda Ray Pratt, who gave me valuable advice during the early stages of the project and shared with me a passionate ambivalence about the South, and James Roberts, who shared with me his knowledge and his love of Faulkner. To Sandra M. Gilbert and to Eric J. Sundquist, who expressed warm interest in my research and offered splendid examples in their own, I am also grateful.

I am most fortunate to have had friends and family members who have known when to inquire and when not to inquire about the progress of the book. They have encouraged me by being enthusiastic about my work and about their own: Gail Galloway Adams, Timothy Adams, Dennis Allen, Temma Berg, Sandra Gabel, Elaine Ginsberg, Laura Gottlieb, Claire Mattern, Kathleen McNerney, Judith Stitzel, Philip Rees, and Linda Yoder. Rebecca Butler Williams and A. Warren Williams, my parents, and Frank Shannon, my son, inspired and challenged me and showed me in various ways that the personal is political.

Dorothy Sedley made an enormous contribution by generously giving me the benefit of her editorial expertise. Her unstinting efforts improved almost every page of the book. As perceptive readers of the original manuscript and its successors, my secretarial assistants, Peggy Briggs, Jackie Seymour, and Sherry Fox, also deserve thanks. Finally, I wish to acknowledge the invaluable assistance of Donald Elfenbein, my husband, who took time away from his own work to critique my argument and analysis and to check and recheck my syntax and citations. Working with such an able and exacting partner has made me look forward to collaborative projects that lie ahead.

· *Women on the Color Line* ·

CHAPTER ONE

· *Stereotyped Women on the Color Line* ·

TEXTS AND CONTEXTS

The "Tragic Octoroon"

In characterizing the woman on the color line, George Cable, Grace King, and Kate Chopin were guided by the conventional treatment of her as the "tragic octoroon" in antebellum fiction. This stereotyped character, whose trials were to provide the background for Cable, King, and Chopin, had emerged early and evolved over the years in works that reflected the idiomatic prejudices of both Northerners and Southerners against blacks and women and the precarious status of free people of color in the United States. Purveyed by authors whom George M. Fredrickson categorizes as "romantic racialists"[1] in the period 1830 to 1861, the period during which slave breeding became a lucrative home industry in the South and freed slaves were in constant peril of seizure and reenslavement, the stereotype was variously depicted in the works of authors such as Richard Hildreth (*The Slave*, 1836), Joseph Holt Ingraham (*The Quadroone*, 1841), Henry Wadsworth Longfellow ("The Quadroon Girl," 1842), Mrs. E. D. E. N. Southworth (*Retribution*, 1849), Harriet Beecher Stowe (*Uncle Tom's Cabin; or, Life among the Lowly*, 1852), William Wells Brown (*Clotel; or, The President's Daughter*, 1853), W. W. Smith (*The Planter's Victim*, 1855), Sydney A. Story, Jr. [Mary Hayden Green Pike] (*Caste: A Story of Republican Equality*, 1856), Mayne Reid (*The Quadroon*, 1856), J. S. Peacocke (*The Creole Orphans; or, Lights and Shadows of Southern Life*, 1856), Van Buren Denslow (*Owned and Disowned; or, The Chattel Child*, 1857), Paul Creyton [John Townsend Trowbridge] (*Neighbor Jackwood*, 1857), Dion Boucicault (*The Octoroon*, 1859), H. L. Hosmer (*Adela, the Octoroon*, 1860), and Metta Victoria Fuller Victor (*Maum Guinea and Her Plantation "Children,"* 1861).

In these tracts and others, the octoroon or quadroon is portrayed as a dark, sweet flower with traces of poison on her lips. Unaware (in many versions of the formula story) and innocent of the toxin she bears, she is fated to suffer social ostracism or slavery for the sins of her white father or male relatives—sins that often include incestuous miscegenetic affairs or desires. In contrast to the restive and rebellious mulatto males also portrayed in these works, the "octoroon" seems remarkably like the prototypical Miss Lily, the white woman destined to be her foil in literature written after the abolition crisis was over. Although the slave narratives that helped shape the story were the "pious pornography of their day, replete with . . . whippings, sexual assaults, and explicit brutality,"[2] this tragic woman of mixed race usually remained pure. Except for faint traces of her ardent past in the sensuous overtones of her description by the writers who employed the stereotype, she possessed none of the lascivious traits associated in the popular imagination with her race. It would not be until the twentieth century and the works of Thomas Dixon, Jr., that the vampirish mulatto woman would become an absolute contrast to that symbol of Southern purity, the Southern lady.

The gradual transformation of the abolitionist's heroine in the post–Civil War period, in the literature of both North and South, was foreshadowed even before the war by hostility to her appearance from those who resented the use to which she was being put. When Dion Boucicault's *The Octoroon* premiered in New York on the evening of December 6, 1859, four days after the hanging of John Brown in Virginia, public sentiment against the production of a play of such topicality ran high. The actress who played Zoe, the octoroon heroine with "flashing dark eyes," said that she feared for her life: "I confess I did feel rather nervous, for I was clad in a long white gown, and so, of course, [was] a mark for every eye."[3] Thus, the emblematic approximation of the attire of the unspotted white ingenue in nineteenth-century fiction merely made the actress an easy target.

Although Cable, King, and Chopin would alter the antebellum stereotype in their portraits of women trapped in a society that hypocritically fostered interracial sex but treated the black woman and her "adulterated" offspring as pariahs, they, like other American writers of the Gilded Age, were fascinated by women of ambiguous racial status: mulattoes, quadroons, octoroons, white orphans whose antecedents were in doubt, women with a tinge of Indian blood like Helen Hunt Jackson's Ramona in her eponymous novel (1884). Their literary presentations of the woman of ambiguous race extended the fictional life of this character, who had become the rage in abolition fiction.

The abolitionists' heroine Cable, King, and Chopin knew was a dark-skinned Hester Prynne who bore what Francis P. Gaines calls "the racial bar sinister in American Romance."[4] Unlike Hester, however, her fate was often to reproduce her own tragedy, for as Whittier emphasizes in "The Farewell of a Virginia Slave Mother to Her Daughters Sold into Southern Bondage" (c. 1837), she could not prevent her daughter from suffering as she had suffered, from "toiling through the weary day" or from serving at night as "the spoiler's prey."[5]

To the Northern antebellum audience for whom she was created, an audience that had shuddered at the visible testimony given by her real-life sisters at antislavery rallies, this staple character was proof of the cumulative sins of the South. She was proof of the North's moral superiority, which needed only to be tapped to put an end to slavery. The product of three successive generations of illicit but enforced miscegenation, the fictional octoroon was the North's favorite emblem of slavery, since her "whiteness" made her "a perfect object for tearful sympathy combined with moral indignation."[6]

In story after story, this near-white ingenue reappears. She is young. She is beautiful. She speaks impeccably and dresses in enviable style. She is raised as a lady in the household of her father, who is, notwithstanding his sexual vagaries, descended from the best blood in the Old South. Her fortune is often irremediably reversed upon her father's death. Her father, like the stereotypical Southern gentleman in the antebellum fiction examined by William R. Taylor's *Cavalier and Yankee: The Old South and American National Character* (New York: George Braziller, 1961), has not seen to things. His concern with attending to pleasure rather than to duties and profit (the obsessions of his Yankee counterpart in fiction of the same period) betrays his daughter, who possesses only the slightest evidence of Negro blood, to the auction block.[7]

In almost all of these stories, the ingenue, upon discovering her "taint," collapses—never to move under her own volition again. In one of the most melodramatic scenes in Boucicault's *The Octoroon,* for example, Zoe, the heroine, gestures toward the bluish tinge in her nails and the faint blue mark in the white of her eyes and exclaims: "That is the ineffaceable curse of Cain. Of the blood that feeds my heart, one drop in eight is black—bright red as the rest may be, that one drop poisons all the flood; those seven bright drops give me love like yours—hope like yours—ambition like yours—life hung with passions like dew-drops on the morning flowers; but the one black drop gives me despair, for I'm an unclean thing—forbidden by the laws—I'm an Octoroon!"[8]

It is difficult, however, to determine whether the ingenue's wilting passivity in the other stories is the result of the spot of black blood or a reaction to the yielding femininity demanded of women in the period. Here, the similarities between some of the features of the stereotype of proper female behavior and the stereotype of black behavior make a distinction difficult. It is not the burden of this chapter to relate the antebellum stereotype of the "nature" of white women to the stereotype of the "nature" of blacks or to attempt to answer the question concerning the priority of sexism or racism that has recently generated so much discussion among black and white feminists. However, it is worth noting that these issues both have long histories. Margaret Fuller, for example, in her plea for legal equity for the married woman—in the nineteenth century still a ward of her husband— saw that women were very commonly depreciated as the enslaved blacks were. She wrote: "[It is well known] that there exists in the minds of men a tone of feeling toward women as toward slaves, such as is expressed in the common phrase, 'Tell that to women and children;' that the infinite soul can only work through them in already ascertained limits; that the gift of reason, Man's highest prerogative, is allotted to them in much lower degree; that they must be kept from mischief and melancholy by being constantly engaged in active labor, which is to be furnished and directed by those better able to think, &c., &c."[9]

If blacks were viewed as feeble mentally, they were viewed as strong physically; white women, on the other hand, were merely feeble, or fragile. Both blacks and white women required looking after. The diaries of Southern women of this period attest to women's perceptions of the parallels between their own situation and that of the slave. "There is no slave after all like a wife," Mary Chesnut wrote in her famous diary. "You know how women sell themselves and are sold in marriage, from queens downward."[10]

Like Mary Chesnut, Sojourner Truth recognized the hypocrisy at the heart of the chivalrous pose of white male supremacists. A woman and a slave, she had never enjoyed the protection that such men conferred on their own women as reparation for their liberty. As she noted eloquently in her famous "Ain't I a Woman?" speech, the fact that she was a woman had never been considered. Since she and other black women had been denied the protections afforded white women, Truth insisted black women should enjoy the right to vote.

Even if they were more nearly white than black, female slaves had no protectors. However, if such women were beautiful according to sexist and racist standards of female beauty, they might enjoy the favor of powerful white males until age made them less attractive and less desirable. The literary appeal of such women also depended on their youth and white beauty. Thus, the octoroon was considered to be more beautiful and more pathetic by virtue of the undetectability of her racial "blemish." She was no doubt also considered to be more feminine and appealing because of her total vulnerability. To white middle-class women, who made up the bulk of the reading audience, the octoroon's story offered little in the way of escape. Forced to rely on male protection and providence and always facing the possibility that their trust would be repaid with disillusionment or destitution, white women perceived the emotional validity of the octoroon's story.

Recognizing that the octoroon was often merely a white woman in blackface, however, black critics have asserted that her story reveals the unwitting racial snobbery of the abolitionists. Sterling Brown, for example, was among the first to notice the disparity between the humanitarian protestations of the abolitionists and their unexamined but deep-seated racial prejudice. Brown notes their assumption that the whiter the Negro the greater the tragedy, quoting John Herbert Nelson's indictment of their "indirect admission that a white man in chains was more pitiful to behold than the African similarly placed. Their most impassioned plea was in behalf of a person little resembling their swarthy protegés."[11]

The equally deep-seated sexism of these tracts, however, has gone unremarked. After all, the tragic heroines are merely white ingenues in blackface. Sexually provocative and paradoxically ladylike, the tragic octoroon gains sympathy not only because of the undetectability of her racial "blemish" but also because of her youth and beauty. To be old or ugly for a woman in a sexist society was a tragedy in its own right, but a tragedy that compelled little sympathy. To be black in a racist society likewise compelled little sympathy, but to be young, beautiful, ladylike, and only technically black was truly pathetic. Qualified on the one hand as lovely objects of sexual desire, the women were disqualified on the other by race from assuming the privileged traditional roles of such attractive women.

Like her lily-white counterparts in eighteenth- and nineteenth-century literature—women who, like Pamela, attain the highest possible goal for a woman, an advantageous marriage—the octoroon, and her story, seldom challenge white male notions of desirable feminine behavior or the literary myth that interracial sex only occurred between white *men* and "black" women. Furthermore, the octoroon's passivity, like Pamela's or Clarissa's, promotes a male supremacist concept of acceptable, docile, virtuous behavior. Her failure to come to grips with herself or her situation after discovering her true identity allows the patriarchal order to prevail, since her salvation rests with the white males in the author's audience rather than with the abolition of white male supremacy.

Describing his mother in words that he confesses might seem more appropriate from her lover, Archy Moore, the light-skinned slave protagonist of Richard Hildreth's *The Slave* (1836), reveals the racism and latent prurience of the typical treatment of the exotic beauty of mixed race. Because Hildreth's novel precedes the abolitionist tract novels that Cable,

King, and Chopin would have known, if only by reputation, and because his description of the tragic octoroon is also representative of the type in many ways, Archy's evocative recollection of his mother deserves notice:

> Yet those who beheld her for the first time, would hardly have imagined, or would willingly have forgotten, that she was connected with an ignoble and degraded race. Humble as her origin might be, she could at least boast the possession of the most brilliant beauty. The trace of African blood, by which her veins were contaminated, was distinctly visible;—but the tint which it imparted to her complexion only served to give a peculiar richness to the blush that mantled over her cheek. Her long black hair, which she understood how to arrange with an artful simplicity, and the flashing of her dark eyes, which changed their expression with every change of feeling, corresponded exactly to her complexion, and completed a picture which might perhaps be matched in Spain or Italy, but for which, it would be in vain to seek a rival among the pale-faced, languid beauties of eastern Virginia.[12]

The racism lurking beneath Hildreth's apparent belief in the passionate nature of the dark woman is no less virulent than the obvious racism in such diction as "degraded" and "the trace of African blood, by which her veins were contaminated." As Jules Zanger notes en passant, the "melodramatic and titillating aspects"[13] of the tragic octoroon's plight were typically emphasized by other writers as they are here by Hildreth with his implied contrast of the dark woman's passionate personality with the languor (frigidity?) of the white woman. Here and elsewhere in literature of the period, the rule is that the tragic octoroon is memorable only as a titillating type in a typical, though moving, situation.

Two novels in the same genre as Hildreth's *The Slave* prove the rule. In William Wells Brown's *Clotel; or, The President's Daughter* (1853) and in Harriet Beecher Stowe's *Uncle Tom's Cabin; or, Life among the Lowly* (1852), neither written by a white male author, tragic octoroons rise above their stereotypical circumstances, above the "melodramatic and titillating aspects" of the narrative, to foreshadow the more realistic heroines of Cable, King, and Chopin.

Brown's *Clotel* provides an interesting commentary on Hildreth's novel, since Brown, a black man, really does what Hildreth in blackface only pretends to do in his tract. Brown, an escaped slave, son of a white father and a mulatto mother, whom he had seen sold into slavery as punishment for an escape attempt he had engineered, describes Clotel as a son might and not with the salacious interest of a lover. Although Brown's filial fervor often exceeds his gifts as a writer, and although, clearly, he too feels that his heroine is more pathetic by virtue of her light skin, Brown, himself a light-skinned black and the first American black novelist, creates a proud, self-contained heroine in stark contrast to the heroines of writers like Hildreth.

The flavor of Brown's prose appears in his presentation of the auction where Clotel is part of a consignment. Quoting the auctioneer but adding his own summary of the proceedings, Brown enumerates Clotel's selling points. Brown's portrait of Clotel is psychologically convincing, since her obliviousness to this scene of degradation suggests her almost comatose response to absolute despair. Frosty rather than fixated on her sexual charms, as Hildreth had depicted his octoroon heroine, Clotel steels herself against the horror that awaits her. Her appearance testifies to her difference from the seductive heroines of Hildreth and other authors, for she dresses down for the occasion, confining her hair neatly instead of "arrang[ing] [it] with an artful simplicity." Clotel does not seem to invite her defloration with the "flashing dark eyes" the stereotype might have provided. She stands frozen on the auction block "with a complexion as white as most of those who were waiting with a wish to become her purchasers; her features as finely defined as any of her sex of pure Anglo-Saxon; her long black wavy hair done up in the neatest manner; her form tall and graceful, and her whole appearance indicating one superior to her position."[14] In this compassionately restrained but subtly sexist portrait, Clotel is not besmirched by the lust her appearance generates. She is, if anything, purer than the tragic octoroons of other abolitionist writers. Gulled by love and by hope, Clotel takes no part in her fall. Unlike the countless unhappy exotic women of mixed blood in other novels of this genre, she does not snivel. Because she is powerless to demand the marriage to which Brown believes her piety and virginity entitle her—powerless to force her lover to fulfill his promise to buy back her mother and sister—Clotel must be satisfied to think of herself as the wife of her caddish master.

Her lofty character, however, initially makes even this submission seem a victory, for to her betrayer's suggestion that he may tire of her, she retorts, "If the mutual love we have for each other, and the dictates of your own conscience do not cause you to remain my husband, and your affections fall from me, I would not, if I could, hold you by a single fetter" (p. 58). This haughty superiority to her circumstances makes Clotel seem more ladylike than her peers trapped in similar situations in other novels. At the same time, however, Clotel's high-mindedness is undercut by the obvious irony inherent in the word *fetter,* for although Clotel is almost woodenly superior to her plight, and therefore undominated by it emotionally, *she* is fettered, and when her lover loses interest, *she* will be auctioned off again.

Although Clotel offers a contrast to the stylized octoroons of other abolitionist writers, her virtues are mostly negative. In order to show that her morals have not been contaminated by her speck of black blood, Brown has substituted an inflexibly sexist view of her nature for the blatantly racist and sexist views of writers like Hildreth. But Clotel cannot be, considering the polemical aims of the novel, a fully realized character because she is fettered by Brown's opinions about what constitutes ladylike behavior. For this reason, Clotel is beautiful, fetchingly attired, soft-spoken, pious, and self-effacing. Exactly the kind of slave or woman a master would be most pleased to possess.

Published just one year before *Clotel*, Harriet Beecher Stowe's *Uncle Tom's Cabin* awakened the conscience of the nation to the evils of slavery and started an avalanche of antislavery polemics. As Helen Waite Papashvily observes in *All the Happy Endings: A Study of the Domestic Novel in America, the Women Who Wrote It, the Women Who Read It, in the Nineteenth Century,* Stowe's novel exploded with "psychic timeliness."[15] But more significantly for the present discussion, in *Uncle Tom's Cabin* Stowe examined the tragic octoroon from a woman's point of view, discarded the salacious elements of the conventional description of the octoroon, and endowed her octoroon with "virtual life."[16]

Few novels have had such far-reaching or profound effects on generations of readers and writers as *Uncle Tom's Cabin*. In *Crusader in Crinoline: The Life of Harriet Beecher Stowe,* Forrest Wilson appraises Stowe's book as antislavery polemic, judging it to be "worth a hundred seductive slave girls standing emancipated beside Henry [Ward Beecher, Harriet's ministerial brother] on the Plymouth stage."[17] Abraham Lincoln's quip that Harriet Beecher Stowe was "the little lady who wrote the book that made this great war" is familiar to every schoolchild. The sentimental death scene of Little Eva has wrung tears from millions, including our contemporary, Ann Douglas, who deplored the effect of the disestablished clergy and the disenfranchised, middle-class woman reader on American literature, but made Harriet Beecher Stowe her muse.[18]

Even after its primary political battle had been won, *Uncle Tom's Cabin* remained a powerful novel. George Washington Cable testified to the effectiveness of Stowe's work and confessed to feeling "widowed by [Little Eva's] death."[19] To the aristocratic Grace King, who observed that Stowe's novel "was not allowed to be even spoken of in [the King] house" but whose presentations of victimized women characters would reveal her in closer agreement with Mrs. Stowe than either woman might have imagined, *Uncle Tom's Cabin* was a "hideous, black, dragon-like book that hovered on the horizon of every Southern child."[20] Its depiction of the realistic details of the tragic octoroon's life and its elevation of the heroine from the stereotype of the abolitionist tracts, however, anticipated Cable, King, and

Chopin's depictions of women caught in the no-man's-land of interracial life.

The character of Uncle Tom, who lingers on as an epithet in the racial controversies of our own period, appropriates many of the "ladylike" virtues usually relegated to the tragic octoroon. Although Tom's character is not distorted to emphasize the salacious, his patience under the lash illustrates the essential feminine virtue of "self-control" urged on every Christian wife and mother of the period by moral pundits like Mrs. Lydia Sigourney, who, in her *Letters to Young Ladies,* a manual of conduct that had gone through sixteen editions by 1849 and was as popular in its way as *Uncle Tom's Cabin,* enjoined her female readers to emulate the martyred Christ. "Self-control," Mrs. Sigourney writes, "is essential to females, because the duties of their peculiar station so often demand its exercise." Mrs. Sigourney would have approved Tom's passivity, resting in the certainty that "even death cannot hurt those who have the passport to a happy immortality." Thus, Tom's willingness to be silent and self-effacing, to be one who "stood aside for all, and came last, and took least, yet was foremost to share his little all with any who needed,"[21] accords with Sigourney's rationalization of woman's unhappy selfless lot as the only path to heavenly bliss.

Through Tom, Stowe addresses the latent martyr in her female audience. Since Tom corners the market on meekness, piety, and endurance—the feminine virtues—Tom's masculinity is more expedient than real, a fact critics have long deplored. The apparent emasculation of Tom, however, is central to the design of Stowe's novel, which pits Tom's redemptive sacrifice against the vengeful maneuvering of Cassy, a quadroon mother whose children have repeatedly been stolen from her. Tom's exalted sentiments, which have frequently been read as a defense of total submission, contrast with Cassy's desire for revenge. Although Tom's overt altruism and disregard for his own welfare make him appear ladylike, Stowe's attitude toward his way of dealing with oppression is more ambivalent than might first appear, and her sympathies are evenly divided between Tom's passive approach and Cassy's active approach to evil.

Stowe's portrait of Cassy as a contrast to Tom reveals Stowe's recognition that intelligence and ingenuity are required to combat the Simon Legrees of the world. Thus, in a world too vile for stainless Little Eva, where "men have learned the art of sinning expertly and genteely [*sic*], so as not to shock the eyes and senses of respectable society"[22] and where woman's only legitimate power depends on her ability to influence such men, Cassy's passion for vengeance and her plot to escape succeed because she is *not* wiltingly feminine.

In naming her defiant octoroon Cassy, Stowe followed convention. Cassy, Kissy, and Crissy were popular names for the fictional octoroon and her darker sisters (perhaps a reflection of the classical erudition of the abolitionists, who by so naming this fictional type were calling to mind *Agamemnon*'s Cassandra).[23] However, Stowe's Cassy possesses more strength than convention would have allowed, though her eventual triumph seems highly unlikely. According to the pattern developed by other writers in this genre, Cassy should share the predictable fate—real or psychological suicide—of her stereotyped sisters.

Cassy's story begins exactly like Clotel's. She, too, has trusted her heart and discovered that white men lie. But Cassy is larger and louder than her chivalrous abolitionist defenders had allowed her to be, and *she* tells her own story with "fierce pride and defiance in every line of her face, in every curve of the flexible lip, in every motion of her body."[24] A tarnished thirty-five rather than a blooming sixteen, Cassy describes being passed from one jaded predator to another. Plotting revenge against her betrayers—the white men who sold her children, the black men who envied and despised her—Cassy manages the big house on Simon Legree's notorious Red River plantation. Stowe's lengthy description of that melancholy place is underscored by Cassy's reply to Tom's suggestion that she pray away her troubles: "The Lord never visits these parts" (p. 362).

When Simon Legree buys a new plaything, sixteen-year-old, high-yellow Emmeline, and, to break Cassy's spirit, sends her down to the cotton fields, she outpicks the most hardened hands. White male writers like Hildreth had warmed to the sedentary concubine and had often portrayed her as recumbent to emphasize her passive availability; Stowe shows Cassy dominating the experienced field hands with her stamina and astonishing them with her compassion when she helps fill the bags of slower pickers.

Demonstrating a toughness never found among other tragic octoroons, Cassy dominates her master just as she dominates her peers. Her power over Legree is strange and singular, for although Legree is Cassy's "owner, her tyrant and tormentor," even "the most brutal man cannot live in constant association with a strong female influence, and not be greatly controlled by it" (p. 410). In addition to making this claim for Cassy's strength, no more at first glance than a reiteration of the nineteenth-century cliché about the intangible but potent spiritual "influence" of woman, Stowe's portrait of Cassy *does* show her controlling her tormentor.

By implication, Stowe juxtaposes Cassy's tempered strength and the pliant fragility of other tragic octoroons. This strength, unlike the pathetic helplessness of the octoroon heroines who preceded Cassy or who were created by the dozens in the wake of the tremendous success of *Uncle Tom's*

Cabin, is, however, the product of Cassy's violated maternity. Cassy's response to this violation made her a compellingly credible character to a society that revered motherhood and believed it to be woman's highest calling.

Rivaling Stowe's depiction of the death of Little Eva for pathos, the depiction of Cassy as a mother helpless to protect her babies still evokes profound sympathy from modern readers. Cassy's degradation is secured through her love for her children, for she must comply with the sexual demands of a series of callous white men in order to protect her young son and daughter. Even after her children are sold at the behest of her lover, Cassy is controlled by his will. "Well, you can do anything with a woman, when you've got her children," Cassy says. "He made me submit; he made me peaceable; he flattered me with hopes that, perhaps, he would buy them back" (p. 374).

Stowe's description of Cassy's loss of her first son justifies but does not prepare the reader for her infanticide upon the birth of another son to another potential betrayer. Cassy says:

> "One day, I was out walking, and passed by the calaboose; I saw a crowd about the gate, and heard a child's voice,—and suddenly my Henry broke away from two or three men who were holding him, and ran, screaming, and caught my dress. They came up to him, swearing dreadfully; and one man, whose face I shall never forget, told him that he wouldn't get away so; that he was going with him into the calaboose, and he'd get a lesson there he'd never forget. I tried to beg and plead,—they only laughed; the poor boy screamed and looked into my face, and held on to me, until, in tearing him off, they tore the skirt of my dress half away; and they carried him in, screaming 'Mother! mother! mother!'" (p. 374)

Torn from her son, Cassy must still play the role of the tragic octoroon, a part assigned her by men. "They made me dress up, every day," Cassy remembers, "and gentlemen used to come in and stand and smoke their cigars, and look at me, and ask questions, and debate my price. . . . They threatened to whip me, if I wasn't gayer, and didn't take some pains to make myself agreeable" (p. 375). In making herself agreeable with that paradoxical combination of ladylike docility and seductiveness, however, Cassy only procures herself another master and more grief.

"Only a woman could forgive Cassie [*sic*]" for killing the baby born to her next white master, asserts Papashvily.[25] Only Harriet Beecher Stowe, who confessed that she composed *Uncle Tom's Cabin* with "no more thought of style or literary excellence than the mother who rushes into the street and cries for help to save her children from a burning house, thinks of

the teachings of the rhetorician or the elocutionist,"[26] could venture beyond the stereotype reproduced in such numbers by other abolitionist
writers to portray sympathetically the octoroon's decision to kill her baby:
"O, that child!—how I loved it! How just like my poor Henry the little
thing looked! But I had made up my mind,—yes, I had. I would never
again let a child live to grow up! I took the little fellow in my arms, when he
was two weeks old, and kissed him, and cried over him; and then I gave
him laudanum, and held him close to my bosom, while he slept to
death. . . . I am not sorry, to this day; he, at least, is out of pain. What
better than death could I give him, poor child!" (p. 375).

Stowe's forgiving female contemporaries had every reason to identify
with Cassy, for the women of Stowe's generation were classed together in
legal documents with Negroes, children, and idiots. Rights for women and
for blacks came to be regarded together as one issue. Wendell Phillips,
spokesman for the abolitionists, for example, promised "first the Negro,
then the woman." Behind the throne or rocking the cradle, the mother in
the nineteenth century was granted merely the illusion that she bestowed
moral "influence" "upon every member of her household, like the dew
upon the tender herb[,] like the sunbeam educating the young flower."[27] In
actuality, Stowe and the mothers in her audience, North and South, had no
more ability to shield their own children than Cassy had to protect hers.
Thus, when Stowe makes Cassy a woman who must obtain freedom for her
child by killing him, she perhaps taps the sympathy and reveals the desperation of her white female audience at the deepest level.[28] A mother herself,
who nursed all seven of her infants at the breast and was nursing one of
them during the frenzied composition of *Uncle Tom's Cabin,* Stowe trans-
forms the tragic sex object, the octoroon, into a pietà. The convincing
depiction of her violated maternity allows Cassy to act authentically as no
tragic octoroon had ever acted.

In a resounding climactic scene at the end of *Uncle Tom's Cabin,* Cassy
recovers her long-lost son and daughter. Motherhood is vindicated, and the
fantasies of the powerless are realized. Simon Legree, who repudiated his
mother's counsel and committed her forgiving last letter and lock of hair to
the flames, is left to madness. When last seen, he is struggling nightly to
escape his "mother's shroud" with Cassy "holding it up, and showing it to
him" (p. 433).

The Louisiana Milieu

It was no accident that Stowe chose Louisiana as the scene of Cassy's
victimization and her victory over Simon Legree, but it is rather amazing
that Louisiana writers like Cable, King, and Chopin would resurrect her

story in the postwar period, for reading or retelling the standard story of the woman of ambiguous race had been considered a betrayal of Southern loyalties before and during the Civil War. In the postwar period, when racial animosities were raging, many Southerners adopted the Northern view that interracial sex in the South had caused God to forsake its cause. William Heyward, a Carolina aristocrat, wrote in 1868, "I believe that God has ordered it all, and I am firmly of opinion . . . that it is the judgement of the Almighty because the human and brute blood have mingled to the degree it has in the slave states. Was it not so in the French and British Islands and see what has become of them."[29]

In *New People: Miscegenation and Mulattoes in the United States,* Joel Williamson describes the hardening of racial attitudes among whites after the war. The mulatto elite that identified in large numbers with the cause of the blacks suddenly lost its status as far as whites were concerned: "[Whites] began to deride mulattoes as 'neither fish nor fowl' and to heap upon them such epithets as 'ring streaked and striped' and 'yellow niggers.' Mulattoes had no race, they taunted, and hence no identity. . . . By the end of Reconstruction, white Southerners were able to condemn the whole of the Negro community as a body, out of hand and without regard to variations in color."[30]

But Louisiana life has always, by its excess of contrasts, encouraged anomalies. In *The Octoroon,* Boucicault, like Stowe, had set the tragic story of his heroine in Louisiana. Against the critics who feared that the play would precipitate war in the streets, *New York Times* critic Henry Raymond asserted Louisiana's atypicality in 1859, urging the public to support the play since it was "not intended to depict the ordinary current of social life [in] the South" but was instead *"a picture of life in Louisiana!"*[31]

In the popular imagination, and to a lesser degree in historical fact, Louisiana was atypical and New Orleans even more so, though Charleston and Mobile competed for honors as sin cities. The immersion of George Cable, Grace King, and Kate Chopin in the ongoing life of New Orleans awakened them to the contradictions of class and caste they saw magnified in day-to-day life in that city, the center of the South's corrupted paradise. The "felt life" of this remarkable city gave license to their artistic imagination and enhanced their grasp of social issues.[32] The contradictory injunctions of the Creole and the American city fathers concerning woman's place may have provoked them to ponder the "woman question" and to think rebellious thoughts about the sexual and racial hypocrisy they witnessed.

White hypocrisy was, of course, an integral feature of American slavery, North and South, from the first. Fanny Kemble's famous *Journal of a Residence on a Georgian Plantation in 1838–1839* (1863) merely confirmed what had been confided to American journals and diaries in secret. Women, especially, revealed to secret day books their irritation with their husbands' and fathers' profligacies. But men, too, were aware of the hypocrisy that shrouded sexual commerce between white men and black women. Josiah Quincy of Massachusetts spoke of his own uneasiness with the common practice in his Journal of 1773:

> The enjoyment of a negro or mulatto woman is spoken of as quite a common thing: no reluctance, delicacy or shame is made about the matter. It is far from being uncommon to see a gentleman at dinner, and his reputed offspring a slave to the master of the table. I myself saw two instances of this, and the company very facetiously would trace the lines, lineaments and features of the father and mother in the child, and very accurately point out the more characteristick resemblance. The fathers neither of them blushed or seem[ed] disconcerted. They were called men of worth, politeness and humanity.[33]

However, institutionalized mulatto concubinage had developed in only one place in the United States, in New Orleans, under the influence of Spanish and French colonists and of Spanish and French refugees from the West Indies. As a result of generations of breeding light-skinned merchandise for a wealthy clientele and of interracial "arrangements" between free women of color and white "benefactors," the word *Negro* was "hardly a fair term, for there were whole rainbow hues of colors" among the prostitutes in New Orleans.[34] The obvious fact of extensive mixing between the white male population and the black female population of New Orleans, however, failed to produce social equality for the near-white offspring of the white dandies, for, as George Washington Cable sympathetically pointed out in *The Grandissimes*, "whatever [was] not pure white [was] to all intents and purposes pure black," even in this environment of toleration for sexual forays across the color line.[35]

As James R. Frisby, Jr., tells the story in "New Orleans Writers and the Negro,"[36] from the time of its settlement in 1699 by the brothers Pierre le Moyne, Sieur d'Iberville, and Jean Baptiste le Moyne, Sieur de Bienville, members of the French Mississippi Company, race relations in Louisiana evolved distinctly, but not distinctly enough to efface racial prejudice, discrimination, or exploitation. Through an oversight, the French company neglected for twenty-two years to import women for the men in Bienville's charge. This oversight ensured miscegenation with the Indian population—which was decimated by the white blight: warfare, disease, and debauchery—and in 1719 with the first African slaves. By 1721, when eighty-eight truant girls were sent from La Salpêtrière, a house of detention in Paris, it was already too late to change what had become accepted practice. The importation of more respectable girls in 1728, the famous "casket-girls" who arrived with their belongings packed in small trunks provided by an alarmed French government, and the introduction of the *Code Noir*,[37] proscribing interracial sexual activity between whites and slaves, could not alter the tacitly condoned facts of life in New Orleans. "Ironically but understandably," Frisby remarks, "there is no record of any of the correction girls ever having borne a child, although the more acceptable casket girls became known as the mothers of now famous Creole families."[38] Similarly, there is no record of the births of half-caste children to the first settlers, although the fact of interracial "mixing" is written on the lineaments of New Orleans natives of the most unimpeachable racial "purity."

Scholars like Herbert Asbury and Stephen Longstreet are amused at Creole genealogical pride and hint that racial purity was, in fact, rare in Creole families. Mere reference to miscegenation would ignite Creoles who maintained their pure white superiority to various admixtures of blacks as well as to crass Yankee intruders into the social life of New Orleans. An interloper himself, Lafcadio Hearn treated the term *Creole* gingerly, giving the etymology of the word, "the diminutive 'criollo,' derived from the Spanish 'criar,' 'to beget,'" and noting the word "primarily signified the colonial-born child of European blood, as distinguished from the offspring of the Conquistadores by slave women, whether Indian or African."[39] Grace King, a defender of Creole honor, acknowledged the ambiguity of the term *Creole*. In *New Orleans: The Place and the People* (1895), she describes the system under which such ambiguities arose and says: "The minute paternalism of the French and Spanish domestic systems was peculiarly favourable to such development; the harmonious results from it can still be traced in the families of Spanish and French coloured Creoles; they themselves base aristocratic pretensions upon their French and Spanish antecedents, and at the time were the first to despise and contemn the laxer regime of the American domestic service."[40] Cable's description of a masked ball in the first chapter of *The Grandissimes* suggests that Creole purity, both racial and ethical, was more myth than reality, since some of the ballgoers, disguised as their own illustrious ancestors, are costumed as priests and Indians. To this injury Cable added the insult of designating the mulatto half brother of Honoré Grandissime "Creole."

The French and Spanish cultural mosaic in Louisiana was further complicated by Anglo-American immigration, by Acadian (Cajun) immigration from Nova Scotia in 1757, and by the immigration of erstwhile French nobility after the French Revolution. Most significantly, the migration of free blacks from Santo Domingo after the insurrection of the 1790s increased the ranks of free people of color in New Orleans and taught New Orleans blacks that they could claim higher social status by virtue of their contact with whites. Since these newcomers of mixed blood were the products of miscegenation, a practice sanctioned in Santo Domingo since 1505, they were attuned to racial distinctions based on gradations of color never before openly acknowledged on such a scale on the Anglo-Saxon mainland. Winthrop Jordan contrasts the racial attitudes of Americans with the racial attitudes of the refugees: "Mulattoes in the West Indies were products of accepted practice, something they assuredly were not in the continental colonies. In the one area they were the fruits of a desire which society tolerated and almost institutionalized; in the other they represented an illicit passion which public morality unhesitatingly condemned. On the continent, unlike the West Indies, mulattoes represented a practice about which men could only feel guilty. To reject and despise the productions of one's own guilt was only natural."[41]

Although the free black refugees from Santo Domingo were unable to alter the prevailing prejudice and hypocrisy of the New Orleanians, they brought with them an already well-established system of caste distinctions based on gradations of color and inherited wealth that would become a striking feature of New Orleans cultural life. On the mainland the custom was to define individuals with the faintest tincture of African blood as black. The Santo Domingans' practice was unable to change the rigidly bifurcated American system; however, they added their own terms to a racial hierarchy that none but they and Louisiana blacks would actually honor, in spite of the apparent genetic predominance of white blood in many American blacks—by 1860, 13 to 20 percent of the black population of the United States had white ancestry.[42]

The influence of Caribbean custom can be seen in the appropriation of the terms *mulatto, sambo, quadroon, mestize, griffe, octoroon,* and even *quinteroon* by Louisiana blacks. To whites, who tolerated these designations, they may have seemed to put a ridiculously fine point on things. However, because white blood was frequently their only passport to freedom and social advancement, many blacks, both enslaved and free, often insisted vehemently upon their share of it. Examinations of records of manumissions, such as those cited by Joe Gray Taylor in *Negro Slavery in Louisiana,* suggest the crucial role played by claims of kinship in increasing the ranks of freed men and women in Louisiana.[43]

In the period from the 1830s, when Louisiana courts passed laws prohibiting manumission, to the 1980s, racial fractions became a fossilized survival of an earlier reality. Occasionally, however, they remind us of the shameful one-drop rule that once prevailed in parts of the South. The lawsuit filed in Louisiana in 1982 by Susie Guillory Phipps, who discovered that her great-great-great-great-grandmother had been black and who was judged to be legally black because of this "taint," proves that issues raised by the one-drop rule still haunt us.

In antebellum Louisiana and elsewhere, however, social distinctions based on gradations of color *were* significant for free women of color and for women slaves, who, if sexually desirable and light-skinned enough, might become the mistresses of wealthy men. Black men, it goes without saying, in Louisiana as elsewhere, had sexual relations with white women only at their peril. Seldom has such a penalty been attached to plainness, since the unattractive female slave, like most of her male counterparts, was destined for the rice or cane fields, where masters and overseers held sway who were at least as callous and brutal as Harriet Beecher Stowe's Simon Legree. In actual fact, the model for Legree seems to have been the father-in-law of Kate Chopin, a man who made a reputation for hard-driving cruelty so typical of Louisiana planters that being sold down the river always implied a death sentence.[44]

For the beautiful mulatto, quadroon, or octoroon woman, whether she was slave or free, a permanent or semipermanent alliance with a wealthy white man was possible. For this reason, these women strove to please. George Washington Cable recalled the exotic, wistfully beautiful women of mixed blood of the antebellum period and proclaimed, as many visitors to New Orleans would also testify, the success of these sirens in pleasing men: "Old travellers spare no terms to tell their praises, their faultlessness of feature, their perfection of form, their varied styles of beauty,—for there were even pure Caucasian blondes among them,—their fascinating manners, their sparkling vivacity, their chaste and pretty wit, their grace in the dance, their modest propriety, their taste and elegance in dress. In the gentlest and most poetic sense they were indeed the sirens of this land, where it seemed 'always afternoon'—a momentary triumph of an Arcadian over a Christian civilization."[45]

Grace King also celebrated the stunning loveliness of these women "in their boxes at the Orleans theatre, rivalling the white ladies in the tier below them, with their diamonds, Parisian head-dresses, and elegant toilets."[46] She notes, in addition, that at the famous balls of the antebellum period, where none but white gentlemen were allowed, they appeared almost white themselves, for "from their skins no one would detect their origin," although "their position in the community was most humiliating," since "they regarded negroes and mulattoes with unmixed contempt" and were so regarded themselves by whites.[47]

At the quadroon balls, free women of color chaperoned their daughters and bargained for extramarital alliances with white men who would become their daughters' *maris*. These alliances, which were called *plaçages*, in many instances became lifetime quasi marriages, with the white man devising a means for his children to be educated as ladies and gentlemen in Paris and for their inheritance of his wealth.[48] However, the humanity and responsibility of individual white men should not be taken as proof of the virtues of the system, for as King notes, the quadroon mother and her octoroon daughter were forced to barter for an advantageous arrangement, "assuming as a merit and a distinction what is universally considered in the civilized world a shame and disgrace."[49] In this respect, certainly, these women were as enslaved as their slave sisters and as their truly white sisters, who were coerced to maintain their chastity both before and after marriage by a standard of conduct that applied only to them. As King remarks perceptively, in the case of the quadroon and octoroon beauties, these balls with their elaborate "negotiations" were "as incredible . . . as the slave marts and the Voudou dances; which, in their way, they seem subtly, indissolubly connected with."[50]

What George Washington Cable regarded with literary nostalgia as a "momentary triumph of an Arcadian over a Christian civilization" and Grace Elizabeth King deplored as an unfortunate and seamy aspect of New Orleans history underwent a metamorphosis after the Civil War. Those black aristocrats who had been insulated by their refinement, intelligence, wealth, or pretension from their black and white fellow citizens lost their ascendancy.

Williamson notes the persistence of relative tolerance of the mulatto elite by whites of the old order after Emancipation and the fury of the outcry against continued miscegenation by the white majority. In his study of the Cane River Creoles of color, Gary B. Mills observes that these aristocrats, who themselves owned slaves, were "soon abandoned by all but their closest white friends, and with the passing of years even these relationships withered."[51] In *Black New Orleans, 1860–1880,* John W. Blassingame surveys the New Orleans press in the postwar years and finds it expressing a "maniacal" feeling against interracial marriage.[52] The rise of the Ku Klux Klan intensified the pressure on all blacks. It is hardly surprising that those who could pass often migrated and were swallowed up in the white majority. Passing as Spanish or Mexican grandees, many of these wealthy quadroon aristocrats may have moved to California or Mexico.[53] There remains, however, a difference of opinion among scholars concerning the size of their exodus from New Orleans. Although the 1890 census identified 70,000 octoroons in the United States, this number represents an undercount, since racial traits in such dilution were seldom detectable.[54]

Those people of color in greater New Orleans who remained to be counted sought refuge from contact with whites and blacks in neighborhoods inhabited solely by those of their own caste. Some of the "ladies" evidently became denizens of New Orleans brothels, whose activities offered tawdry versions of the glamorous quadroon balls of yesteryear. These balls continued to entrance men like Lafcadio Hearn, who confessed his infatuation with a woman seen at a quadroon ball in 1880. Hearn's description of this infatuation is cast in the language of courtly love: "I have suffered the tortures of a thousand damned souls. I went too near the flame and got cruelly burned. . . . I got caught in a terrible net. . . . I became passionately in love before I knew it. . . . You think I am writing folly and madness. But you could never understand me further unless you lived in this accursed city. Still I love it so much. I love New Orleans!"[55]

By the time of Hearn's description, interracial liaisons were less expensive to maintain than in the prewar years because they were by now most often temporary. By 1902, one generation after Hearn's fantasy infatuation with an exotic beauty, many of the pretty children produced by such liaisons had also been corrupted in the "sporting houses" that made New Orleans a Mecca for the dissolute and necessitated the publication of an underground guidebook of vice entitled *The Blue Book*.

In this period, 1870–1900, as Edmund Wilson observes in a different vein concerning the earlier period, New Orleans offered "a kind of international experience which . . . could hardly . . . [be] got anywhere else in the United States." Herbert Asbury aptly summarizes the situation in the New Orleans of these years and implies, with a noticeable trace of Southern chauvinism, that the responsibility for the cultivation of sin on a grand scale belonged to the Yankee entrepreneur and the Yankee connoisseur of illicit pleasures: "It was under the rule of the United States that New Orleans embarked upon its golden age of glamour and spectacular wickedness and attained its full stature as a city of sin and gayety unique on the North American continent."[56]

Late in the nineteenth century, the "Yankees" confined the demimonde to Storyville, a section adjacent to the French Quarter. Racial lines, hardening elsewhere in the South in the eighties and nineties with the passage of Jim Crow laws, did not eliminate Storyville, where, according to Longstreet, "when it came to orgying and making money there wasn't (and is not today) any color line."[57] Whether because of the Latin laissez-faire attitude about the pursuit of pleasure or because of the economic upheavals brought about by the Civil War defeat, sexual commerce between the races continued almost unabated there.

The Genteel Tradition

In this milieu, where integration after dark was an immutable fact of life, Cable, King, and Chopin shared a sometimes keen, sometimes barely conscious, awareness of the contradictions underlying white supremacy. Frisby is surely correct in stressing the racial sophistication of these authors and in maintaining that they show that they did know what was going on, not only in the parlors but in the kitchens, the bedrooms, the sheds, and the whorehouses. All three would demonstrate an acute awareness of the nuances of racial problems, an awareness seemingly inevitable in writers who had constant contact with these problems or their implications.

Cable and Chopin transgressed the genteel commandments of their editors and their audience in confronting these problems, and Grace King also demonstrated her concern with the racial and sexual hypocrisy she witnessed. A member of the White League, who proclaimed that she wrote all her fiction from the "standpoint of a white lady,"[58] and a Southern white lady at that, she also confronted the facts that linked kitchen, bedroom, shed, and whorehouse in her beloved city. In her nonfictional *New Orleans: The Place and the People*, King wrote of the social instabilities caused by extensive racial "mixing" in her New Orleans. She clearly wished that the facts she reported were not so; but although she interpreted these facts in a racist fashion by pronouncing that "in regard to family purity, domestic peace, and household dignity" the mulatto women of the city were "the most insidious and the deadliest foes a community ever possessed," King described what she saw.[59]

Perhaps because she was much less graphic than Cable and Chopin in her descriptions of the realities of class, sex, and caste in New Orleans, Grace King was spared the repeated rejections they experienced. But whatever the individual impulses that directed these authors in their choices of fictional subject and technique, all three were inhibited in these choices by prudish editors and readers. In a biographical essay on Lafcadio Hearn, who proved himself more open to direct exploration of interracial experiences than Cable, King, or Chopin, Malcolm Cowley sheds light on the excessive nicety of the respectable publishers of the genteel tradition:

> American daily journalism gave Hearn a chance he would have found in no other field. He had come to this country at a time when many serious writers, after fleeing to Europe, were complaining from a distance that American books had to be written and American magazines edited for a genteel audience composed chiefly of women. They forgot the newspapers, which were written for men and therefore retained more freedom of speech, besides a touch of cynicism. The newspapers of the time discussed dangerous topics like prostitution, adultery and miscegenation.[60]

Writing under the constraints of book and magazine publishers of the day, Cable, King, and Chopin were inhibited in their treatments of taboo topics such as miscegenation. They were inhibited by editorial assumptions about what an audience "composed chiefly of women" might want to read. Since Margaret Fuller at the *Dial* and Sarah Josepha Hale at *Godey's Lady's*

Book were the only notable women editors during this period, men were mainly responsible for decisions about feminine taste. Today, such decisions seem at their best to have been patronizing and prudish. Examples of the extreme Victorian nicety and solicitude of the gentlemanly editors of this period abound.

Sensing the potential for offense in one of Grace King's stories, Richard Watson Gilder asked her in a letter dated September 24, 1891, to drop the word *red* from her description of a priest's nose, since readers might assume this detail denoted drunkenness and "was an attack on the priesthood."[61] The rejection of "Posson Jone'," one of Cable's best early stories, on similar grounds by *Scribner's*, the *New York Times*, the *Galaxy*, and *Harper's* in close succession demonstrates the prudery of the editors of these representative publications. Although its subsequent acclaim may have led these editors to rue their decisions, Cable's "Posson Jone'" was refused repeatedly because it dealt humorously with a drunken preacher who gambles away his church's money. Justifying his rejection of "Posson Jone'," Henry Mills Alden, editor of *Harper's*, wrote sanctimoniously to Cable that "the disagreeable aspects of human nature are made prominent, and the story leaves an unpleasant impression on the mind of the reader." Alden's later statement that stories for *Harper's* "must be of a pleasant character and, as a rule, must be love tales"[62] suggests that Cable's story was also unacceptable because it possessed no "love interest." Ironically, "'Posson Jone'" when published proved to be the most widely commended of all of Cable's stories, and was praised by Charles Dudley Warner for showing that actual life, even low life, could be heightened to gain an idealistic effect."[63]

If a tipsy clerical character repelled genteel editors, how much more might they have been revolted by the fallen woman, her procurer, and her client? Cable's sensitivity to the genteel limitations of his editors and many of his readers no doubt persuaded him to cast the events of *Madame Delphine* and "'Tite Poulette," his two most famous stories dealing with miscegenation, in the safe and romantic past and to pass over the morganatic character of Madame Delphine's marriage with a phrase indicating the less said the better.

Although it is pointless to bemoan what might have been in literature, many critics have already reviled the Victorian taboos and the feminine audience that stifled the writers of this period. Van Wyck Brooks's lament for the Twain lost to posterity through genteel editing at home and in his editor's office is a well-known case in point. Edmund Wilson's regretful epitaph for Cable is less well known but speaks to the same issue: "The slow strangulation of Cable as an artist and a serious writer is surely one of the most gruesome episodes in American literary history."[64]

The countervailing common sense of William Dean Howells of the

Atlantic Monthly notwithstanding, the editors of *Scribner's, Harper's, Century, Lippincott's,* and *Appletons'* insisted on presenting an idealized world for their subscribers. In this world, religion prevailed and sectional bitterness could be effaced by the love affairs and marriages of Southern belles and Northern officers. The blight of physical passion was absent. The deadly seriousness of the literary love affairs produced under the aegis of editors like Alden, who had determined that the stories chosen for his magazine "as a rule, must be love tales," can be measured by the hostile reactions of many serious writers to love as a topic for their fiction. For although in *Anna Karenina* (1873–77) Tolstoy had shown that passion, realistically portrayed, was a topic of many dimensions, American writers under the relentless pressure of genteel editors of the Gilded Age seemed frequently to agree with Minister Sewell in Howells's *The Rise of Silas Lapham* (1885) that the insipid love affairs current in the fiction of the day were painted "in a monstrous disproportion to the other relations of life."[65]

Grace King, for one, embraced the tenets of a realism of the "commonplace" espoused by Howells. Claiming "I am not a romanticist, I am a realist à la mode de la Nlle Orléans,"[66] King, like Cable and Chopin, was sensitive to the pressure of genteel editors who wanted the sweetness and light of the standard love story in the work she presented them. Later, long after she had abandoned the writing of fiction, King blamed the "romantic" requirements of her editor, George P. Brett of Macmillan, for the long neglect of her Reconstruction novel, *The Pleasant Ways of St. Médard,* which deals with the grueling postwar experiences of a destitute patrician family like King's own. Brett had evidently hoped for a sensational but coyly asexual romance of Reconstruction like Thomas Nelson Page's *Red Rock* (1898) or Thomas Dixon, Jr.'s, *The Leopard's Spots* (1902), for he refused King's fifth and final proof of *St. Médard;* and the novel languished for ten years until its serendipitous discovery in manuscript by Edward Garnett, who, assuming that it had been published, ranked it superior to Willa Cather's *O Pioneers!* in his *Atlantic Monthly* review of February 1916.

King wrote Garnett that his praise had "created quite a sensation" in New Orleans, where some people also assumed that her novel had been published. Some people, she reported, had even sent her orders for it. Garnett's praise, however, did not budge George Brett at Macmillan, who perhaps guessed that the public would not buy King's realistic depiction of Reconstruction life. Henry Holt and Company, which published *The Pleasant Ways of St. Médard* in 1916, issued only three small printings, despite favorable reviews.

When she met Thomas Nelson Page four years later, King lamented the fate of her novel, perhaps echoing her earlier observation that it had consumed years of her life, bleeding her of spirit and energy. Page gave her his formula for literary success, the very formula Brett had insisted she employ if she wanted Macmillan to publish her book. As King reports the encounter, Page admitted that he too had once run afoul of an editor who wanted him to write saleable formula stories. Page had learned the secret and was eager to tell King how to succeed as he had done. "Just rip the story open and insert a love story," he said. "It is the easiest thing to do in the world. Get a pretty girl and name her Jeanne, that name always takes! Make her fall in love with a Federal officer and your story will be printed at once!"[67]

As her *Memories of a Southern Woman of Letters* repeatedly attests, King was often appalled by the bad manners of Northerners, and would hardly have allowed "Jeanne," her Southern belle, to dally with a Federal officer. Instead of changing her novel by making the expedient insertion, King waited until a change in the literary climate gained *St. Médard* the audience it deserved. In *Grace King of New Orleans: A Selection of Her Writings*, Robert Bush asserts that King had chosen to preserve her story of the "cruel memories of economic struggle and humiliation" rather than submit to the pressure to reproduce another trite love story between Northerner and Southerner.[68]

Cable, King, and Chopin experienced similar editorial pressures. Cable's biographers agree that Cable's art was marred by his response to the coercion of his editors, who urged him to strike from his writings "the iron-sinewed handling of social and moral problems which supplied its strength."[69] If Cable's art was debilitated by his willingness to embrace the "love motif" and to neglect a more serious treatment of the complicated social world of New Orleans, his situation was typical. In *John March, Southerner* (1894), for example, a novel published after an almost ten-year hiatus in his literary career, Cable introduced the boring, syrupy love affair of John March and Barbara Garnet in what he proclaimed to be his most ambitious novel. Was this affair, asks Louis D. Rubin, Jr., "developed to such interminable length by Cable in a desperate effort to please his editor [Richard Watson Gilder]?" We do not know, answers Rubin rhetorically, but it is clear that "the John March–Barbara Garnet relationship is in the novel not merely because of Gilder, but because of the whole Genteel Tradition; it is typical magazine material, no better and no worse than most of the fictional romances of the period, written by a man who wrote willingly and eagerly for a magazine audience."[70]

Editorial hostility to the peopling of sentimental love stories with realistic heroines can be seen in the critical furor caused by the publication of Kate Chopin's *The Awakening*. So terrible was the outcry occasioned by Chopin's poignant presentation of Edna Pontellier's adultery and self-discovery that more than sixty years after its publication, *The Oxford Companion to American Literature* entry on Kate Chopin still resonated with much of the disapproval of *The Awakening*'s original readers: "Mrs. Chopin's last novel, *The Awakening* (1899), caused a storm of criticism that ended her literary career, because readers of the time were shocked by the realistic treatment of morbid psychology in this objective account of mixed marriage and adultery."[71]

Ironically, the hostility of the genteel reading public and the genteel editors and critics of the Gilded Age to heroines who strayed from the norms prescribed for white women in this period may have helped push Cable, King, and Chopin toward depiction of women who could be interesting by virtue of birth and situation rather than by virtue of their unladylike behavior. Because interracial love was so far removed from the actual experience of most of the reading public and because the woman of color was often regarded as the "sunkissed embodiment of ardency,"[72] Cable, King, and Chopin could resurrect the tragic octoroon of their abolitionist predecessors to imply what they could not safely say about the erotic basis of human love. By recasting the standard love story, giving the female lead to a woman of ambiguous racial status, these three authors in some measure freed themselves from Victorian constraints imposed by editors who insisted on replication of the standard love story. Although miscegenation was a topic surrounded by taboos and only Cable would finally depict violations of these taboos in a positive light, King and Chopin, spurred by his example, attacked the sexual and racial double standard through their characterizations of women trapped on the color line.

Immersion in the mixed racial milieu of New Orleans and sensitivity to editors who urged them to eschew dangerous topics like interracial love but to embrace insipid topics like the sexless love of chivalrous young men for spotless young women interacted in determining the artistic choices available to each of these authors. Resurrecting a familiar female stereotype in a group of stories quite distinct from most of the magazine fiction of the period 1870–1900, each created women characters of greater depth and more dimension than the heroines admired by genteel critics and readers of this period. Although the life stories of their characters are usually no happier than those of their prototype, the octoroon, they are more often survivors. The realism with which they are depicted, moreover, distinguishes them from both the antebellum stereotype that gave them origin and its commercial counterpart in the popular fiction of our day. Through their treatment of these racially marginal women characters, Cable, King, and Chopin disclose the multiple personal and political guises of sexism, classism, and racism, which together fix the life chances of all women.

CHAPTER TWO

· George Cable ·

THE STEREOTYPE RESURRECTED

Cable's Rise

George Washington Cable's stories of New Orleans whetted the national appetite for Louisiana local color in the 1870s. Publication of Cable's "'Sieur George: A Story of New Orleans" by *Scribner's* in October 1873 launched a career that would span four decades. The publication of "Belles Demoiselles Plantation" in April 1874 and "'Tite Poulette" in October 1874 gave the first indication of the direction Cable would take in exploring the problems created by slavery and the long history of covert miscegenation in the South. The publication of these and Cable's other stories in *Old Creole Days* in 1879 assured Cable a national following.

The Northern readers of *Old Creole Days* were charmed by Cable's depiction of old New Orleans and awakened only slowly to the implicit criticism of the Southern verities already apparent in his treatment of the "tragic octoroon" in "'Tite Poulette." With the exception of the reviewer of *L'Abeille*, the French-language newspaper of New Orleans, who was affronted by Cable's "slighting" treatment of Creoles, Southern reviewers initially approved Cable's stories. They even failed to respond as negatively as might have been expected to Cable's frontal attack on racism in *The Grandissimes* (1880) and *Madame Delphine* (1881). Although *The Grandissimes* fulfilled Cable's stated intention to make it "as plain a protest against the times in which it was written as against the earlier times in which its scenes were set," Cable continued to have a following in the South.[1]

Reviews by the Southern press of the works published in the first decade of Cable's career, 1874–84, for the most part ignored the rising intensity of his social commentary in these works, focusing instead on the new era in Southern literature that they augured. Mrs. William Malone Baskervill, a

134,629

cultivated Southern lady, read *Old Creole Days*—one of the later editions of the collection included *Madame Delphine*—and reported: "I said to myself, with profound feeling: 'It has come at last!' I meant the day of the South's finding her expression in literature. Such a moment of overwhelming conviction and satisfaction can come only once, I know. I realized then that the South had the material in her old past, and that we had the writers with the art to portray it."[2]

In a sense, such optimism was well-founded. The demand for Southern stories stimulated by Cable's "discovery" in the Mardi Gras season of 1873 by Edward King, a Northern correspondent on assignment for *Scribner's*, did have far-ranging effects on Southern literature. In *The Mind of the South* W. J. Cash wrote of the phenomenal blossoming of Southern letters during this period. "The multiplication of Southern writers," says Cash, "would go on at such a pace until in 1939 the South actually produced more books of measurable importance than any other section of the country, until anybody who fired off a gun in the region was practically certain to kill an author."[3] But when asked about the simultaneity of his literary rise and the rise of local-color fiction from the South, Cable (who had been writing for ten years before Edward King "discovered" him) said, perhaps too modestly, that the events were probably just coincidental.[4]

Reflecting the North's interest in the literature of the conquered, Edward King's "The Great South" series and Cable's rapid rise to national prominence strengthened the local-color impulse in the South. Northern critics of the 1870s and 1880s quite predictably praised the early productions of Cable and his Southern contemporaries at the expense of Southern writers of the antebellum period, and new Southern writers emerged in increasing numbers under the Northern patronage that followed Cable's success.

Discussing the proliferation of Southern writers during this period in *Southern Life in Fiction*, Jay B. Hubbell asserts that "the War between the States may be said to have emancipated not only the slaves but the Southern writers as well."[5] Unfortunately, however, an understandable desire to glorify the Lost Cause and to sell their fiction to New York and Boston harnessed most of Cable's contemporaries to commercial production. Even the most talented and most dedicated of the postwar generation suffered a swift decline in artistic power. Perplexed by this phenomenon, Hubbell notes in *The South in American Literature, 1607–1900*, that "in nearly every instance the writer's first book is his best." Hubbell joined Van Wyck Brooks, who had noted a generation earlier that "the chronic state of our literature is that of a youthful promise which is never redeemed" and had further lamented that "the blighted career, the arrested career, the diverted career are, with us, the rule."[6]

As is characteristic of many writers of the postwar generation, Cable's early fictional works are his best. Unlike the ephemeral productions of many Southern writers of this period, however, Cable's fiction used history to comment on conditions of his own day. What Cable read in the New Orleans archives and in the back issues of the New Orleans *Picayune* he saw confirmed every day on the street. Shaped by the material mined from Louisiana history, shaded by details gleaned by his close observations of ongoing city life, and controlled by a penetrating moral vision, Cable's early stories expose those historical injustices that are still a part of the flesh and blood of the South and of the nation.

In his early works Cable already demonstrates his mature ability to use history to illuminate contemporary problems. In "George W. Cable's Use of the Past," Arlin Turner makes the familiar comparison of Cable with Hawthorne and concludes: "Cable saw his city and state and region to be products of historical circumstances and forces. . . . He found in the historical past clues he thought valuable for understanding the present and for resolving current issues."[7]

In *Patriotic Gore: Studies in the Literature of the American Civil War,* Edmund Wilson recognizes the brilliance of Cable's early works, those completed before his publishers gained a stranglehold on his talent, and perceives also that Cable's real point of view "is not fundamentally romantic but historical and sociological." Wilson suggests the specific nature of Cable's abilities as a realist when he notes Cable's "striving for accuracy of observation, his naturalist's interest in varied types, in the eventual objectivity of his judgments."[8]

In *George W. Cable: The Life and Times of a Southern Heretic,* Louis D. Rubin, Jr., also takes Cable's measure and finds "almost nowhere else in the literature of his time . . . an image of the South—or, for that matter, of American society—and the place of the Negro in it, that today seems of compelling truth and even urgency." Edmund Wilson believes that the effectiveness of Cable's early fiction "depends on the startling relationships, the unexpected courses of action that result from the queer situation of two races living side by side, entangled with one another but habitually ignoring this fact, proceeding more or less at cross-purposes but recurrently brought up short by love, sympathy or consanguinity."[9]

These assessments of Cable reflect the growing awareness and approval of the central role that an indictment of racism played in his fiction. Regrettably, however, admiration of Cable for his courageous fight against racism tempts us to see his art principally in terms of his attack. And perhaps inevitably, we tend to see Cable, not as an artist, but as a historical anomaly—a protester born too soon.

During a period that saw a rise in the overt expression of racial hysteria

North and South, Cable's reasoned assault on racism was heretical. In "Black Stereotypes as Reflected in Popular Culture, 1880–1920," J. Stanley Lemons describes the white backlash that began building to a climax after the betrayal of the promises of the Civil War and Reconstruction in the Compromise of 1877. By the 1890s, when the climax was reached, Northern and Southern whites were for the most part reconciled to each other and were determined or willing to deprive blacks of their newly won constitutional rights. The Supreme Court endorsed segregation in 1896 with its "separate but equal" decision, ratifying the popular will. In comic and horrific rituals, the oppression of blacks and the repression of blackness unified whites across class lines. Popular culture made the black "the principal comic figure in the 1890s, replacing the Irishman as the butt of America's jokes,"[10] and mob insanity made blacks the scapegoats of lynching and burning rituals. As Trudier Harris notes in *Exorcising Blackness: Historical and Literary Burning Rituals*, after the Civil War the term *lynching* took on a new and more sinister meaning, reflecting the demented reality of white violence against blacks. Statistics confirm the testimony of semantics. Between 1882 and 1903, 2,060 blacks were lynched. Many of them were burned or "roasted alive" while members of the mob tore trophies of clothing or flesh from them.[11]

In his fiction Cable captured the psychology of white racism; and, as the central figure and catalyst of what Warner Berthoff calls "a New Orleans renaissance in the '70s, '80s, and '90s," he attempted to stem the racist tide with fiction grounded in the New Orleans milieu he shared with Grace King and Kate Chopin. His portraits of women of mixed blood prove his "firm interior grip on [the] actual social order" and his awareness of the plight of women in general.[12] His intuitive understanding of the complex interactions of class, race, and sexual attractiveness in fixing a woman's chances for life validates his portraits of women without male protectors, women whose hardships he had ample opportunity to observe. He cannot have been unaffected by the long, dependent widowhood of his mother, Rebecca Boardman Cable, who lived intermittently with him or her daughters after her husband's death in 1859 until her own death in 1890, and he must have been acutely aware of the limited chances of his sisters, Mary Louise Cable, a spinster, and Antoinette Cable Cox, a penniless widow with three children, who made up a second dependent household, which Cable called his "other house."[13] And finally, the invalidism, after repeated childbearing, of his wife of thirty-five years, Louise Bartlett Cable, who bore five daughters and three sons, must have worked on Cable and influenced his perception of women and their problems.

Cable's concern for women and his understanding of their situations were not confined to women of his own race and social class. In "The

Freedman's Case in Equity" (*Century,* 1885), the essay that signaled his irrevocable break with the dominant, racist attitudes of his region, Cable explains that the origin of his commitment to fight for Negro rights was his concern for a black mother and her daughter who were humiliated by being forced to ride in a crowded railway coach with nineteen chained, filthy convicts on their way to the mines. (Cable was also acutely conscious of the plight of the prisoners, as his work against the convict-lease system shows.) Sensitive to the injustice accorded to this woman in the name of racial supremacy, Cable noted that if the woman had been traveling as the nurse of a white child, she would have ridden in the nearly empty white car. His deduction about this woman's plight would become the thematic foundation of his early fiction, for he believed that "the whole community is sinned against in every act or attitude of oppression, however gross or however refined."[14]

Cable's sensitivity to oppression and his hatred of it are apparent in his fictional presentations of the victimization of women on both sides of the color line. Although he used conventional formulas to extricate some of his women characters from hopeless situations, and although the modern reader may wish on occasion that he had omitted genteel coyness or sentimental excess, Cable's heroines are in general much more believable and attractive as human beings than his heroes; and the realism with which his heroines are depicted contrasts and occasionally conflicts with the standard romantic situations in which they are cast.

Anyone reading all of Cable's fiction, however, will be struck by the disparity between the excellence of Cable's early characterizations of women and the banality of those in his later works. This disparity seems especially marked in Cable's depictions of women of mixed blood because his return to a lifeless treatment of the tragic octoroon coincides with a shift in his views on miscegenation. Although the evidence of his nonfictional writings suggests that Cable never completely rejected the notion that blacks were inferior, only in his later works do his unexamined, unresolved racist attitudes infect his characterizations. Similarly, the unexamined sexist views that cloud Cable's characterizations of women and that emerge early in his moralizing on "true womanhood" (a catchphrase of the day) and his voyeuristic descriptions of the voluptuous charms of his heroines become pervasive and fatal to his later characterizations of women.[15] Because they are the focus of Cable's ambivalent notions about blacks and about women, his early characterizations of women of mixed blood provide proof of his gifts as a realist and his ability to transcend the prejudices of his culture in his art. Because Cable treated the tragic octoroon at the beginning and the end of his career, the deterioration in his portrayal of this female character indicates his rise and fall as a literary artist.

Cable's promising, anonymous beginnings as a published author coincide with the appearance of "A Life-Ebbing Monography" in the New Orleans *Picayune* on December 24, 1871, a story often credited to Cable's pen. Although the role of the woman of mixed blood is minimal, the story itself is of interest because it suggests the author's potential as a social critic. In effect, the narrator of the story exposes the absurdity of the obsession with purity of blood by claiming to recount from old records the story of a white man who attempted to bypass the law against intermarriage by opening a vein in his arm in order to mingle his blood with the blood of the beautiful mulatto he wanted to marry.

"A Life-Ebbing Monography" may be attributed to Cable with even greater certainty than is usually the case. On the basis of striking thematic parallels, Arlin Turner argues that the story "seems . . . to belong to the ancestry of" "'Tite Poulette" and *Madame Delphine*.[16] But there are, in addition, historical reasons to believe that Cable is in fact its author. In *Black New Orleans, 1860–1880*, John W. Blassingame reports that his research in the archives of New Orleans uncovered what purports to be a true account of a white cashier of a New Orleans bank who married a black woman after transfusing some of her blood into his own body in order to share the stigma and legal disability of her race.[17] Since we know that Cable based his *Strange True Stories of Louisiana* (1889) on historical episodes he had culled from the New Orleans archives, it seems quite possible that he had come upon the very same account and made it the basis of this story of star-crossed love on the color line.

Cable's realistic technique and his concern with racism evolve with the creation of "'Tite Poulette," *The Grandissimes*, and *Madame Delphine*. Although *The Cavalier* (1901), Cable's historical novel of the Civil War, sold well, by 1890 Cable had written the works on which his reputation as a literary artist rests. When Edmund Wilson observes that Cable was finished as a literary artist in the early 1890s, he voices the critical consensus.[18]

The precipitous decline of his art in the 1890s reflects in large part Cable's disillusionment with fiction as a vehicle for his vision. It was frequently asserted by critics of the period that Cable's failing powers display the artist destroyed by the advocate. However, Kjell Ekström notes in *George Washington Cable: A Study of His Early Life and Works* that Cable's later works suggest conscious efforts to refrain from expressing his views. Whether Cable had decided to alter the tone of his fiction to keep from further antagonizing the South as he had done in the 1880s, or whether he had completely revised his views concerning the functions of literature in society, as some of his statements imply, his loss of passionate interest in creating an imaginatively valid world was devastating to his art.

At the time he wrote "'Tite Poulette," *The Grandissimes*, and *Madame*

Delphine, however, Cable believed that literature had a duty to present and defend truth "even though it shake the established order of things like an earthquake."[19] In these works Cable's characterizations of women reveal his growth as a literary artist. And in these works Cable's portraits of women are functional as well as decorative, for his realistic characterizations of women carry much of the implied criticism of the social order.

In "'Tite Poulette," *The Grandissimes,* and *Madame Delphine,* Cable's transformations of the traditional stereotype of the tragic octoroon reveal his concern with issues of gender and race and his growing involvement with the human dimensions of social problems. In *Gideon's Band* (1914), a much later work, however, Cable's art is contaminated by the conventions his best fiction had abandoned. One indication of the dismal quality of this novel is Cable's characterization of Phyllis, a lifeless, formula, mulatto heroine, who resembles Palmyre Philosophe of *The Grandissimes* in superficial detail but has none of Palmyre's troubling complexity or vitality. Phyllis, a quadroon whose tragic history becomes central to Cable's plot in *Gideon's Band,* is described safely and in terms of the stereotype. While her sexual victimization by her master and his overseers recalls the tragic imbroglio of Cassy's history in *Uncle Tom's Cabin,* and while Phyllis has the most eventful and dramatic life of any of the characters in Cable's novel, she does not develop through her own actions, as his earlier heroines like Palmyre had done. She never becomes the exciting character Cable guardedly, but repeatedly, claims she is.

Before we examine Cable's earlier works, it is helpful to consider *Gideon's Band* because of the light it sheds on his avowed attitudes toward miscegenation. Cable's published responses to the accusations that he had urged racial mixing all insist on his opposition to miscegenation. However, the shaky logic embedded in the responses seems inconsistent with Cable's realistic presentations of the problems posed by interracial love in "'Tite Poulette," *The Grandissimes,* and *Madame Delphine.*

As early as 1885 in "The Freedman's Case in Equity," Cable wrote, the "occasional mingling" of the Negro's blood with that of "a superb race of masters" improved the Negro, who "was brought to our shores usually a naked, brutish, unclean, captive, pagan savage." Yet, having conceded the existence of an improved mixed stock in the South, Cable later asserted, perhaps defensively, in "The Silent South" that the "two antipodal races . . . have no wish to, and for all we know never will, mingle their two bloods in one stream."[20] This is the tack Cable took in his nonfictional writings and the one he also takes in *Gideon's Band* to resolve the problem of miscegenation. But Cable's claim that the races are antipodal is contrary to all the evidence he confronted on any street in New Orleans, where there were many shades of skin color in the passersby. It is therefore difficult to believe that Cable really imagined that racial mixing, already a fait accompli, would halt because of what he called the "natural abhorrence" of the races for each other. Cable's continuing need to explain what he meant when he argued for civil equality for the Negro drew him to this issue repeatedly, for many Southerners equated civil equality with interracial sex. In "The Negro Question," for example, he reasserts by implication the fundamental, and presumably natural, separation of the races: "Dissimilar races are not inclined to mix spontaneously. The common enjoyment of equal civil rights never mixed two such races; it has always been some oppressive distinction between them that, by holding out temptations to vice instead of rewards to virtue, has done it; and because slavery is the foulest of oppressions it makes the mixture of races in morally foulest form."[21]

In *Gideon's Band* Cable's plot perpetuates a false view of history and of human nature. In this late work Cable resolves with deceptive ease the dilemma that in his early stories is fraught with anguish for his characters on both sides of the color line: Old Joy, Phyllis's black cousin, confirms the Panglossian view that "social confusion" will be averted by the good sense of individuals.[22] Old Joy insists on the ability of "race conscience" to keep the races separate, predicting and approving Phyllis's refusal of the proposal of a white preacher who has promised to take her to the Western frontier, where she will be able to pass as white.[23]

Old Joy's response to the notion of Phyllis's passing, of course, was exactly the kind of response Cable's readers would have been most comfortable hearing. In *George W. Cable*, Philip Butcher notes Cable's chariness in dealing with the theme of miscegenation and mentions that Cable became so careful to avoid anything that might smack of an interracial alliance or of the sanctioning of such an alliance that he made a celibate of Fortune in *The Flower of the Chapdelaines* (1918) because Fortune, a white girl held illegally as a slave, assumes she has black blood. According to one of the other characters in the novel, Fortune is "too good and high-mind' to be marrie' to any white man wha'z willin' to marry a nigger."[24]

Although both these late works reiterate Cable's standard answer to the questions posed by his racist critics about his attitudes toward miscegenation, these confirmations of "race conscience" seem to be recantations of the messages of "'Tite Poulette," *The Grandissimes,* and *Madame Delphine.* Today, Cable's admirers who read *Gideon's Band* or *The Flower of the Chapdelaines* will very likely be shaken by such an answer, by the correspondingly marked deterioration in Cable's art, and by the apparent shift in Cable's racial attitudes. The conflict between Cable's arresting presentations of the love of women of mixed blood and white men in his early fiction and his ambivalence, lack of candor, or confusion about miscegenation reveals only one aspect of the problem Cable poses for the critic. For in

"'Tite Poulette," *The Grandissimes,* and *Madame Delphine,* his realism discloses a more faithful and more consistent view of racial issues than he ever achieved in his nonfiction discussions of these issues. His moving descriptions of women in these stories lead the reader beyond consideration of race alone to consideration of the shared oppression that is women's lot.

Because "'Tite Poulette," *The Grandissimes,* and *Madame Delphine* reveal the crushing impact of sexism and racism on women, it is tempting to assume that Cable was making a conscious attack on sexism as well as racism in these works. But whether Cable was consciously approving of the strong current of feminist protest of the period or not, his early characterizations of women reveal that he was buffeted by that current. Despite his weakness for describing his heroines in ravishing and, on occasion, quite conventional detail, his early portraits of women are charged with life. And he depicts the allure of women on both sides of the color line with amazing, even daring, impartiality.

Focusing on the seeming incongruity between Cable's lavish descriptions of beautiful women and his rigid, inhibiting Presbyterian values, Louis D. Rubin, Jr., finds that Cable's women characters lack the indomitable, sterling traits of Cable's mother. Cable's morally inferior Creole women, Rubin writes, are "indicative of the kind of attraction that the sensuous and the voluptuous held for Cable."[25] Rubin thinks it unfair that Cable renders such harsh judgments of male Creoles for their moral laxity, indolence, and arrogance while seeming to excuse, if not condone, equally undesirable traits—financial impracticality, lassitude, superstitiousness, and reliance on romantic love even when love has failed them tragically—in the Creole women and women of color he delights in. What Rubin fails to notice is that Cable finds the women less deserving of harsh judgment because their immaturities are the crippling effects of female conditioning in a racist and sexist society.

In *Southern Honor: Ethics and Behavior in the Old South,* Bertram Wyatt-Brown speculates about the conditioning that produced pliant behavior in the abused Southern wives of the antebellum period:

Southern males sometimes believed that a little home violence went a long way to ensure loyalty and inspire healthy respect. If it worked with blacks, it surely would help with meddlesome women. . . . the women rarely prosecuted their abusive husbands, who claimed that they had apologized once arrest had sobered them. Besides, they were the women's sole support in so many cases. The real reason, though, for the women's acquiescence was the same then as it is today: the woman's feeling of inferiority, no matter how addicted her husband was to alcohol, no matter how violent he became in self-

despisement and anger. Not surprisingly, the Southern cultural emphasis upon total masculinity, total femininity encouraged male abuse
and female submission that stimulated even more violence. Constantly urged to prove his manhood as he was growing up, the male
used alcohol and physical violence to overawe his wife with a male
superiority that he did not altogether feel. Convinced from childhood
that she was always to defer, being less worthy of attention than her
brothers, and dependent first on father, then on husband, the woman
felt duly chastened by a beating, but remained resentful of it any-
how.[26]

There is an almost indefinable poignance in Cable's early descriptions of
his women characters. Compounded of empathy, attraction certainly, and
close observation of living models, these descriptions capture more than
pose and ambience. Cable's description of the Grandissime women gathered together for their *fête de grandpère,* a patriarchal celebration of the
ancien régime, for example, reveals much more than Cable's "connoisseur's
eye for feminine beauty."[27]

> You note the exquisite pencilling of their eyebrows, here and there
> some heavier and more velvety, where a less vivacious expression
> betrays a share of Spanish blood. As Grandissimes, you mark their
> tendency to exceed the medium Creole stature, an appearance height-
> ened by the fashion of their robes. There is scarcely a rose in all their
> cheeks and a full red-ripeness of the lips would hardly be in keeping;
> but there is plenty of life in their eyes, which glance out between the
> curtains of their long lashes with a merry dancing that keeps time to
> the prattle of tongues. You are not able to get a straight look into
> them, and if you could you would see only your own image cast back
> in pitiful miniature; but you turn away and feel, as you fortify your-
> self with an inward smile, that they know you, you man, through and
> through, like a little song.[28]

This tribute to the many shades of Grandissime beauty conveys more
about the status of the women themselves than at first appears. Although
the Grandissime women in this description are seen momentarily and from
an inviolable distance by a narrator who confesses his limitations as an
observer, in this fleeting glimpse of their beauty, Cable manages to suggest
both the antagonistic distance between Creole and American culture and
the accompanying fascination of Americans with Creoles. But perhaps
what the ladies themselves would call the je ne sais quoi of Cable's tribute
to their elusive loveliness is the ironic reflection of male scrutiny Cable
allows them in this description. The self-fortifying "inward smile" of the

male outsider shows that they have put him in his place. The reciprocal nature of this exchange suggests that the ladies also know their place.

The description of the Grandissime women is quite characteristic of Cable's caressing, minutely sensitive, physical descriptions of women. Such descriptions almost always reveal more than they may have been consciously designed to reveal about the "abyss of inequality" separating the sexes.[29] Frequently, a gesture or a glance brings the portrait to life, revealing the static nature of the role that woman must play, her self-awareness, and her understanding of the limitations placed on her. In later descriptions of the Grandissime women, Cable suggests the price these white women pay for their pedestals. For although these aristocratic Creoles sparkle with "plenty of life" at the *fête de grandpère,* their aspirations as well as their friendships are circumscribed—their constraint belies their merriment. Cable later remarks that "the ladies of the Grandissime mansion . . . asked passengers' questions, got sailors' answers, retorted wittily and more or less satirically, and laughed often, feeling their constrained insignificance" (p. 316).

In their roles as passengers on the family vessel, the Grandissime women carry the family virtues as baggage to be jettisoned at the first warnings of choppy water. When the "ladies" pray for mercy for a "treacher[ous]" negro, "the male Grandissimes were not surprised at this exhibition of weak clemency [a pointedly ironic echo of their victim's name, Clemence] in their lovely women; they were proud of it; it showed the magnanimity that was natural to the universal Grandissime heart, when not restrained and repressed by the stern necessities of the hour" (p. 316).

Clemence exposes the double standard implicit in this white male attitude when she begs for her life: "You ain' got no mo' biznis to do me so 'an if I was a white 'oman! You dassent tek a white 'oman out'n de Pa'sh Pris'n an' do 'er so!" (p. 322). The different standards applied to white and black women by white men, however, do not disguise the powerlessness these women share despite their racial differences. Both the plea of the Grandissime "ladies" for mercy and Clemence's appeal for justice are ignored by the Grandissime men. Because the Grandissime women are guardians of the virtues their men revere when they have time, their dismissal, like Clemence's murder, seems to constitute a plain protest against male supremacy.

"'Tite Poulette"

Whether angry, despairing, or cynical about their places in a white man's world, Cable's women characters are hostages to male supremacy. The women of the aristocracy suffer the protective tyranny of their men. The sham of chivalry requires their dependence, but their knowing glances and shared laughter suggest that they are fully acquainted with the weaknesses of the strutting white men around them. Black women and women of mixed blood are preyed upon by these same white men. The presentation of this bitter division of oppression emerges in "'Tite Poulette," Cable's first acknowledged story to deal with the situation of women and the topic of miscegenation.

According to Kjell Ekström, "'Tite Poulette" was ready for publication by the end of 1873. It is probable that Cable had already broached the topic in publishing "A Life-Ebbing Monography" in the winter of 1871 and that he continued pondering the subject through the summer of 1872. Cable mentions in "My Politics" that he had started doing research in the New Orleans archives following a request to write a column for the *Picayune* dealing with local history. In the archives Cable read hundreds of old newspapers; and he says, "Here I got my inspiration for ' 'Tite Poulette,' written in sympathy for the fate of the quadroon caste."[30] A diary entry dated January 10, 1889, recalls this beginning. Cable wrote: "I found a certain satisfaction in *writing* that public avowal of my views which I found it so painful publicly to speak."[31]

Through the veil of fiction, Cable broached the topic of miscegenation, but more delicately than this diary entry suggests. In "Cable and the Theme of Miscegenation in *Old Creole Days* and *The Grandissimes*," William Bedford Clark notes Cable's timidity in "'Tite Poulette," remarking, "It is little wonder that ''Tite Poulette' was well-received in Cable's native New Orleans. . . . It is fundamentally a love story in which the problem of racial oppression is only a temporary frustration. The only real miscegenation takes place long before the story begins, and, by ultimately asserting that his heroine is white, Cable effectively sidesteps all controversy."[32]

But if Cable's method in "'Tite Poulette" is less direct than in *The Grandissimes* and *Madame Delphine*, "'Tite Poulette" reveals, nevertheless, the hallmarks of Cable's genius—its haunting effects, achieved through delicacy of shading and ambiguous revelation. It is clearly only in relation to Cable's later treatments of the themes introduced in "'Tite Poulette" that this beautiful story appears to be inferior.

Subordinate to the realistic setting and characterization, the romantic plot of "'Tite Poulette," which some critics have characterized as a fairy tale, unfolds in a residence on Doumaine Street in New Orleans just after the Louisiana Purchase. In an article entitled "The Scenes of Cable's Romances" (*Century*, November 1883), Lafcadio Hearn identifies this landmark and affirms the realism of Cable's rendering of the scene for those who made the understandable inference that Cable's exotic settings were a figment of his imagination. Hearn described the locations of Cable's stories so vividly that these locations became the sites for pilgrimages from the North. Today, one of the houses on Doumaine Street, known as "Madame John's Legacy," testifies to Cable's realism and his popularity.

In contrast to the realism of its setting and characterizations, the plot of "'Tite Poulette" seems contrived and unoriginal. It involves three major characters: a still-attractive, thirtyish, quadroon woman named Zalli, who calls herself Madame John; her breathtakingly beautiful "daughter," nicknamed 'Tite Poulette, whose real name is never given; and a naive, unemployed young Dutchman named Kristian Koppig, who watches the corruption that threatens 'Tite Poulette with more and more concern through his dormer window directly across the street from the women's apartment.

Koppig falls in love with 'Tite Poulette. Ordinarily a white man like Koppig might make an arrangement to possess the woman of "caste" he desired. But Koppig is poor and pure, and in any event Madame John has been resisting making just such an arrangement for her seventeen-year-old daughter. Koppig pities the women and fears the worst for the girl. In an attempt to help, Koppig visits the ballroom where Madame John works as a paid dancer and is stabbed. 'Tite Poulette and her mother nurse Koppig back to health, and 'Tite Poulette and Koppig fall more deeply in love. Both are tormented by the law against their marriage, but when Koppig finally asks 'Tite Poulette to marry him despite the law, Madame John produces the papers that prove 'Tite Poulette's Caucasian parentage and make the marriage possible.

The conventionality of some aspects of "'Tite Poulette" and of the racial and sexual views it implies cannot be denied. At the same time, the story illuminates the strength of Cable's sympathy for women on the margins of society. Its forced happy ending cannot erase the vivid impression Cable creates of the "purgatory" of their daily lives.[33] Through the use of suggestion, ambiguity, and veiled allusion, Cable portrays Madame John and 'Tite Poulette's plight, allowing them to reveal themselves through their own actions. Cable's juxtaposition of scenes between the women and scenes in which Kristian Koppig watches them, moving from ignorance to understanding of their danger, establishes the even pace of partial disclosure in the story.

The selective economy of Cable's scene painting in "'Tite Poulette" suggests a decaying society where conventional values have little relevance. For despite their gentility women like Madame John and 'Tite Poulette can expect no protection from white "gentlemen." Only an outsider like Koppig can save them. To Cable's readers and to Koppig, the women's beauty and humanity seem poignantly out of place. Looking at the building where the harried women once lived, Cable directs attention to the windows of their apartment. These windows, which had once been huge and open, have been walled up and later reopened slightly with the addition of small, latticed peepholes in their batten shutters. Through the lattices, which suggest the limited view of the confined lives of 'Tite Poulette and Madame John that the story will provide, Cable's characters survey their neighborhood. The narrator's speculation about the building stresses the furtive, makeshift appearance of these windows and the correspondingly furtive or guarded personalities of the residents: "I do not know who lives there now. You might stand about on the opposite *banquette* for weeks and never find out. I suppose it is a residence, for it does not look like one. That is the rule in that region."[34]

Implying, perhaps, disapprobation of the night lives of the residents, Cable's reference to one of the rules in *that* region introduces the first of several questions about disclosures and appearances in this world of deceptive values. The detailed treatment of the windows of Madame John's and 'Tite Poulette's apartment suggests that life had continued in this neighborhood with a steady, imperceptible decline, but with more and more concern that certain activities remain hidden. "In the good old times of duels, and bagatelle-clubs, and theatre-balls, and Cayetano's circus," Cable remarks with pointed irony, since *good* quite obviously does not mean good at all in this region of the city, "there lived in the portion of this house, partly overhanging the archway, a palish handsome woman, by the name—or going by the name—of Madame John" (p. 214).

The hesitation over Madame John's name reinforces the cautionary description of Madame John's neighborhood and implies that some questions about Madame John may never be answered satisfactorily. Her good humor, her intelligence, and her pride, however, are evident in her appearance: "Though fading, she was still of very attractive countenance, fine, rather severe features, nearly straight hair carefully kept, and that vivid black eye so peculiar to her kind. Her smile, which came and went with her talk, was sweet and exceedingly intelligent" (p. 214).

The observation "You would hardly have thought of her being 'colored'" is fitting. For while Madame John's tinge of color helps explain her solitude, her sadness, her protectiveness of 'Tite Poulette, her anger and her defensiveness, she still seems like any other mother in her love for her daughter. Madame John's flashing smile and her witty conversation suggest her social gifts, but "something told you, as you looked at her, that she was one who had had to learn a great deal in this troublesome life" (p. 214).

The impression that Madame John has had a sad life is deepened by the immediate juxtaposition of her knowledge of "this troublesome life" with 'Tite Poulette's blithe innocence. 'Tite Poulette reveals what Madame John once was. Madame John reveals what 'Tite Poulette must become in the ordinary course of events in the racist, sexist society in which they live. The Creole wolves in the neighborhood call the saints to witness the striking difference between the two women: "'But!'—The Creole lads in the street would say—'—her daughter!' and there would be lifting of arms, wringing of fingers, rolling of eyes, rounding of mouths, gaspings and clasping of hands" (p. 214). Madame John recognizes the danger for 'Tite Poulette and hides her at home.

"And who was this Madame John?" Cable asks. She is a woman who has long been the subject of malicious gossip, he suggests obliquely through her neighbor, the wigmaker. Bending Kristian Koppig's ear with insinuations that, out of coyness or decorum, are not reported fully, the wigmaker says sotto voce: "'Why, you know!—she was'—said the wig-maker at the corner to Kristian Koppig—'I'll tell you. You know?—she was'—and the rest atomized off in a rasping whisper. She was the best yellow-fever nurse in a thousand yards round; but that is not what the wig-maker said" (p. 215).

The wigmaker's character assassination reveals little about Madame John's history, but it reinforces the impression Cable creates of Madame John's unusual alienation from her neighbors. The known facts and her behavior hint at the reasons she is envied and hated. For it is known that Madame John, who resists the acquaintance of her neighbors, received her house as a legacy from an unmarried gentleman named John who protected her while he lived. During Monsieur John's life, Madame John was never called Madame John, for according to custom, while Monsieur John's mother lived, only his wife would have been entitled to be called Madame John. When Monsieur John dies, Zalli, who at that time seems to have her residence elsewhere, brings 'Tite Poulette, an infant, to his bedside. Monsieur John addresses Zalli as though she had been a faithful wife deserving the title Madame John and gives his house to her.

Zalli can move into Monsieur John's house and take his name only upon his death. But she has relied on his protection and is unprepared to deal with the sordid realities of the world of business, for "with the fatal caution which characterizes ignorance, she sold the property and placed the proceeds in a bank, which made haste to fail. She put on widow's weeds, and wore them still when 'Tite Poulette 'had seventeen,' as the frantic lads would say" (p. 216). Thus, since Monsieur John's death, Madame John has steadily been losing ground. A crisis looms before her because 'Tite Poulette now requires more protection than ever. Cable suggests the threat to 'Tite Poulette by alluding to the familiar street-corner scene with the adolescent male pack not yet daring to approach the young woman, who ignores them. At this age, of course, 'Tite Poulette's animated entourage is relatively harmless. However, through cagey denial, Cable implies the universality of the scene, noting that "theirs were only the loose New Orleans morals of over fifty years ago." Although 'Tite Poulette is safe from her adolescent admirers, her status obviously depends upon her mother's status. The next contrasting observation therefore sounds an ominous note: "And yet the mother was soon to be, as we shall discover, a paid dancer at the *Salle de Condé*" (p. 217).

Dancing for pay brings down the curtain on the courtesan's career. Now she must perform for the many what was once reserved for the one. Madame John's recollections of the tawdry heyday of the quadroon balls and of her first lover, however, are poignantly romantic. She does not repent her "happy days" (p. 217) on the margins of polite society, but her feelings about her days of "glory" are, nevertheless, pathetic—not because she has sinned, but because except for that tarnished, transient, happy time, now past, she has known no happiness:

> To Zalli, of course, as to all "quadroon ladies," the festivities of the Condé-street ball-room were familiar of old. There, in the happy days when dear Monsieur John was young, and the eighteenth century old, she had often repaired under guard of her mother—dead now, alas!—and Monsieur John would slip away from the dull play and dry society of Théâtre d'Orléans, and come around with his crowd of elegant friends; and through the long sweet hours of the ball she had danced, and laughed, and coquetted under her satin mask, even to the baffling and tormenting of that prince of gentlemen, dear Monsieur John himself. No man of questionable blood dare set his foot within the door. (p. 217)

Despite Madame John's uncritical memories of the balls "in the happy days when dear Monsieur John was young," her reflections on the festivities of the quadroon ballroom offer a critical perspective on the system she remembers. Significantly, Madame John is not the object of this critical perspective. She is pathetically proud that "many noble gentlemen were pleased to dance with her." Her boasting about the social status of her partners, "Colonel De—— and General La——: city councilmen and officers from the Government House" (p. 217), reveals, instead, the complicity of the rulers of the city in maintaining the demimonde as a relief from the "dull society" of their constrained, pious wives. The Gallic surnames of Madame John's anonymous admirers of bygone days and the masking of the revelers reinforce the suggestion that the men "*slip* away from the dull play and dry society of Théâtre d'Orléans." Madame John's memory that she had been led into this hidden, gay world for the amusement of white males suggests the long history of debasement women on both sides of the color line have suffered at the hands of these men. The fact that many fine gentlemen at the ball now ask about 'Tite Poulette emphasizes the continuity of that history.

Madame John thinks that everything was "decorously conducted indeed!" (p. 217) at the quadroon balls of her youth. Madame John's attachment to Monsieur John explains her rose-colored recollections, for when he dies, she puts on mourning, and "her glittering eyes never again looked through her pink and white mask, and she was glad of it; for never, never in her life had they so looked for anybody but her dear Monsieur John" (p. 218). The depth of Madame John's love for Monsieur John is without question. His attitude toward her is less certain. While he lived, he protected her jealously. Madame John proves her uncritical attachment to her possessor by happily asserting that Monsieur John had often "knocked down some long-haired and long-knifed rowdy, and kicked the breath out of him for looking saucily at her" (p. 217). We sense, however, that the violent Monsieur John may not have been quite the gentleman Madame John believes he was.

Madame John's delusions of former grandeur heighten her sense of shameful decline. Now she works in the ballroom where she was formerly a guest. Madame John's decline as the result of Monsieur John's death, of course, is not peculiar to her or to the other quadroon ladies who were more frequently abandoned than "widowed." White ladies forced to rely on their fleeting beauty for security also found themselves looking back with a sense of loss and confusion on the pretty dresses and flattery of the past. Cable suggests a parallel between Madame John and white women in the only overt social criticism in the story: "Living was hard work; and, as Madame John had been brought up tenderly, and had done what she could to rear her daughter in the same mistaken way, with, of course, no more education than the ladies in society got, they knew nothing beyond a little music and embroidery" (p. 218). Fleeting beauty and a smattering of decorative skills cannot maintain Madame John and 'Tite Poulette any more than they can maintain Cable's white ladies in *The Grandissimes*.

Grinding poverty and social ostracism force Madame John back to the *Salle de Condé* to earn a living for herself and 'Tite Poulette. There she dances the *Danse du Shawl* beautifully; and, whether the shawl drops or not, Cable emphasizes the nobility of Madame John's sacrifice in taking off her mourning costume, in touching her face with powder and paint to restore the appearance of her former freshness, and in working on Sunday. Madame John's rationalization, "It had to be done. It brought some pay, and pay was bread" (p. 220), states the extremity of the women's situation.

The emotional cost of the decision to return to the ballroom appears in the women's behavior on Sunday nights, when 'Tite Poulette paces for hours until her mother, "like a storm-driven bird, came panting home" (p. 220).

Having no friends, Madame John must consort with the enemy, personified by Monsieur de la Rue, the proprietor of the *Salle de Condé,* a man Kristian Koppig recognizes as instinctively "as one knows a snake" (p. 219). Here, the symbolic associations of the snake with sin, specifically with unrestrained sexuality, are obviously exploited, and the implication that Monsieur de la Rue may be a procurer is obviously to be drawn. The images of Madame John as a "storm-driven bird" and of 'Tite Poulette as her "little chick" caught in the toils of an unctuous male predator are sustained by the precision of Cable's description of Monsieur de la Rue. Monsieur is "a smooth man, with his hair parted in the middle, and his cigarette poised on a tiny gold holder," and he carries a sword cane (p. 218). But it is Monsieur de la Rue's attitude and the social approval of that attitude that define the threat he poses for Madame John and 'Tite Poulette. Knocking insistently at their door, cursing the dust, and wiping the inside of his hat with his handkerchief, Monsieur de la Rue asserts his seigneurial privileges. Monsieur's arrogance is seconded and compounded by a neighborhood boy, who eggs him on by saying, "Knock hard!" (p. 228). Clearly, except for Kristian Koppig, all the men in 'Tite Poulette's world are predators or their accomplices.

Monsieur de la Rue brings about the crisis in the lives of Madame John and 'Tite Poulette when he sees the girl for the first time and attempts to arrange to have her join her mother at his ballroom. Monsieur is just going home after a night of debauchery; Madame John and 'Tite Poulette are entering the cathedral. The confrontation between Madame John and Monsieur de la Rue with 'Tite Poulette silent in the background captures the inflections and intentions of the mother and the procurer:

> "Madame John," whispered the manager.
>
> She courtesied.
>
> "Madame John, that young lady—is she your daughter?"
>
> "She—she—is my daughter," said Zalli, with somewhat of alarm in her face, which the manager misinterpreted.
>
> "I think not, Madame John." He shook his head, smiling as one too wise to be fooled.
>
> "Yes, Monsieur, she is my daughter."
>
> "O no, Madame John, it is only make-believe, I think."
>
> "I swear she is, Monsieur de la Rue."
>
> "Is that possible?" pretending to waver, but convinced in his heart of hearts, by Zalli's alarm, that she was lying. "But how? Why does she not come to our ball-room with you?"

Zalli, trying to get away from him, shrugged and smiled. "Each to his taste, Monsieur; it pleases her not."

She was escaping, but he followed one step more. "I shall come to see you, Madame John."

She whirled and attacked him with her eyes. "Monsieur must not give himself the trouble!" she said, the eyes at the same time adding, "Dare to come!" (pp. 224–25)

This episode convincingly presents the underlying attitudes of Monsieur de la Rue and Madame John. Monsieur can afford to be polite and to press his point later, sure of winning as he always does. Madame John cannot afford to be impolite, although Monsieur de la Rue threatens her. The manager's demands and Madame John's defiance remain tacitly understood. The realistic treatment of Madame John's Gallic shrug and her turn of phrase when she says, "Each to his taste, Monsieur; it pleases her not" and "Monsieur must not give himself the trouble"—literal translations of French idiom—reinforce the realism with which she is depicted. The understated responses here illuminate the real terror of Madame John's situation and explain why she barricades 'Tite Poulette in the apartment and refuses to return, even to collect her salary, to the ballroom where Monsieur presides.

In the scene with Monsieur de la Rue in the cathedral and throughout the story, Madame John upstages 'Tite Poulette. But an attempt to emphasize the inevitability of 'Tite Poulette's becoming a Madame John herself seems to motivate Cable's change of emphasis from the conventional story of the pristine tragic octoroon to a more realistic story of her sinned-against mother. Even 'Tite Poulette, however, is treated more realistically than her prototypes in earlier fiction. For, although she resembles the tragic octoroons of earlier fiction and although this resemblance must be attributed in part to Cable's conscious exploitation of the sentimental stereotype in order to obtain sympathy for 'Tite Poulette and her plight, 'Tite Poulette's character may also be seen quite realistically as the product of Madame John's knowledge of the realities in their world and her attempt to shield her daughter from these realities.

Cable might have treated 'Tite Poulette with saccharine sentimentality, but he handles her with restraint. Kristian Koppig, who has a romantic bias, writes her mother in the Netherlands about 'Tite Poulette and summarizes her situation: "In this wicked city, I see none so fair as the poor girl who lives opposite me, and who, alas! though so fair, is one of those whom the taint of caste has cursed. She lives a lonely, innocent life in the midst of corruption, like the lilies I find here in the marshes, and I have great pity for her. . . . I know there is a natural, and I think proper, horror of mixed blood (excuse the mention, sweet mother), and I feel it, too; and yet if she were in Holland to-day, not one of a hundred suitors would detect the hidden blemish" (pp. 222–23).

The "tint of color in her Southern cheek" (p. 216) and the "magnifi-cen[ce]" (p. 220) of her "flashing" (p. 221) dark eyes may or may not lend a racial cast to the description of 'Tite Poulette. Notwithstanding such am-biguous details, the racist attitudes Koppig reflects in this letter do not contaminate the narrative; for 'Tite Poulette's beauty, sweetness, and purity do not depend on her race. Cable stresses the similarity of all young women without regard to their race in his treatment of her. Watching the world go by from the small lattice openings in the windows of her apartment, 'Tite Poulette behaves like many other young women in confined situations; she falls in love with the first nice young man in the vicinity and dreams up ways to be where he will be and ways to be seen by him.

She plants a hanging garden at her window directly across from Kop-pig's dormer and waters her garden incessantly until the plants develop root rot. Her "cigar-boxes with wretched little botanical specimens in them trying to die" (p. 226) show her interest in Koppig, her love for beauty, her deprivation in her narrow world, and her desire for escape. The cultivation of flowers, of course, is a familiar pursuit of the stereotyped, chaste hero-ine, but in New Orleans, a city famous for the profusion of its exotic flowers and plants, a pathetic, makeshift garden such as this one testifies to poverty and isolation as well as to stereotypical purity and sweetness. Fur-ther, in describing 'Tite Poulette as an inept gardener, Cable is playing against the horticultural emphasis in descriptions of the "good" woman in nineteenth-century literature. In *All the Happy Endings*, Helen Waite Pa-pashvily notes that such a woman had an infallible way with flowers. She "wore a few violets at her throat, some jasmine tucked in her belt; she dropped pansies . . . as she went, on graves, in sickrooms, at balls, at meet-ings and partings." The "influence" of her floral presence or remembrance "was enough to keep a good man on the right track or bring the most hardened sinner to repentance."[35]

That Madame John has the larger role in "'Tite Poulette" is evidence of Cable's daring in suggesting in a nonjudgmental way the tragic dimensions in the character of a woman with a past. But beneath her sweetness, 'Tite Poulette has a sense of mischief and a strength of will appropriate in the cherished, beautiful, only daughter of a widowed mother. The discussions between 'Tite Poulette and Madame John provide insight into the injustice of Madame John's and 'Tite Poulette's suffering and intensify the ambiguity surrounding 'Tite Poulette's true racial identity. Cable maintains the ambi-guity of these scenes without sacrificing the credibility of either 'Tite Poul-ette or Madame John until the end. He controls the tendency of such scenes to veer toward melodrama by the delicacy of his treatment and by the brightness of his characterizations. Thus, he closes one scene by having Madame John and 'Tite Poulette look out of their window to see whether they have been overheard by their Dutch neighbor. Madame John quiets 'Tite Poulette's alarm by saying lightly "He speaks—oh! ha, ha!—he speaks—such miserable French!" (p. 224). In her Gallic chauvinism, Madame John anticipates Cable's white Creole heroine, Aurora Nancanou, who infuriates her young Creole husband with her linguistic ineptitude when he attempts to coach her in English. As a woman, she has far fewer opportunities to talk with the enemy than he. But perhaps her inability to learn is also a kind of passive resistance to his dominance, for she scorns the language of the *Américains*. Cable depicts her scorn by having her take a letter written to her in English and hold it out "as if she was lifting something alive by the back of the neck."[36]

Clearly, if 'Tite Poulette is white, as Madame John insists she is, Koppig is not the answer to Madame John's prayers for her. This fact and the thread of racial ambiguity so conveniently unraveled by Madame John's final disclosure raise questions about the truth concerning 'Tite Poulette's race. Two consecutive scenes between mother and daughter sustain the ambiguity about 'Tite Poulette's race, allowing for Madame John's climactic confession but throwing doubt on its truth. In the first scene, the women discuss 'Tite Poulette's prospects. Madame John thanks God that her daughter has no lover. However, she forecasts 'Tite Poulette's future and predicts to her that "you will be lonely, lonely, all your poor life long." "There is no place in this world for us poor women. I wish that we were either white or black!" Madame John says (p. 221). The impact of this wish resides in its ambiguity. Whether Madame John regrets that she and her daughter are not of the same race or that they are both so fatally "mixed," Madame John's lament that there is no place for women like her is a moving appeal for acceptance as a human being regardless of race.

Madame John's despair becomes anger when she imagines an escape for 'Tite Poulette and sees that escape closed off by legal prohibitions. In the next scene between the two women, Madame John attempts to make her daughter promise to accept a proposal from a white lover without confessing her "taint." Impatiently, 'Tite Poulette reminds her mother of the law. "But the law is unjust," urges Madame John. "I would surely tell him!" 'Tite Poulette rejoins (p. 223).

We feel the depth of Madame John's love for 'Tite Poulette in these scenes and doubt that she would have concealed 'Tite Poulette's true racial identity for so many years for selfish reasons. Furthermore, the consistent high quality of the narrative, dialogue, and characterization in "'Tite Poulette" makes the *ex machina* production of the documents proving 'Tite Poulette's white parentage problematic. However, the problem posed by the ending cannot be denied or dismissed entirely, for Cable wrote of the plan of " 'Tite Poulette": "I portrayed a white girl *falsely* supposed to be of negro extraction, suffering the semi-outlawry to which quadroons and octoroons were condemned by society and the laws in Louisiana during the early years of the present century. But the situation was chosen for its romantic value, a value always recognized in that condition, throughout the South as well as elsewhere."[37]

Through its melodramatic ending Cable's story fulfills this intention. However, Cable came to recognize the inadequacies and the possibilities of " 'Tite Poulette." A letter from a woman of the quadroon caste who had read the story and had been moved by the essential truth and compassion of Cable's writing begged him to rewrite it. Cable explains that this woman urged him to change the story "if you have a whole heart for the cruel case of us poor quadroons" because "Madame John lied! The girl was her own daughter; but like many and many a real quadroon mother, as you surely know, Madame John perjured her own soul to win for her child a legal and honorable alliance with the love-mate and life-mate of her choice."[38] This appeal inspired Cable some six years later to write a truer account of the quadroon's dilemma in *Madame Delphine* (1881).

The delay between Cable's commitment to the reworking of the story of " 'Tite Poulette," begun on his first trip North in 1875, and its completion for serialization in 1881 may reveal Cable's sensitivity to the genteel limitations placed on writers of the period. We tend to forget that Cable's refusal to condemn Madame John for her past on the illicit fringes of genteel society was daring for its time. Moreover, Cable and his family were still living in New Orleans. Cable's caution in releasing a story that would make explicit the social criticism implicit in " 'Tite Poulette" in this potentially hostile community seems understandable. His hesitation to delve more deeply into the ethical problems that emerge in " 'Tite Poulette" may also reflect Cable's inability to resolve his ambivalence about miscegenation. In explaining why *Madame Delphine* remained unfinished so long, Arlin Turner mentions Cable's desire for more pay for his fiction, but speculates that the delay may also indicate Cable's reluctance to argue the cause of the quadroons as directly as he planned in the story.[39]

The Grandissimes

Whatever the reason for the six-year hiatus between the inception and the publication of *Madame Delphine,* Cable did not drop the cause of the quadroons after finishing " 'Tite Poulette." He had an early outline of *The Grandissimes* by March 17, 1877, when H. H. Boyesen wrote him praising his proposed novel and predicting that it would be "the kind of novel which the Germans call 'Kulturroman,' a novel in which the struggling forces of opposing civilizations crystalize & in which they find their enduring monument."[40]

Set in the period just after the Louisiana Purchase in 1803, when political dissension between Creoles and intruding Americans was at its most intense, *The Grandissimes* exposes the tension between contending civilizations and the conflict over the place of the Negro in a phobic, paranoid, slaveholding society. The historical backdrop of *The Grandissimes* includes colonial exploitation and corruption, the founding of rival patriarchal dynasties, duels, quadroon balls, voodoo rituals, slave insurrections, racial hysteria, the failure of the indigo planters, the resulting switch to large-scale cultivation of sugarcane, recurrent yellow-fever epidemics, floods, cultural dissension, massive immigration, and commercial expansion.[41] Through this dramatic backdrop, which he had also employed in " 'Tite Poulette," Cable provided a historical analogue for the political and social conflicts of the Reconstruction period.

In his presentations of Creoles, Americans, quadroons, and Negroes at work and at play, at home and in public, Cable creates a realistic picture of ongoing life that Edmund Wilson calls an "anatomy" of Southern society. The novel's hero, Joseph Frowenfeld, is a twenty-six-year-old American newcomer who tries to understand this seemingly chaotic, alien culture by recording temperature, barometric pressure, and other quantifiable facts of his experience in New Orleans in his daybook. Ultimately, however, Frowenfeld's attempts to objectify his experiences fail, for he cannot maintain his detachment in the face of the brutal treatment of blacks that is sanctioned and carried out according to the terms of the *Code Noir* or in the face of the strange blend of reticence and flirtatiousness of Creole women. Frowenfeld's Puritan ambivalence, which reinforces the complexity of tone in the novel and suggests the characteristically intense love-hate relationship of Southerners and acculturated Northerners with the South, is nowhere more apparent than in his attitude toward the women characters on both sides of the color line.

The novel's central thematic concern with oppression is sustained by Cable's characterizations of three representative, dispossessed women characters—Aurore ("Aurora") De Grapion Nancanou, an aristocratic, impoverished Creole lady who cannot work to support herself because ladies are only supposed to be ornamental; Clemence, a streetwise slave merchant who conceals her angry observations about racism in audacious badinage with her customers and leads the ancient Calinda dance and the songs of derision directed against the whites of the ruling class at night; and Palmyre Philosophe, a brilliant quadroon who has learned many Negro dialects and practices the voodoo arts as a means to insurrection.

Cable's realistic presentation of these women's situations is strengthened by his characterizations of the women themselves. His characterization of Palmyre Philosophe, though flawed, suggests the militant black women of our own time. In "The Serpent of Lust in the Southern Garden: The Theme of Miscegenation in Cable, Twain, Faulkner, and Warren," William Bedford Clark evaluates Cable's departure from the stereotype of the mixed-blood heroine in *The Grandissimes* and writes: "In his creation of Palmyre Philosoph [*sic*], Cable has transformed the usually passive heroine of the 'tragic mulatto' tradition—more sinned against than sinning—into a terrifying physical realization of the spirit of righteous wrath."[42]

Cable's other women characters are more subdued than Palmyre but equally vivid. Aurora Nancanou is generally admired although superficially understood. Clemence, the *marchande des calas* (cake vendor), has also been praised. Philip Butcher, for example, notes Clemence's significance among the wide range of racial types portrayed in *The Grandissimes* and says she is "not unworthy of comparison with Jim, the slave Mark Twain's genius provided as foil and companion for the immortal Huck Finn."[43]

Cable's presentation of the bonding of these women, for protection from and in defiance of the authority of white males, forms a counterpoint to his presentation of the treacherous behavior of white men toward the women dependent on them. The lynching of Clemence, who had nursed one of her murderers as an infant, is a terrifying instance of such treachery. But repudiations of human ties of all kinds are shown to be characteristic of the males of the ruling class, for even Numa Grandissime, who, it is said, was more humane than most of his male kin, "nobly sacrificed a little sentimental feeling" (p. 108) by deserting the quadroon mother of his illegitimate son Honoré in order to marry a white woman and to perpetuate the "pure" Grandissime line. The Grandissime women are not blameless, for they comply or submit as they have been taught to do.

Perhaps because he recognized the powerlessness of these women, Cable is relatively, if not completely, sparing of them. In an aside to the reader that betrays contradictory talents for insight and cant, Cable describes the social order of New Orleans in *The Grandissimes* by observing that "the community recognized the supreme domination of the 'gentleman' in questions of right and of 'the ladies' in matters of sentiment. Under such conditions strength establishes over weakness a showy protection which is the subtlest of tyrannies, yet which, in the very moment of extending its arm over woman, confers upon her a power which a truer freedom would only diminish; constitutes her in a large degree an autocrat of public sentiment" (p. 160).

Taken together, Cable's insight into the subtle tyranny of chivalry and his rationalization of such tyranny seem quite extraordinary, especially considering his hatred of oppression, "however gross or however refined" ("The Freedman's Case in Equity," p. 78). The singular of "gentleman" and the plural of "the ladies" may be significant—the sentiments of one lady would presumably have little weight in public deliberations. Furthermore, when seen in the light of his convincing presentations of repeated, shocking violations of the "sentiment" women are supposed to wield in the novel, Cable's facile, perhaps complacent, rationalization of the subtle tyranny of chivalry, which never, in any case, extends to nonwhite women, lacks conviction.

The common enemy of the heroines of the novel on both sides of the color line is Agricola Fusilier, who, as his name implies, represents both the farmer and the soldier aristocracy of the South. He speaks for the "undivided public sentiment" in the novel (p. 59). Agricola's prejudices may be shared in large measure by the unconsulted women of the white aristocracy, but Cable ridicules Agricola's intellectual pretensions and his presumption in speaking for the whole community. A fleeting allusion to the fact that Agricola accosted and slapped a man with whiter skin than his own at a quadroon ball (p. 15) suggests his sexist and racist prejudices. But Cable allows Agricola to expose himself to Frowenfeld at length aloud:

> "H-my young friend, when we say, 'we people,' we *always* mean we white people. The non-mention of color always implies pure white; and whatever is not pure white is to all intents and purposes pure black. When I say the 'whole community,' I mean the whole white portion; when I speak of the 'undivided public sentiment,' I mean the sentiment of the white population. . . . What is that up yonder in the sky? The moon. The new moon, or the old moon, or the moon in her third quarter, but always the moon! Which part of it? Why, the shining part—the white part, always and only! Not that there is a prejudice against the negro. By no means. Wherever he can be of any service in a strictly menial capacity we kindly and generously tolerate his presence." (p. 59)

The racist sentiments Agricola supports here with malapropos allusions to the moon suggest how faint a voice white women actually have in expressing their views, since he tolerates women only when they are at home and in their place. Here and elsewhere in the novel, it is clear that white women count for little with Agricola except as they reflect his prejudices.

In this characterization of Agricola and elsewhere in *The Grandissimes,* Cable discloses the subordinate status of women in Creole society, illuminating the distinct, yet complementary, experience of women on both sides of the color line and establishing a context in which both racial and sexual oppression can be seen as features of complex social processes that support patriarchy. The conflict between what Cable says on occasion and what he shows repeatedly throughout *The Grandissimes* when describing the subordinate status of his women characters, however, creates a problem for the reader. Significantly, this problem has not concerned critics, who have suggested that there are contradictory impulses in the novel and have measured its blending of romanticism and realism. In the introduction to his 1957 edition of *The Grandissimes,* for example, Newton Arvin perceives that the novel "made a sharp break with the central tradition of Southern fiction, as it then was and was long to be" and notes Cable's contradictory impulses, observing that even a fairly responsive reader might come away from *The Grandissimes* with "a sense of having been breathing the warm, soft air of the romantic, and even the sentimental."[44] The interplay in the novel between Cable's contradictory impulses toward women, though previously unexamined in any depth, is quite evident, since these women are often reflections of the contradictory values and desires of their creator—of his chivalrous impulses and artistic empathy and of his salacious and voyeuristic drives.

Cable, however, was not alone responsible for the contradictions apparent in *The Grandissimes.* Any ultimate decision about responsibility for flaws in the novel or its characterizations must take into account the long, painful period of revision that followed Cable's completion in August of 1879 of the manuscript first outlined to H. H. Boyesen more than two years earlier. The protracted editing of *The Grandissimes* and Cable's subsequent works has become a scandal in literary history.[45]

Arlin Turner notes Cable's justifiable irritation with the treatment the manuscript of *The Grandissimes* received in the rush to prepare it for the first installment of serialization in the November 1879 issue of *Scribner's.* For almost two years, batches of the manuscript were mailed back and forth between New Orleans and New York: in the final year, Cable continued to revise copy down to the final galley proofs of the last installments. The editors' meddling, Turner suggests, was unusually intense during this time; they "proposed changes with such urgency that the novel as finally published contained touches from the editors' hands which the author accepted only reluctantly."[46]

The editing of the novel was more exasperating and severe than it might have been, for *The Grandissimes* was Robert Underwood Johnson's first editorial assignment, and although he was sympathetic with Cable, Johnson saw his own career in the balance. Johnson, a Southerner, wrote Cable of his feelings of close identification with the project: "You must remember that my reputation as an editor is involved as well as yours as a writer."[47] Two more Southerners, Mrs. Sophia Bledsoe Herrick, the daughter of the slavery apologist Albert Bledsoe, and Irwin Russell, the Mississippi poet remembered for "Christmas Night in the Quarters," reinforced its conservative tone. Johnson's postcard to Cable of August 18, 1879, implied that the editors anticipated intense labor on the manuscript to ready it for serialization. Johnson wrote: "Your MS *contains* a superb story, overlaid with too much purpose. A story without a purpose is an absurdity, but you have enough for three."[48] The zeal of Johnson, Herrick, and Russell may have introduced contradictions and inconsistencies into the novel as well as expunging them from it.

One telling example of the minutiae that the editors debated appears in Russell's objection to the scene in which Palmyre Philosophe, a quadroon, embraces Honoré Grandissime, a white gentleman, upon his return from ten years of schooling in Paris. "Alteration is imperatively required," Russell wrote. But Russell apparently did not understand that different customs concerning interracial public displays prevailed in New Orleans, for Cable replied with an extended explanation and concluded, "I must beg you not to omit it."[49]

Notwithstanding the problems *The Grandissimes* poses for both the literary scholar and the reader, it is the first novel from the South to attack Southern racial attitudes so directly, and it is among the first Southern novels to make women significant in its treatment of Southern society. For while white women may have been central to the plantation legend, as William Taylor maintains in *Cavalier and Yankee,* women had inhabited the shadows in most Southern literature of the antebellum period. In the literature of popular postbellum women authors such as Augusta Evans [Wilson] and Mrs. E. D. E. N. Southworth, though the issue of woman's place was repeatedly broached, women characters were only nominally Southern.[50] In "Frivolity to Consumption: or, Southern Womanhood in Antebellum Literature," John C. Ruoff surveys Southern literature of the nineteenth century and finds that the women portrayed in Southern novels of the postbellum period are not identifiably Southern at all but rather "are typical of the women portrayed in sentimental novels of the latter half of the nineteenth century without regard to region."[51]

Cable, however, departed from the pattern in delineating women in the society he examined. His women characters are not merely adjuncts to standard love plots, since he chose to make them both humanly detailed and distinctively Louisianian. The violent, oppressive milieu that shapes the characters of these women and the characters of all of the individuals in the novel is distinctively, frighteningly Southern. "Hints, allusions, faint unspoken admissions, ill-concealed antipathies, unfinished speeches, mistaken identities and whisperings of hidden strife" (p. 96) surround the violent events of the story, which include a lynching, a suicide, two stabbings, two shootings, a scene of vandalism, and a gruesome mutilation.

Inevitably, the romantic counterpoint to the violence of *The Gran-dissimes* seems trite and unrealistic. Although three love stories in *The Gran-dissimes* were a selling point of the serialized story for a growing but not particularly discriminating magazine audience, and although women characters are necessary for these standard love stories, Cable's women characters are a much more significant part of the social texture and the thematic concern of the novel than has usually been supposed. While these women characters are somewhat circumscribed by the love stories, so too are all the male characters between the ages of eighteen and forty.

Despite editorial meddling, sentimental effusion, inconsistent authorial commentary, and formulaic handling of numerous love stories, *The Gran-dissimes* is filled with characters who are vivid, substantial, and dramatically self-validating. Almost all of these characters are new to fiction. Even among the Creoles of New Orleans, Cable found defenders who admitted the painstaking accuracy of his portraits of Creoles. The broken English of Cable's Creole characters infuriated many in the Creole community, but G. H. Clements, who had Creole relatives and was well acquainted with New Orleans Creole society, praised Cable's rendering of their accent and their idiom. Amused, Clements reported that his aunt was beside herself because of Cable's "ridicule" of Creole speech and that she asserted angrily: "'Tees not so, he naver hyar peeple talk so."[52]

Moreover, in his reproduction of the dialect of the Creole ladies, Aurora and Clotilde Nancanou, Cable implies the irrelevance of their "sentiments" to men like Agricola through a realistic presentation of their "charmingly" broken English. Unlike the white Honoré, whose opinions count in Creole society and who as a white male possesses the power to confer privilege on the woman or women he chooses, Aurora and Clotilde are cloistered with one another. Their voices are as indistinguishable as the notes of two caged birds. It is no accident certainly that the quadroon Honoré, the half brother of the white Honoré, also speaks broken English. Emasculated by racism, the quadroon Honoré also "stands at the opposite end . . . of the dialect continuum" in relation to his white brother.[53] The oppression he suffers marks his speech as surely as it marks that of the white ladies.

Many critics approved the accuracy of Cable's record of Creole speech in *The Grandissimes;* some of them perceived the subversive nature of his message. Objecting to Cable's portrait of the mulatto Honoré Grandissime and commenting that he feared *The Grandissimes* would appeal most to admirers of *Uncle Tom's Cabin,* the reviewer of the New Orleans *Democrat,* for example, admitted that Cable's characters "were and are living, breathing men and women, transferred from actual life to his pages, made immortal by their repeating everyday speech and manners."[54]

In "After-Thoughts of a Story-Teller," Cable confirmed that he had, indeed, drawn his characters in *The Grandissimes* after living models: "In *The Grandissimes* every prominent character is drawn from a model—including Frowenfeld—except Clotilde, who, I think, any reader will say, is both more real and more attractive than the apothecary. Aurore's model was at least as beautiful and charming as she is portrayed, and in the same ways."[55]

Everyone in the society that had been the model for *The Grandissimes* is implicated in or victimized by the violence and injustice such a social order generates. In "Literature in the Southern States" (1882), one of his first public addresses, Cable described the stifling effects of the closed Southern system and said that the order of society was "fixed, immovable, ironbound. . . . No moral question was open for public discussion. All was isolation. The whole South, except in the cities, was turned by the plantation idea into a vast archipelago of patriarchal estates whereof every one was a complete empire within itself and looked to its neighbors for little else than to supply matrimonial alliances to its imperial family."[56]

In *The Grandissimes*, Palmyre Philosophe becomes the indictment of the sexism and racism of this static world, for Palmyre possesses dynamism, strength, and intelligence—qualities necessary for the survival of any society but devalued and ultimately lost if they appear in a black or a woman. But Palmyre is more than "a terrifying physical realization of the spirit of righteous wrath,"[57] although she is finally reduced to this symbolic single dimension. Initially, she is a self-conscious, complex character, possessed by and possessing the duality of experience and motivation of a woman stranded between antagonistic races. In "That Outward Existence Which Conforms: Kate Chopin and Literary Convention," Emily Toth recognizes Palmyre's importance in *The Grandissimes* and perceives that "only Palmyre sees the tie between patriarchy and racism, two caste systems in which an individual's possibilities are defined at birth."[58]

Joseph Frowenfeld acknowledges the justice of Palmyre's hostile response to white men who degrade her because of her sex and her race. Discovering through one of Palmyre's baleful glances that she "hated men" (p. 134), Frowenfeld cannot resent her hostility. He understands that "this woman had stood all her life with dagger drawn, on the defensive against what certainly was to her an unmerciful world. . . . So far as Palmyre knew, the entire masculine wing of the mighty and exalted race, three-fourths of whose blood bequeathed her none of its prerogatives, regarded her as legitimate prey" (pp. 135–36). Cable's development of Palmyre's silent, brooding character is consistent with Frowenfeld's first impression of her. By refusing to define herself as patriarchal society defines women of her caste, Palmyre becomes the "final, unanswerable white man's accuser" in the novel (p. 134). Significantly, Palmyre exempts white women from her rage. Having made the connection between racism and sexism, she recognizes the enemy and bides her time.

Palmyre's insurrectionary rage makes her an obvious departure from the passively virtuous tragic octoroons and quadroons of earlier fiction. Like Harriet Beecher Stowe's Cassy, Palmyre is bent on revenge, but Palmyre's rage remains unsoftened by Christianity or by contrition. It is truly terrifying because it is convincingly and unapologetically motivated. The frisson of the unwary spectator in response to the adolescent Palmyre's menacing appearance of great passion and great coldness prepares for Frowenfeld's reaction, many years later, to her unsettling adult personality:

> While yet a child she grew tall, lithe, agile; her eyes were large and black, and rolled and sparkled if she but turned to answer to her name. Her pale yellow forehead, low and shapely, with the jet hair above it, the heavily pencilled eyebrows and long lashes below, the faint red tinge that blushed with a kind of cold passion through the clear yellow skin of the cheek, the fullness of the red, voluptuous lips and the roundness of her perfect neck, gave her, even at fourteen, a barbaric and magnetic beauty, that startled the beholder like an unexpected drawing out of a jewelled sword. . . . To these charms of person she added mental acuteness, conversational adroitness, concealed cunning and noiseless but visible strength of will; and to these, that rarest of gifts in one of her tincture, the purity of true womanhood. (pp. 59–60)

Clearly, Palmyre possesses the fierce strength of will and intelligence to preserve her purity rather than the conferred, unapproachable status that helped the white woman preserve hers. Subsequent descriptions of Palmyre's adult beauty, however, sustain the disturbingly sensationalistic tone evident in this description by exploiting new chilling paradoxes to imply Palmyre's "cold passion" and her quiet fury. Such paradoxical formulations are a familiar racist way of perceiving the presumably antagonistic impulses of a character with a divided racial inheritance. But Palmyre, in contrast to the women characters created by racist writers, manages to preserve her purity and her dignity against the predatory society she confronts.

Cable's emotion-charged diction and imagery in describing Palmyre have bothered his critics. James R. Frisby, Jr., quotes Cable's description of the "feline" Palmyre, who "with all her superbness [is] a creature that one would want to find chained," attributing sadomasochistic fantasies to Cable. Frisby writes: "Evidently, the author wishes he had the chains, but clearly he does not mean the chains of slavery. The passage is as overtly sexual as any popular American writer could get in the period."[59] Equally gratuitous comments from other critics reveal the current predisposition to look for the libidinal tensions in literary works, a predisposition that may seriously hamper our understanding of Cable and Palmyre.

A close examination of Palmyre's interaction with Joseph Frowenfeld sheds light on this confusion about Cable's unconscious motives in his treatment of Palmyre. For Cable's dramatization of Palmyre's and Frowenfeld's responses to each other is consciously calculated to show first Frowenfeld's susceptibility to a Latin view of the quadroon woman despite his inhibiting, puritanical Anglo-Saxon views and then Palmyre's vulnerability and her need to be accepted as a human being despite her hostile pose. The suppressed sensuality that many critics detect in Palmyre's and Frowenfeld's interviews betrays Frowenfeld's unacknowledged attraction to this woman whom society has tarred with lascivious availability.

In the mounting tension of the first and second encounters between Palmyre and Frowenfeld, he, to his dismay, becomes increasingly conscious of her strong sensual appeal. At the same time, Palmyre's attitude toward Frowenfeld changes from suspicion to trust. The irony of this situation is that Frowenfeld's superior morality does not prevent him from responding to a quadroon woman as other white men have also been conditioned to respond. Palmyre's misfortune is that she will always be misunderstood in this way, despite her need for understanding and respect.

Louis D. Rubin, Jr., takes note of the disturbingly ambiguous nature of the first temptation scene between Frowenfeld and Palmyre: "The scene in which Joseph Frowenfeld goes to her quarters to tend her wound in place of the ill Doctor Keene, and administers to her as she lies in her bed, is full of a repressed sexuality made only more smoldering by Cable's claim that Frowenfeld, almost alone of the men she knows, does not look upon the quadroon woman as a sexual object."[60]

The close of this initial intimate scene shows Frowenfeld's as yet unacknowledged physical attraction to Palmyre. It is worth noting that Cable has not said that Frowenfeld does not or cannot see what other white men see—the vulnerability of Palmyre and its attractiveness. What Cable says is that Frowenfeld differs from the men Palmyre has known because he does not regard her as "legitimate prey." Frowenfeld's subsequent confusion about his feelings for Palmyre is foreshadowed by his troubled departure at the end of this first interview: "It was many an hour after he had backed out into the trivial remains of the rain-storm before he could replace with more tranquillizing images the vision of the philosophe reclining among her pillows, in the act of making that uneasy movement of her fingers upon the collar button of her robe, which women make when they are uncertain about the perfection of their dishabille, and giving her inaudible adieu with the majesty of an empress" (p. 136).

For the moment, and only because of Frowenfeld's humanity toward her, Palmyre lets down her guard. Earlier in this same scene, Palmyre behaves with the same kind of self-disclosing naturalness when she visibly warms to the apothecary because he respectfully removes his hat when he sees her. The candor and vulnerability of Palmyre's reactions on both occasions suggest that for all her imperiousness she is starved for those signs of courtesy that white women receive as though by right.

Frowenfeld's uneasiness in the presence of Palmyre and her contrasting acceptance of him are reemphasized in the scenes between them that follow. Palmyre comes to rely more and more on the pure, disinterested friendship of Frowenfeld, while he comes more and more to mistrust his own reactions to her. At the opening of the novel, the white Honoré Grandissime observes to Frowenfeld that those who move to New Orleans eventually go native: "You must get acclimated, . . . not in body only, that you have done; but in mind—in taste—in conversation—and in convictions too, yes, ha, ha! They all do it—all who come. They hold out a little while—a very little; then they open their stores on Sunday, they import cargoes of Africans, they bribe the officials, they smuggle goods, they have colored house-keepers. My-de'-seh, the water must expect to take the shape of the bucket; eh?" (p. 37).

In his final encounter with Palmyre in her bedchamber in a chapter pointedly entitled "Another Wound in a New Place," Frowenfeld begins to comprehend his own potential for becoming acclimated to the seductions of the South. When Palmyre seizes Frowenfeld's hand to beseech his help, he experiences and recognizes the surge of his own repressed desire. Frowenfeld's overt, sexual response is unconcealed even by genteel literary evasion: "However harmless or healthful Joseph's touch might be to the Philosophe, he felt now that hers, to him, was poisonous. He dared encounter her eyes, her touch, her voice, no longer. The better man in him was suffocating. He scarce had power left to liberate his right hand with his left, to seize his hat and go" (p. 201).

Misinterpreting the violence of Frowenfeld's reaction to Palmyre's touch, Palmyre's slave maid comes to her rescue with a blow that stuns Frowenfeld and sends him out into the street hatless and bleeding. In the brief scandal that ensues, Frowenfeld defends himself vigorously against the slander that he has been visiting a quadroon, while his neighbors, in contrast, are vaguely entertained at this piece of gossip only because they had assumed that Frowenfeld was a cold fish.

Cable stages the interviews between Palmyre and Frowenfeld to show the pull of the culture on Frowenfeld. Palmyre's stigmatized beauty rather than her seductiveness elicits the response from Frowenfeld, who is described experiencing a "thrill of disrelish" (p. 290) when he again confronts her. At the same time, however, the interviews between Palmyre and

Frowenfeld reveal the underlying complexity of Palmyre's character and the pathos of her situation. In spite of her understandable hatred of most white men, Palmyre is still capable of making exceptions, but she will never find the pure friendship she longs for.

Palmyre's sad history, told throughout the novel in *Rashomon*-like fragments, explains why she is the guarded character she is. Of all the characters in *The Grandissimes*, Palmyre is the least talkative. Lacking the Latin volubility of the other characters, she makes her presence felt through her gestures and her majestic and ominous silences. Frustrated in her love for the white Honoré Grandissime and relegated to the pariah status of the quadroon woman, Palmyre meditates on revenge. The details of her history justify her commitment to vengeance. Palmyre's rage, however, seems not to be merely personal. Her connections among the other blacks in the novel, her command of many Negro dialects, her political awareness of slave insurrections elsewhere, and her plans to use the African slave prince, Bras-Coupé, to foment a bloody rebellion evidence her political aims.

Palmyre's need for autonomy appears from the first. A member of the De Grapion family, whose last remaining legitimate heir is Aurora De Grapion Nancanou, Palmyre possesses the suicidal pride of the De Grapions. As a child Palmyre was precocious and proud, and when she was given to Aurora to be her slave maid, Palmyre soon took charge of her mistress, since of the two little girls, Palmyre was the "ruling spirit" (p. 60). Palmyre remains the dominant of the two women, although the De Grapions soon send her away in order to protect Aurora from being ruled by her.

At the Grandissime mansion, where she lives on loan from the De Grapions, Palmyre also becomes an embarrassment, first because of her arrogance and strange power and her unwillingness or inability to "present herself in the 'strictly menial capacity'" (p. 61), and then because of her passion for the white Grandissime princeling, Honoré. Palmyre's passion for this exceptional member of the white ruling class temporarily holds her violence in check.

Palmyre's longstanding unrequited love for the white Honoré becomes a wretched, interracial triangle with the addition of the older Honoré, a free man of color and the "dark sharer" (p. 279) of the dishonor of the Grandissime family. Cable's racial ambivalence may be reflected in the demoralized mulatto Honoré's inferiority to his younger brother of the same name, for the two men attended the same Parisian schools, but the mulatto brother speaks and writes like an inferior. Cable exploits the confusion over the identities of two characters of the same name and uses the mulatto Honoré's diffident behavior and his thick dialect to distinguish between them. The constraints on the male quadroon appear in the mulatto Honoré's behavior in the presence of whites. When he visits Frowenfeld, the mulatto Honoré never sits down with the apothecary. When other white people come into the pharmacy, the mulatto Honoré invariably departs.

Characterized by Cable as a "man of strong feeling and feeble will (the trait of his caste)" (p. 197), Honoré, f. m. c. (free man of color), becomes a contrast to Palmyre, who rejects him because she seeks strength in the man she loves. Palmyre's attraction to the kind of strength and stature she herself possesses can be seen in her response to Bras-Coupé. The memory of Bras-Coupé's shipment from Africa on a ship ironically named *Egalité*; his purchase by the brother-in-law of the white Honoré; his refusal to demean himself by work; his passion for Palmyre; and his being maimed after striking his master in defiance of the *Code Noir*—the memory of all this is still vivid for everyone Frowenfeld meets. The suspenseful allusions to Bras-Coupé, which build until the middle of the novel, when his story is told at length on three separate occasions to three distinct audiences, emphasize the centrality of his story and its message that "all Slavery is maiming" (p. 171).

From their first meeting, Palmyre identifies with Bras-Coupé. After his death she is transformed by this identification. "He seemed to her the gigantic embodiment of her own dark, fierce will, the expanded realization of her lifetime longing for terrible strength" (p. 175). The nexus of Bras-Coupé, Palmyre, and all the women in the novel becomes explicit through Bras-Coupé's sympathy for the "ladies" and their sympathy and identification with him.[61] Palmyre is joined to the African prince in her desire to liberate her people and her desire for revenge. Clemence is joined to him through the horrifying death she suffers at the hands of his murderers. And Aurora Nancanou is joined to him through the appropriation of her property. Aurora asserts her connection to Bras-Coupé with gay despair. "There are many people who ought to have their rights," she says. "There was Bras-Coupé; indeed, he got them—found them in the swamp. Maybe Clotilde and I shall find ours in the street" (p. 260). She fails to understand in her childlike perplexity why the spells on her behalf and the basil she rubs on her doorsill fail to bring money to pay the rent. Palmyre, in contrast, is determined to seize her rights. But while Aurora and Palmyre respond in different ways to the expropriation of their rights, they are both victimized by the social order, and they are therefore sisters under the skin. In fact, like the brothers Honoré and like real-life siblings of antithetical races described by Eugene Genovese and other historians of the Old South, Aurora and Palmyre may have the same father.[62] Appropriately, Palmyre is unguarded and loving in Aurora's company; and we see Palmyre's humanity rather than her protective facade when she and Aurora meet.

In an early scene in which Aurora ventures out alone to visit Palmyre to obtain a love charm, Cable suggests the sisterly relationship between the two women who are unknowingly in love with the same man. The moment Palmyre sees that Aurora is her caller "her whole appearance changed," "[a] girlish smile lighted up her face, and as Aurora rose up reflecting it back, they simultaneously clapped hands, laughed and advanced joyously toward each other, talking rapidly without regard to each other's words" (p. 71). The joy of meeting again after a separation of only a few days subsides, and Palmyre begins to mother Aurora, though the two women are very nearly the same age. Palmyre's spontaneity and her affectionate openness at the beginning of the scene offer insight into the depths of the character she shields from a hostile world.

Mere friendship, however, has not brought Aurora to visit Palmyre, as both women know. Aurora desires a charm to bring love or money or both. Palmyre seizes a letter Aurora carries in her hands. Interrogating Aurora like a parent still supporting a wayward adult child, or an older sister left with the responsibility for a younger sibling, Palmyre looks at the demand for the rent from Aurora's landlord and asks:

"Have you not paid it?"
The delinquent shook her head.
"Where is the gold that came into your purse? All gone?"
"For rice and potatoes," said Aurora, and for the first time she uttered a genuine laugh. . . . Palmyre laughed too, very properly.

(p. 72)

Aurora pretends that she desires a spell only to bring money, but Palmyre gives Aurora the spell she really wants: "She saw that though Aurora might be distressed about the rent, there was something else,—a deeper feeling, impelling her upon a course the very thought of which drove the color from her lips and made her tremble" (p. 72). Aurora fears the magical powers of Palmyre, as do many of the white people in New Orleans. Palmyre's instructions to Aurora at the close of the scene emphasize the contrast between Aurora, who is terrified by magic, regrets appealing to Palmyre's powers for help, and prays "to Fate for Clotilde to come and lead her away as she had done at the apothecary's" (p. 74), and Palmyre, who stages a spell to placate Aurora and to find out what is really on Aurora's mind.

In the scenes between Palmyre and Frowenfeld and this scene between Palmyre and Aurora, Palmyre comes alive through the presentation of her many dimensions: her pride, her magestic beauty, her intelligence, her capacity for deep loyalty and love, her sorrow, her anger, and her consciousness of the role she must play to protect herself. To Cable (who grew up in a community that still remembered the frenzied dances and the exotic rituals of the Place Congo, where the last famous or infamous practitioner of voodoo rites, Marie Laveau, had communed with her followers in the late 1840s) the machinations of a woman conscious of playing this role were entirely conceivable.[63] Palmyre's melodramatic exterior reveals her careful management of the illusion she must project in order to preserve her autonomy.

Therefore just as Clemence affects a "professional merry laugh" (p. 252) and sings her satirical songs, full of political insight and double entendre, to the French, the Spanish, and then the American occupiers of New Orleans, Palmyre puts on outlandish protective coloration for self-defense. Palmyre's anger and defiance are quite as believable as Clemence's anger and Aurora's anger, but Palmyre's means of self-preservation differ from Clemence's and Aurora's because she is a quadroon woman and her dilemma and her character differ from theirs.

Unlike Clemence, who assumes that she has the license of the fool to speak her mind and be ignored, and Aurora, who chatters charmingly and whose charm disguises the unconscious astuteness of her observations, Palmyre is menacingly silent. But, Cable writes, "so, sometimes, is fire in the wall" (p. 175). Palmyre knows how to manage her silences to create fear and respect in other people. Cable shows her manipulative pauses in the scene in which she engineers a "favorable" divination for Aurora. Yet Palmyre's conditioned, calculated ways of dominating events and other people ultimately fail her because, for all her skill, she is a quadroon woman. Thus, in the spell she makes for Aurora, Palmyre unknowingly strengthens Aurora's determination to win the white Honoré Grandissime for a husband. Aurora, of course, succeeds with Honoré where Palmyre has failed, in part because Aurora is white. Similarly, in an earlier attempt to curry favor with the fiancé of her Grandissime mistress, Palmyre unwittingly precipitates the tragic sequence of events that ends in Bras-Coupé's death when she dresses up to meet the African with the fatal result that he falls in love with her and demands her for his wife. Her characteristic behavior appears in her calculations before she meets Bras-Coupé: "It was Palmyre's habit to do nothing without painstaking. 'When Mademoiselle comes to be Señora,' thought she . . . 'it will be well to have Señor's esteem. I shall endeavor to succeed'" (pp. 173–74).

To persuade Bras-Coupé to work, the Señor promises him Palmyre as a mate; and Palmyre becomes one of the unwilling or soon-to-be disillusioned brides in the novel. The promise demonstrates the cavalier attitude of white males toward the rights of black women, for Palmyre pleads against the marriage. It is ironic that her only salvation from this loveless marriage is that she still belongs to the De Grapions, who have merely loaned her to the Grandissime family. Despite her unique experience of sexual coercion, Palmyre is only one of the women in the novel who find a flaw in society's romantic myths about marriage. And although all these women eventually marry—even Palmyre, who miscalculates, pretending to consent to marry Bras-Coupé because she assumes that Agricola Fusilier will stop any wedding he believes she wants—they all question the romantic verities established by the patriarchal order. Even the foremothers of the Creole families in *The Grandissimes* are shown to suffer from the sexist expectations of their societies. The Indian queen Lufki-Humma, the ancestress of the Grandissime family, is killed after presenting her husband with a female infant, for "he was as fully prepared as some men are in more civilized times and places to hold his queen to strict account for the sex of her offspring" (p. 18). The casket-girl who is the ancestress of the De Grapions refuses to marry as she is expected to do and is told, "If you want to live easy and sleep easy, do as other people do—submit" (p. 26).

Because she is basically a romantic soul herself, Aurora Nancanou's witty observations on marriage are the most striking. Aurora epitomizes all the qualities sought after in the traditional lady described by George Fitzhugh, one of the most impassioned advocates of slavery and the subordination of women. Fitzhugh wrote:

So long as she is nervous, fickle, capricious, delicate, diffident and dependent, man will worship and adore her. Her weakness is her strength, and her true art is to cultivate and improve that weakness. Woman naturally shrinks from public gaze, and from the struggle and competition of life. . . . in truth, woman, like children, has but one right and that is the right to protection. The right to protection involves the obligation to obey. A husband, a lord and master, whom she should love, honor and obey, nature designed for every woman. . . . If she be obedient she stands little danger of maltreatment.[64]

Aurora, however, has not fared particularly well by depending on male protection. Her pathetic reminiscences of better days cast doubt upon the protection of marriage as she and the other women in *The Grandissimes* know it: "If we had here in these hands but the tenth part of what your papa often played away in one night without once getting angry! But we have not. Ah! but your father was a fine fellow; if he could have lived for you to know him! So accomplished! Ha, ha, ha! I can never avoid laughing, when I remember him teaching me to speak English; I used to enrage him so!" (p. 66). Here, Aurora's lack of critical perspective about her irresponsible husband, who lost large sums of money with sangfroid but was eventually killed in a duel over a card game, is a telling comment.

In this slaveholding society the institution of marriage was a mockery. Thus, Palmyre can never marry into the white aristocracy, although she bears the blood of the De Grapions. But when she is promised to Bras-Coupé, a letter arrives, presumably written by Aurora's father, who promises that he will "have the life of the man who knowingly had thus endeavored to dishonor one who *shared the blood of the De Grapions*" (p. 176). This means that marriage was often not an option under any circumstances for a woman like Palmyre. Aurora, on the other hand, must marry to survive.

Consequently, although Aurora's betrothal to the white Honoré Grandissime is a happy event, it is also her escape from an unthinkable life without a male protector. Aurora's half-serious advice to Clotilde suggests the absolute dependence of women like Aurora on remaining attractive to men and on surviving by being protected by them: " 'Clotilde, my beautiful daughter,' said Aurora, pushing her bedmate from her and pretending to repress a smile, 'I tell you now, because you don't know, and it is my duty as your mother to tell you—the meanest wickedness a woman can do in all this bad, bad world is to look ugly in bed!' " (p. 288).

Here, Aurora conveys the facts of life with a certain practical acuity consistent with her character. However, in a double-edged conversation between Aurora and her solemn, responsible daughter, Clotilde, later in the novel, Cable suggests the futility of depending on beauty alone. The rent problem still presses upon Aurora and Clotilde in spite of their extraordinary loveliness. Aurora has sought out Palmyre and done everything that might be imagined of an ineffectual nature to procure the necessary money. The more down-to-earth Clotilde has attempted to sell her heavy gold bracelet. They have both tried living on the earnings from guitar and embroidery students but have failed because their pride will not allow them to demand payment. In contrast to Palmyre Philosophe, who is barred from the man she loves but can work to support herself as a hairdresser and a voodoo medium, Aurora and Clotile cannot scrape together enough money to eat. Clotilde complains:

> "It is not so hard to live, . . . but it is hard to be ladies. . . . After all, . . . what troubles us is not how to make a living, but how to get a living without making it. . . . we are compelled not to make a living. Look at me: I can cook, but I must not cook; I am skillful with the needle, but I must not take in sewing; I could keep accounts; I could nurse the sick; but I must not. I could be a confectioner, a milliner, a dressmaker, a vest-maker, a cleaner of gloves and laces, a dyer, a bird-seller, a mattress-maker, an upholsterer, a dancing-teacher, a florist—"
> (p. 255)

Aurora, who has not yet broken the glad tidings to Clotilde that she has snared the white Honoré and solved their financial problems at a single stroke, responds with cynical good humor:

"My angel daughter, . . . if society has decreed that ladies must be ladies, then that is our first duty; our second is to live. Do you not see why it is that this practical world does not permit ladies to make a living? Because if they could, none of them would ever consent to be married. Ha! women talk about marrying for love; but society is too sharp to trust them, yet! It makes it *necessary* to marry. I will tell you the honest truth; some days when I get very, very hungry, and we have nothing but rice—all because we are ladies without male protectors— I think society could drive even me to marriage!" (p. 255)

Although part of Palmyre's tragedy is that she cannot gain the love of the white Honoré, her inability to marry the man she loves is really the least of her problems. In the intrigue to keep from marrying Bras-Coupé (and elsewhere in the novel), Palmyre stands poised and silently plotting. Cable shows her pain at the rejection she experiences as a woman and as a human being. Ultimately, however, Cable's unwillingness to explore fully Palmyre's plans for revenge or revolution deprives her of her complex, exciting dimensions as a character. But it is only after her discovery of the white Honoré's love for someone else that Palmyre devotes herself completely to vengeance and thereby deteriorates as a character. Driven by one motive, she becomes incapable of love, loyalty, gratitude, or complexity of thought. Only then does she become a "physical realization of the spirit of righteous wrath."[65] Her problem is to kill Agricola Fusilier and, Cable implies, to mastermind a slave rebellion. But Cable's treatment of Palmyre the revolutionary possesses a vagueness that his treatment of her personal suffering does not have.

Early in *The Grandissimes,* Cable prepares for the subsequent transformation of Palmyre into an avenging angel by mentioning her fantasies of using Bras-Coupé to wreak vengeance on her enemies. Before the ill-fated wedding when Bras-Coupé fells his master with a single blow of his fist, Palmyre imagines Bras-Coupé sitting docilely at her feet, learning "the lesson she had hoped to teach him" (pp. 183–84). "She had heard of San Domingo, and for months the fierce heart within her silent bosom had been leaping and shouting and seeing visions of fire and blood" (p. 184). When Bras-Coupé stands and curses his master's house before vanishing into the bayou, Palmyre watches his curse decimate the white man's family and destroy his crops as though the working out of their tragedy fulfills her dreams of terrible power. Significantly, Bras-Coupé singles out the white males of his master's family for destruction, saying, *"Mo cé voudrai que la maison ci là et tout ça qui pas femme' ici s'raient encore maudits!* (May this house and all in it who are not women be accursed)" (p. 187).

After Bras-Coupé's death as a result of his maiming in accordance with the grim provisions of the *Code Noir,* Palmyre becomes a voodoo. Among the credulous whites and blacks of the community, it is supposed that Palmyre is possessed by the spirit of Bras-Coupé; and the fear of the Grandissimes and the guilt of her real owners procure her manumission. Although Palmyre plays upon this fear in a calculated way, she knows the limitations of her magic. For when she wants a spell herself, she seeks out Joseph Frowenfeld, who she and many others in New Orleans assume is a sorcerer. Thus, if they exist, Palmyre's magical powers are minimal. But Palmyre has charismatic power. Because she is capable of bending other people to her will and using them to carry out her designs, Palmyre is more dangerous than the African prince ever was.

While Palmyre's violent response to her oppression is not directly condemned, Cable's failure to explore fully her political aims suggests that he may have been uncomfortable with this facet of her character. Cable has Joseph Frowenfeld propose a nonviolent approach to the problems Palmyre attempts to resolve with violence. Frowenfeld's long-winded appeal to the mulatto Honoré to become an antebellum Booker T. Washington may suggest Cable's uneasiness with the threat of bloody revolution. Frowenfeld declaims: "I have no stronger disbelief than my disbelief in insurrection. I believe that to every desirable end there are two roads, the way of strife and the way of peace. I can imagine a man in your place, going about among his people, stirring up their minds to a noble discontent . . . as in each case might seem wisest, for their enlightenment, their moral elevation, their training in skilled work; . . . using all his cunning to show them the double damage of all oppression, both great and petty—" (p. 196).

The anachronism of this post–Civil War appeal to reason to solve the problems of slavery and of the disenfranchised free people of color is apparent. Frowenfeld's beliefs about insurrection simply do not fit the world Palmyre knows. Perhaps because her reactions to oppression clash with such appeals, Palmyre is treated ambivalently throughout the novel. She becomes a "poisonous blossom of crime growing out of crime" (p. 134) and "a creature that one would want to find chained" (p. 71). But Cable's ambivalent treatment of Palmyre falls short of censure; her credibility as a character is weakened but not destroyed. Cable's final refusal either to sanction or to moralize Palmyre's use of the violent tactics of white society places the responsibility for her crimes on the oppressive order that created her. Presumably sheltered under a new and undisclosed name, Palmyre Philosophe as "Madame Inconnue—of Bordeaux" survives to reject the system that defined her as inferior. The last white man to see her reported that she lived alone, insisting on her privacy, and that "he tried to scrape acquaintance with her, but failed ignominiously" (p. 331).

In Palmyre Philosophe, Cable shows a woman divided against herself, not because she possesses the warring impulses of one with a divided racial inheritance, but because of the injustice she suffers. Palmyre must detach herself completely from her society in order to attain a measure of peace. Palmyre's final rejection of the well-intentioned gestures of the white man who seeks her acquaintance implies condemnation of the white men who rule and of the white men who merely go along.

Madame Delphine

Although the message Cable conveys through Palmyre Philosophe is a significant aspect of the thematic concern of *The Grandissimes*, Cable's view of Palmyre and of the women of her caste was neither simplistic nor doctrinaire. Unlike some modern historians who posit one typical reaction to racial oppression, Cable seems to have been aware that individuals respond differently to discrimination. In *Madame Delphine*, the work generally conceded to be Cable's masterpiece, Cable illuminates another convincing yet representative woman of mixed blood. In the character of Madame Delphine, Cable shows the psychic toll inflicted on a woman being held responsible and assuming the responsibility for her own victimization.

Beleaguered by racist opponents who accused him of urging racial "mixing," Cable, who had postponed completing *Madame Delphine* for six years, asserted in the preface to the 1896 edition: "I have a notion I shall always be glad I wrote it." The risk Cable ran in allowing and apparently sanctioning miscegenation in the story suggests the boldness of this assertion; for until 1967, when *Guess Who's Coming to Dinner* announced the media's acceptance of (or rather willingness to exploit) the still shocking idea that there might be a happy ending for an interracial couple, the few interracial affairs or marriages in literature, drama, or film had been implicitly condemned by the psychic pain they produced or by the convenient death of the nonwhite woman, whether she was Eurasian, American Indian, black, or Hispanic.[66]

Madame Delphine challenges racial prejudice by presenting a deeply consistent view of racial questions. The artistic quality of the story strengthens the challenge it issues. The subtlety of Cable's treatment of theme, setting, and characterization helps ensure the readers' response whatever their racial biases. Arlin Turner recognizes the power of *Madame Delphine* and notes the lightness of Cable's touch in allowing "a figure of speech, an ironic turn of thought, a hint of feelings only half expressed" to evoke this response.[67]

Unlike "'Tite Poulette," which introduces a wrenching improbability at its climax, *Madame Delphine* is all of a piece. The title of the story may have been suggested to Cable by the title of Madame de Staël's *Delphine*, the story of a woman who finds her passion for her lover more important than the world's condemnation of that love. Cable's plot, which contains unusual events, is the frame to which his realistic setting and characterizations are inextricably joined. The antecedent action of the story is romantic: on her journey home to live with Madame Delphine, Olive, the beautiful near-white daughter of Madame Delphine's morganatic marriage to a white man, meets, converts, and falls in love with the pirate who boards the vessel she is on; the pirate, Ursin Lemaitre-Vignevielle, leaves the sea and becomes a banker with the proceeds of his piracy; Vignevielle roams the streets of New Orleans at night in hopes of meeting the unknown girl who gave him her missal and converted him. The current problems of the characters in the story, however, are realistic: Olive must adjust to life in the quadroon quarter after being educated as a white girl by her father's relatives. And Madame Delphine must attempt to solve the dilemma of how to keep Olive and yet liberate her from the restrictions placed on women of their caste. The characterization of Madame Delphine, who ultimately fails to resolve conflicting demands placed on her by her desire to be with her daughter and her desire to obtain a better life for her, verifies and informs the whole story. In *Madame Delphine* the pity Cable had shown for 'Tite Poulette and Madame John is transformed into empathy for women stranded between antagonistic races, denied their basic rights as human beings, and victimized by sexism and racism.

The setting of *Madame Delphine* establishes what Henry James called "a palpable imaginable *visitable* past," thus serving to suggest the truth of the events that occur.[68] Cable's subtle control of tone appears from the first lines, when he introduces his reader to the region of New Orleans where Madame Delphine and Olive once lived, approximately sixty years before. Cable establishes rapport with his readers by addressing them directly and by giving them a special tour of the sites usually missed by other tourists. By according his readers this privileged position, Cable sets them up to assume a share of the responsibility for the injustices they witness.

Entering an off-limits region, Cable stresses the cramped, dirty nature of life here: "Many great doors are shut and clamped and grown gray with cobweb; many street windows are nailed up; half the balconies are begrimed and rust-eaten, and many of the humid arches and alleys which characterize the older Franco-Spanish piles of stuccoed brick betray a squalor almost oriental."[69] The contrasts to this scene of exterior decay appear through batten shutters, "opened with an almost reptile wariness," which reveal glimpses of antique lace, brocade, silver and the astonishing appearance outside on the street of a few women of surpassing "patrician beauty." With knowing emphasis Cable adds that the name of the street cannot be remembered, since "names in that region elude one like ghosts" (p. 2).

The initial suggestiveness of this opening is reinforced when Cable focuses on a residence closed off from its neighbors so that "you would say the house has the lockjaw." The shutters at windows and door and the heavy bolt on the garden wall without "are shut with a grip that makes one's knuckles and nails feel lacerated" (p. 3). Later in the story the symbolic appropriateness of this opening becomes clear when we learn that Madame Delphine's disposition more than sixty years before was to lock herself away from the world: "Even in those days the house was always shut, and Madame Delphine's chief occupation and end in life seemed to be to keep well locked up in-doors" (pp. 6–7).

The "simple key to the whole matter" (p. 3), which links past and present in this region of the city and explains the behavior of its inhabitants, is offered by one of the present residents: "Dey's quadroons" (p. 4). Descendants of the "patrician" quadroon beauties who were celebrated in letters and diaries of foreign visitors to New Orleans confirm Cable's description and suggest the misery of the caste that had been glamorized by naive or insensitive writers. Cable describes them in real terms: "Nor, if we turn to the present, is the evidence much stronger which is offered by the *gens de couleur* whom you may see in the quadroon quarter this afternoon, with 'Ichabod' legible on their murky foreheads through a vain smearing of toilet powder, dragging their chairs down to the narrow gateway of their close-fenced gardens, and staring shrinkingly at you as you pass, like a nest of yellow kittens" (p. 5).

Cable's leisurely, realistic introduction to the decline of the quadroon quarter in the 1880s shades all subsequent descriptions of places and persons of the earlier period recreated in *Madame Delphine*. The community's continuing jaded acceptance of interracial liaisons appears in the fact that the tourist's curiosity is answered with blasé local disbelief. In this regard, it would seem *plus ça change, plus c'est la même chose,* for "it would have passed all Creole powers of guessing to divine what you could find worthy of inquiry concerning a retired quadroon woman; and not the least puzzled of all would have been the timid and restive Madame Delphine herself" (p. 4).

The "golden age" (p. 4) of the free quadroon caste of the 1820s, when racial mixing had produced a kind of "splendor" through "a survival of the fairest through seventy-five years devoted to the elimination of the black pigment and the cultivation of hyperian excellence and nymphean grace and beauty," was a time of rampant sexism, Cable implies. The sexist bias in the exploitation of the African is apparent in Cable's hint that only women were singled out for "favor." For this reason, Cable writes of "the *quadroones* (for we must contrive a feminine spelling to define the strict limits of the caste as then established)" (p. 5).

That the white male elite was alone responsible for the creation and perpetuation of this caste system is evident in Cable's passing but pointed observation about the quadroon balls: "The magnates of government,—municipal, state, federal,—those of the army, of the learned professions and of the clubs,—in short, the white male aristocracy in every thing save the ecclesiastical desk,—were there. Tickets were high-priced to insure the exclusion of the vulgar. No distinguished stranger was allowed to miss them." The other unconsidered point of view toward these exclusively white-male pastimes is evident in Cable's suggestive inclusion of Madame Delphine's perspective on the quadroon-ball era: "Madame Delphine, were you not a stranger, could have told you all about it; though hardly, I suppose, without tears" (p. 6).

Through the depiction of two atypical white men, Père Jerome, a Creole priest whose humanitarian tolerance provides a contrast to the irresponsible apathy of his community, and Captain Ursin Lemaitre-Vignevielle, a pirate, Cable provides the social context for an understanding of Madame Delphine's character and her dilemma. Emphasizing the role that social conditioning plays in determining the individual's moral choices, Cable recalls Vignevielle's early training by a martinet grandfather who despised Ursin's gentleness and benevolence and attempted to transform them. "The labors of his grandfather were an apparent success. . . . He had cultivated [Ursin] up to that pitch where he scorned to practise any vice, or any virtue, that did not include the principle of self-assertion. A few touches only were wanting here and there to achieve perfection, when suddenly the old man died" (pp. 8–9).

Considering his training, Lemaitre-Vignevielle's choice of piracy as a profession is as predictable, Cable implies, as Madame Delphine's alliance with a white "protector." Père Jerome recognizes the similarity between the conditioned choices of the pirate and those of the quadroon and provides the text that asserts the community of all sinners in his discussion with his childhood friends about the absent Vignevielle, in fragments from a sermon he preaches, and in his talks with Madame Delphine. Père Jerome's talk about his friend who has turned pirate begins the action of the story and establishes everyone's involvement in the paths taken by Vignevielle and, by extension, Madame Delphine. Père Jerome says: "It is impossible for any finite mind to fix the degree of criminality of any human act or of any human life. . . . There is a community of responsibility attaching to every misdeed. No human since Adam—nay, nor Adam himself—ever sinned entirely to himself. And so I never am called upon to contemplate a crime or a criminal but I feel my conscience pointing at me as one of the accessories" (p. 13).

Later, Père Jerome, whose concern is more about how he should feel than about what he should say, preaches a sermon about corporate responsibility, taking his text from the dying words of the martyr, St. Stephen, who prays for his tormentors: "Lord, lay not this sin to their charge" (p. 19). "Oh, where is there any room, in this world of common disgrace, for pride?" Père Jerome asks his congregation. "Even if we had no common hope, a common despair ought to bind us together and forever silence the voice of scorn!" (p. 20).

Père Jerome perceives the applicability of his text to Madame Delphine and Olive immediately, just as he perceives their caste at a glance. The contrast between the women is pronounced. Madame Delphine is "a small, sad-faced woman, of pleasing features, but dark and faded"; and Olive is "a girl still in her teens, though her face and neck were scrupulously concealed by a heavy veil, and her hands, which were small, by gloves" (p. 20). Père Jerome understands the "simple key" to their problems: they are "quadroons."

In the story that follows Père Jerome's introduction to the women, Olive becomes more and more alien to the world of the quadroon quarter, because it is Madame Delphine's intention that her daughter be protected from that world. The heavy veiling and gloves are only one suggestion of Madame Delphine's scrupulous care of the girl. Cable's lyrical paean to Olive's beauty justifies Madame Delphine's fear for her daughter. Spied on by her lover unawares, as 'Tite Poulette and Clotilde Nancanou had been spied on by Kristian Koppig and Joseph Frowenfeld in Cable's earlier stories, Olive seems the pristine heroine of convention:

> From throat to instep she was as white as Cynthia. Something above the medium height, slender, lithe, her abundant hair rolling in dark, rich waves back from her brows and down from her crown, and falling in two heavy plaits beyond her round, broadly girt waist and full to her knees, a few escaping locks eddying lightly on her graceful neck and her temples,—her arms, half hid in a snowy mist of sleeve, let down to guide her spotless skirts free from the dewy touch of the grass. . . .
> . . . She approaches the jasmine. . . . That neck and throat! Now she fastens a spray in her hair. The mockingbird cannot withhold; he breaks into song. (pp. 42–43)

Here, rhapsodic tone and predictable but sensuously lush imagery disclose how thoroughly Cable delights in the image he has created and in his ability to translate that image into prose. Cable continues in familiar Victorian clichés: "when the heart of the maiden still beats quickly with the surprise of her new dominion," "the holy coronation of womanhood," "the openness of child-nature mingled dreamily with the sweet mysteries of maiden thought" (pp. 43, 44).[70]

Olive's ripe and languorous beauty, her uneasiness in her new home, and her wistful passion for the pirate she met on her voyage home to New Orleans, however, help explain Madame Delphine's reentry into the world. For she can no longer ignore or deny the prohibitions, dangers, and problems of her caste. Cable's brief glimpses of Madame Delphine are much more revealing than his lengthy descriptions of her daughter. She appears to be unusually dispirited even for her age and her caste; but "against a fierce conventional prohibition, she wore a bonnet instead of the turban of her caste" as a courageous gesture of self-assertion (p. 31).

Despite her anger at the degradation she is subject to as a quadroon woman, Madame Delphine feels responsible for the degradation she has suffered. Capturing and conveying Madame Delphine's feelings about her caste with sensitivity, Cable shows her ritual gestures of self-consciousness and shame. In a moving scene with Père Jerome, Madame Delphine's dialogue is subordinated to her revealing hesitation in saying what she really feels. Held in check by shame and impeccable manners, Madame Delphine's conflicting emotions surface and grow in intensity. She begins to speak to Père Jerome almost as though against her will: "She rose bashfully and gave her hand, then looked to the floor, and began a faltering speech, with a swallowing motion in the throat, smiled weakly and commenced again, speaking, as before, in a gentle, low note, frequently lifting up and casting down her eyes, while shadows of anxiety and smiles of apology chased each other rapidly across her face. She was trying to ask his advice" (p. 25).

Madame Delphine's statement of her problem to Père Jerome confirms her conviction that she should be blamed for her suffering. Madame Delphine confesses first that she has done a "cruel thing" by falling in love with Olive's father—when obviously the cruelty, if there was any cruelty, was her lover's—and then that she has done a wicked thing by letting Olive come to live with her. Père Jerome offers a more rational view of Madame Delphine's decisions and tells her that God will make an exception since "sin [was] made easy to her—almost compulsory" (p. 26); Madame Delphine listens gratefully in disbelief.

Madame Delphine's insistent and persistent sense of her own inferiority and evil reappears when Père Jerome asks whether Olive looks like her. Madame Delphine answers: "Oh, thank God, no! you would never believe she was my daughter; she is white and beautiful!" (p. 27). Earlier Madame Delphine has spoken of her "husband" in a similar way, absolving him of all responsibility for their relationship: "He was an American, and, if we take her word for it, a man of noble heart and extremely handsome" (p. 6). The impression created by Madame Delphine's involuntary revelations is reinforced at the close of this scene with Père Jerome, when the priest has another caller and Madame Delphine leaves: "Madame Delphine's eyes ventured no higher than to discover that the shoes of the visitor were of white duck" (p. 30).

Because of her feelings of worthlessness, Madame Delphine cannot be angry on her own behalf. In a scene between Madame Delphine and Vignevielle, she is dismayed at discovering that she has presented his bank with a bogus bill. Yet when Vignevielle shows her the telltale marks of counterfeit but refuses to give back the bill she has given him, Madame Delphine leaves, "loving the ground beneath the feet of Monsieur U. L. Vignevielle," with no thought of seeking police aid to capture the person who has passed her the bill (p. 34). To be certain, the law offers no protection for women like Madame Delphine, for when she discovers that someone has broken into the walled garden behind her house, she and Olive flee into their house, and bar it everywhere against intruders, and fall asleep, "holding each other very tight, and fearing, even in their dreams, to hear another twig fall" (p. 47).

Although Madame Delphine has always fled confrontation, her love for Olive forces her to vent her rage for the first time. Her final discussion of her status and Olive's with Père Jerome brings her nearer to a conscious understanding of racism and sexism. Olive now has a chance to escape the quadroon quarter, for Vignevielle wants to marry her. Demonstrating her force of character, Madame Delphine insists on Olive's right to marry whom she wants. She startles Père Jerome "with a loud, harsh, angry laugh," quite out of character for a woman who has an unusually pleasing, musical, low voice, and launches into a tirade about the law that is harming her child: "Separate! No-o-o! They do not want to keep us separated; no, no! But they *do* want to keep us despised!" . . . "But, very well! from which race do they want to keep my daughter separate? She is seven parts white! The law did not stop her from being that; and now, when she wants to be a white man's good and honest wife, shall that law stop her?" . . . "No; I will tell you what that law is made for. It is made to—punish—my—child—for—not—choosing—her—father!" (p. 62).

The gestural accompaniment to this impassioned rejection of the law against miscegenation prepares for Madame Delphine's last battle and for her collapse at the end of the story; her temporary strength only proves the extremity of her situation. Her tension appears in her savage jerking of a single thread in the fabric of her skirt (p. 60); and her physical weakness, which has already been suggested when Père Jerome asks her whether she has made a will, appears in her grimace of pain as she begins her attack on the law that perpetuates illicit, interracial relationships.

The accumulated details of Madame Delphine's tense gestures are even more eloquent than her angry outburst in conveying the picture of a genteel woman beset by injustice. Her distracted, compulsive folding of the skirt of her faded, dark dress discloses her agitation repeatedly in the story. Her understandable fear of strange men when she ventures out alone and hears a man's footstep behind her or when she sees a man's shoe track in her garden implies the baseness of many white men in the society in which Madame Delphine and Olive live.

When Vignevielle's friends forbid his marriage to Olive, Madame Delphine pushes herself past endurance to provide an escape for Olive from the life she has known. In the penultimate scene of the story, Madame Delphine perjures herself to free Olive. The determination and uncharacteristic boldness of her behavior in this scene and the levity of Vignevielle's friends, who recognize that she is in a "state of high nervous excitement" but are insensitive to her real feelings, are juxtaposed. The humorous observation that Madame Delphine "walks like a man" and the rejoinder, " 'She must not forget to walk like a woman in the State of Louisiana,'—as near as the pun can be translated" (p. 71), recall Cable's definition of the *"quadroone"* caste established for the amusement of white men at the expense of women—whether black, white, or racially mixed. Clearly, Vignevielle's friends can only see the stereotype their community has accepted, for they react in a conditioned way to Madame Delphine. Thus, when one of them asks Madame Delphine to be seated because she is obviously feeling faint, "the ladies rose up; somebody had to stand; the two races could not both sit down at once—at least not in that public manner" (p. 73).

When Madame Delphine produces the fraudulent evidence to prove Olive's white parentage, Vignevielle's friends again reveal their unthinking concern with appearances by believing her lie immediately because Olive is so visibly white. The understated manner of Madame Delphine's lie contrasts to the melodrama of Madame John's confession. To the assembled white people, she says: " '*C'est drôle'*—it's funny . . . with a piteous effort to smile, 'that nobody thought of it. It is so plain. You have only to look and see. I mean about Olive.' She loosed a button in the front of her dress and passed her hand into her bosom. 'And yet, Olive herself never thought of it. She does not know a word' " (p. 74).

With this Madame Delphine produces photographs of an anonymous couple (her dead "husband" and her "sister-in-law"), claiming that they are the parents of Olive. Vignevielle's friends are relieved. But Olive herself is less easy to convince. In the patois Madame Delphine tells Olive that she is not her real mother. Cable underlines the separations created by arbitrary racial distinctions in the total separation of Madame Delphine and Olive at the end of the story. Emphasizing the irony of this loss for Madame Delphine, Cable shows Vignevielle's friends treating her with humane concern only now that it is too late.

In the denouement Madame Delphine witnesses the marriage she has lied to ensure. Staring out from under the rim of her faded, dingy, defiant little bonnet at Olive's wedding, Madame Delphine is a sad, affecting picture: "She sat as motionless as stone, yet wore a look of apprehension, and in the small, restless black eyes which peered out from the pinched and wasted face, betrayed the peacelessness of a harrowed mind" (p. 79).

Père Jerome's compassion for Madame Delphine and his complicity in her lie (for he joins Olive to Vignevielle after testifying to Madame Delphine's "unimpeachable" veracity) give Cable's sanction to the marriage. Because of the perspective the story offers on the tragic life of the quadroon, Madame Delphine's sacrifice seems well worth making; and Madame Delphine's death in the confessional, which has been prepared for throughout the story, seems a blessed deliverance from the guilt society forces on its victims. Cable's indirect indictment of society appears in Père Jerome's final plea on Madame Delphine's behalf: "Lord, lay not this sin to her charge!" (p. 81).

With Père Jerome's plea, Cable powerfully restates his attitude toward Madame Delphine, Palmyre Philosophe, and Madame John. Although we have tended to see Cable principally as a lone crusader against racism, his presentation of the situations of these women of mixed blood and his depiction of the psychological effects of such situations on these women prove the complexity and comprehensiveness of his perspective. The thematic chord that joins the stories of these women reminds us that Cable knew that social injustice ultimately destroys not only the oppressed but also the oppressor. This perception of the mutual dependence of all members of society informs " 'Tite Poulette," *The Grandissimes,* and *Madame Delphine.* It is this perception that allows for Cable's fresh exploration of the problems of the color line.

In " 'Tite Poulette," *The Grandissimes,* and *Madame Delphine,* the early works that establish Cable's importance as a realist, the violated humanity that women of mixed blood share with white women shows that Cable was more deeply conscious of the inequities all women suffer than has been supposed. Cable's presentation of the range of women's responses to oppression in these works redeems worn stereotypes, confirming his grasp of the authentic human problems of all women in a man's world.

CHAPTER THREE

· *Grace King* ·

INGENUES ON THE COLOR LINE

King's Realism

Like George Cable, Grace Elizabeth King drew the inspiration for much of her fiction from the mixed racial milieu of New Orleans. In such works as "Monsieur Motte," "Madrilène; or, The Festival of the Dead," "Bonne Maman," and "The Little Convent Girl," King created women characters whose complexity transcends sexual and racial stereotypes.[1] Cable had found a means to protest the racial inequities of his day covertly by locating his fiction in the romantic past. King joined the issues of race and gender in post–Civil War New Orleans, venting her resentment of Yankee fiat and of male privilege in an ironic examination of the world she knew. Her occasionally inconsistent, but always compelling, treatment of distinctions based on gender, race, and class contains this irony in full measure; for in King's fictional world of the defeated South, black and white males are inept or absent, and black and white women must struggle together to survive with dignity.

King was prompted to set the record straight by her irritation with what she felt were Cable's slighting descriptions of New Orleans Creoles. In *Memories of a Southern Woman of Letters* (1932), King hints at the basis for her resentment of Cable's work when she recalls her meeting with Richard Watson Gilder, Cable's Northern editor, in 1885. In this encounter, King said, she had "hastened to enlighten [Gilder] to the effect that Cable proclaimed his preference for colored people over white and assumed the inevitable superiority—according to his theories—of the quadroons over the Creoles," noting that Cable "was a native of New Orleans and had been well treated by its people, and yet he stabbed the city in the back, as we felt, in a dastardly way to please the Northern press."[2]

Notwithstanding King's initial irritation with Cable, she would add

74

greater depth to the picture he had drawn. Within her "paradigmatic com-munity" of women on both sides of the color line, the rites of passage for girls are perilous.[3] Without a stable patriarchal order to assign women their place, problems of sexual identity for girls entering womanhood inevitably impinge upon problems of racial identity, raising implicit questions con-cerning racial as well as sexual injustice. Considering her credentials as a white supporter of the old order, it is hardly surprising that King was largely unconscious of or confused about the symbiotic relationship be-tween racism and sexism in the society she renders in such detail. But as was the case with George Cable and Kate Chopin, the achievement of King's fiction exceeded her conscious grasp of social issues, confirming the trans-gressive and transformative power of literary art.

Though she mourned the passing of tradition, King was ambivalent about many traditional values. She was particularly suited to recognize the stunting effect of Victorian attitudes toward women. A cultured, bilingual member of an aristocratic but impoverished New Orleans family, King was able to adopt a detached point of view toward the artificiality of the treat-ment of American women in much of the fiction of her day. European literature, which she knew with great familiarity, demonstrated contrasting ways of perceiving and presenting women. So too did the urbane, Euro-peanized culture of her city, where "respectable women took wine with their dinner and brandy after it, smoked cigarettes, played Chopin sonatas, and listened to the men tell risqué stories."[4]

Grace King's cultural sophistication is evident in her first article, "Hero-ines of Novels." This study in comparative literature was undertaken for the Pan Gnostics, a literary society in New Orleans revived by Julia Ward Howe during the Cotton Centennial Exposition in 1885, and was published in the *Times-Democrat* literary page for Sunday, May 31, 1885. It reflects the serious-ness of Grace King's research and, perhaps, the constraint she felt as a woman against acknowledging her authorship. Robert Bush explains that "Heroines of Novels" was signed P. G. because anonymity "was entirely proper for a young woman of New Orleans, where the achievement of newspaper publicity was sometimes frowned upon."[5] Within this society, in which hostility toward the accomplishments of women was disguised as gallantry or indulgence of their "frivolous" pursuits, Grace King was excep-tional because she later came out in the open to strive for the literary success that she ultimately achieved.

"Heroines of Novels" announces King's early dissatisfaction with the way women characters had been handled in literature, a dissatisfaction that would inevitably influence her own characterizations of women. In this tyro effort, Robert Bush says, King "exhibited a wide learning in the four literatures which she was considering, indicating that she had prepared herself in her subject as well as if she had been expecting to pursue a professorship." At this, the outset of her career, Bush continues, "her interest was women in literature, and this was to be her main theme for fiction. . . . she was establishing herself as a kind of advocate, interpreter, and apologist of womankind."[6]

Demonstrating her wide, sympathetic reading of French, English, German, and American writers, King nevertheless finds almost everywhere in the literature she treats a lack of fidelity to woman's experience. Thus, she admires the heroines of German writers for their spiritual values, but finds them dull. When she generalizes about German heroines, King sees their exalted lives as a stark contrast to the worldly lives of their husbands: "We see in German novels a continuous, if monotonous, exalted type of woman. The rigid domesticity of their lives is the first striking point, and this seems to have been always thus. Old chronicles describe them sitting in lonely towers, faithful *hausfrauen,* taking care of their children and dependents, while their husbands are off fighting, plundering, crusading, hunting, getting up religious wars or political excitements, staying away from their homes, as husbands still are apt to do, months at a time."[7]

There is truth here in the German presentation of woman, King seems to say, but she turns from the long-suffering German heroines in whom she recognizes an "indorsement of her own heart" to a consideration of French heroines. Although, as she admits, the French heroines of novels "have never been considered very proper acquaintances for ladies," King shows that she has more than a passing acquaintance with French heroines herself by hinting at their repellent attributes while at the same time pronouncing that they are a "consommée of all that the French sensorium of a century has discovered to be the most alluring physically, the most charming mentally." In contrast to the German male author, who imagines a domestic world of *Kinder, Kirche, und Küche* for his heroines, the French novelist "seeks his [heroines] anywhere but in the regions of his family." These male authors, King finds, "have exposed every conceivable heroine to every divisible temptation, and noted the hundredth part of a shade in her conduct." King concludes: "When the heroine dies suddenly, as French heroines have a fashion of doing, one craves an autopsy, just to know if really the novelist were quite correct in his diagnosis" (p. 9).

King sees both the French and the German treatment of the heroine as static, stereotyped. The scandalous fondness of the French writers for women characters they would never consent to marry is something King does not attempt to explain. Instead she ends her discussion of the relative merits of French and German heroines with an invocation of cultural relativism: "The state of a society which produces such heroines and tolerates them must be studied before any verdict can be reached." Through this evasion of any moral judgment, King allows her aesthetic judgment, which betrays more than a trace of Gallic chauvinism, to stand. Ignoring the great Russian novelists in her discussion, King opines: "Artistically the novel has reached perfection in France alone" (p. 9).

Later in her career King's commitment to truth in art led her to ignore genteel prudery in an attempt to tell something of the true story of a French woman who had lived by the "supreme arts" she had mentioned in her "Heroines of Novels." On her first trip to Paris in 1891–92, she translated some letters attributed to the passionate pen of George Sand, and found later that in sending them to Charles Dudley Warner, her mentor, she had herself blundered. King's faux pas does not appear to have originated in the indiscretions that must have been confessed or exposed by the letters themselves, but rather in her insensitivity to the extreme nicety of the literary proscriptions at the time, perhaps especially the literary double standard that prohibited a woman writer from treating certain subjects. Warner's negative response shocked King back into an awareness of the conventions in genteel America.

King recalls the incident in her *Memories of a Southern Woman of Letters*, minimizing the rejection that caused her to abandon the project "meekly" and noting that "in comparison with what magazines publish at the present time they [the letters] are mere icicles." At the time, however, she writes, she had been "transported" by the beauty of the letters and felt eager to share her find with Warner. Warner's reaction reveals how far in advance of her American friends Grace King was at the time, for he "jumped away from them [King's translations] as from a fire, and wrote me a severe scolding for translating them. No magazine would publish such things, he wrote, and he was ashamed that I should even think of submitting them to an editor."[8]

In retrospect at the end of her career, King recalled Warner's rejection of her literary efforts with mellow equanimity; however, her debut discussion of English and American heroines in "Heroines of Novels" had shown her irritation with the Victorian notion that the only fitting female character for a woman writer to be concerned with was the "ideal" woman, a sexless, self-denying paragon. Produced in quantities by English and American writers and indistinguishable from one another, these women characters, King asserted, are "perfectly transparent illusions—magic-lantern reproductions of an infinitely small ideal in the minds of the authors, who do not seem to be satisfied with the women they know and see about them." Such false "ideals," King knew, have an impact on life; she lamented this fact, observing that American women "ape with American facility the novelist's affectation" (p. 9).

The exceptions King sees to the dismal rule among English and American authors reveal her preference for realistic depictions of women. Only Charlotte Brontë and George Eliot emerge unscathed by criticism that touches even William Dean Howells and Henry James. King's approval of Brontë and Eliot foreshadows the direction she would take in portraying women who departed from the "ideal." Both Brontë and Eliot, King thought, "felt the injustice of necessarily beautiful heroines" (p. 9). Eliot, King perceived, felt the injustice of necessarily and unrealistically virtuous ones.[9]

For Grace King, writing a survey of American literature in her 1885 "Heroines of Novels," the absence of a Jane Eyre or a Maggie Tulliver was a significant problem. King perceived in the lack of believable female characters in American literature an injustice to the American woman, who "must find very little comfort for herself and sisters in the reading of novels prepared by her compatriots." The real woman who is poor, King says, finds in real life "none of the compensations necessary to make poverty interesting in a novel. No perfect beauty—no pre-eminent talents—she cannot hope to clear the ditch which separates obscurity from fame, any more than to catch the millionaire hero" (p. 9).

King's perception of the terrible, frustrating disparity between the world of novels and the real world of American women readers continued to animate her when she began writing fiction. In a letter to Charles Dudley Warner dated September 17, 1885, King discusses her first story and proclaims her determination to redress what she had found to be a deplorable literary fact. She writes: "It seems to me, white as well as black women have a sad showing in what some people call romance. . . . as I recollect little things, I think I shall try and write them. If no one else does it better, one of these days they may prove a pleasant record and serve to bring us all nearer together blacks and whites."[10] In an unpublished notebook dated 1886–1901, King reiterated her commitment to setting the facts straight on behalf of women. She wrote:

> Romance with its glasses rose or jaundice colored is peering around anxious to draw a little profit from a situation which was interesting and thrilling. Caricaturists and fun-mongers are searching new clothes for their old wit and are helping to perpetuate distorted characteristics & impossible vernacular. All the while, the persons most interested, the heroines so to speak are trudging their way out of this life with very much the same calm indifference as one fine morning they trudged their way out of slavery into freedom and their mistresses trudged (not so indifferently however) out of wealth into poverty.[11]

Although some literary historians have seen King as an adversary of Cable, King's complaint about the "sad showing" of black and white women in "romance" quite clearly places her among those writers of the Gilded Age who were determined to strip the gilt off the sentimental heroine of American romance. However, King was ahead of many of her contemporaries, for she recognized and commented in her notebook that the historical contributions and the contemporary circumstances of black women were being ignored, while "the negro men have had their wrongs & rights blazoned from one end of the country to the other."[12]

In "The Literature of Impoverishment: The Women Local Colorists in America, 1865–1914," Ann Douglas Wood treats King briefly, perhaps because King's cosmopolitan background is something of an embarrassment to the thesis that the women local-color writers lived "impoverished" lives in the cultural backwaters of America and that their work reveals this impoverishment. In her examination of King's "A Crippled Hope," which appeared in the July 1893 *Century*, however, Wood acknowledges the distinctly optimistic quality of King's vision, while placing her among women authors, most notably Sarah Orne Jewett and Mary E. Wilkins Freeman, who "debunked and exposed the falsities for post Civil War America of the sentimentalist tradition they inherited." Wood emphasizes the significance of all of these women authors in creating "a literature of protest, of protest and deep resistance against a male-dominated technological society which was isolating, ignoring and crippling its women."[13]

The similarity of King's vision to that of Northern women writers is implied in Wood's identification of King as one of the second generation of American women authors after the Civil War who still wanted to believe in conventional feminine virtues but "had lost faith in their potency"[14] and who therefore spurned the slick stereotypes that maintained a false view of woman's place in American society. Certainly, the lingering neglect King suffered until the 1960s reveals her kinship with all the women local-color writers of this period—North and South. Although she was acknowledged in her own time as a writer of distinction and ability, today her work remains in partial eclipse. But because her literary christening occurred after Richard Watson Gilder, Cable's Northern editor, challenged her to write better, "if Cable is so false to you,"[15] King was guaranteed a footnote, at least, in works on Cable. In these entries King's racial views, if not her work, were derogated and dismissed by implication. The assumption that King was a dramatic contrast to Cable in her racial attitudes also fostered slighting mention of her in histories of Southern culture such as Clement Eaton's *The Growth of Southern Civilization, 1790–1860* (1961), Jay B. Hubbell's *The South in American Literature, 1607–1900* (1954), Jay Martin's *Har-*

vests of Change (1967), and to a lesser extent Edmund Wilson's *Patriotic Gore* (1962). An exception to the rule, Richard M. Weaver acknowledged in *The Southern Tradition at Bay* that Grace King was "perhaps the best historian of the breakup of the old class system."[16] Weaver placed King among those Southern writers who withheld unqualified allegiance to Southern values and "were continuously disturbed by an inner voice of social justice." He discovered in the work of King and these others "sympathetic pictures of the vanishing order and a general endorsement of those virtues on which the South prided itself, but . . . also many uneasy questions, either direct or implied."[17]

Despite the complexity of King's work; her possible significance as a realist in the French tradition; her fictional and nonfictional contributions to the recording of Southern history; and her attempt to preserve "experiences, reminiscences, episodes, picked up as only women know how to pick them up from other women's lives . . . and told as only women know how to relate them,"[18] despite all this, Grace King long continued to be misunderstood by critics, who regarded her as an unsympathetic antithesis to Cable.

A case in point is Merrill Maguire Skaggs. *The Folk of Southern Fiction*, her response to the cry for research into Southern writing at odds with the plantation myth, attempts to trace a literary tradition surrounding "plain folk," the respectable Southern yeoman, in Southern local-color fiction. Skaggs's insightful discussion of Cable's treatment of the Creole suggests that King and Cable were in closer agreement than had been supposed. However, Skaggs's misinterpretation of King's attitude toward race surfaces when she remarks disdainfully that "Miss King confirms the existence of 'the steady detestation' [that Cable said] righteous white women felt towards the quadroons." When she proceeds to generalize incorrectly that, with the exception of King's heroine in "The Little Convent Girl," "Miss King's quadroons and mulattoes are prostitutes," Skaggs's misreading of King is even more apparent.[19]

Such hasty generalizations appearing in otherwise persuasive and excellent scholarship helped perpetuate the neglect of a gifted writer. The troubling appearance of racist sentiments in King makes it easy to dismiss her along with writers who glorified the mythic South. King contributed to this problem by her intense Southern partisanship, what Robert Bush calls her regional *"pietas,"*[20] which Edmund Wilson said she maintained in her public utterances by resorting to Orwellian "doublethink," putting the best face on things for the outsider *pro patria*.[21] For this reason, although King demonstrated a critical command of contemporary literature unusual for a person of her time and a hostility to stereotyped characters in fiction, she once affirmed her Southern loyalties by praising Thomas Nelson Page for giving the nation Southern stories of "ineffable grace" and depicting the Negro as "humorous, shrewd, and loyal to his master and his family as it has been stereotyped in fiction."[22]

Despite her inclination to doublethink, King's racial perspectives were more complex than her statements about Page and Cable might indicate. Recent studies, such as Helen Taylor's examination of the personal and professional networks that sustained Grace King as an artist and an intellectual and Anne Goodwyn Jones's exploration of King's development within a rigidly racist patriarchal society, have recognized that the racial ambivalence King expresses is further complicated by her unconscious identification with oppressed blacks in her fiction.

King's historical writing on New Orleans also reveals her knowledge of the complexities of race and caste. In *New Orleans: The Place and the People* (1895), justly praised as one of the best popular local histories of the period, King evaluates the negative effects on the family produced by a population of beautiful, sought-after quadroon women. She recognizes the desperation of these women to attach themselves to white men, admitting that the need to find a male protector was something that white women felt as well.[23] She appears to be validating Cable's portrait of Madame Delphine when she writes: "The great ambition of the unmarried quadroon mothers was to have their children pass for whites, and so get access to the privileged class. To reach this end, there was nothing they would not attempt, no sacrifice they would not make." "Many of the quadroon belles, however, attained honourable marriage, and, removing to France, obtained full social recognition for themselves and their children."[24]

In France, King was well aware, distinctions of color were not as significant as in New Orleans. In *Memories of a Southern Woman of Letters,* she recalls having seen a Negro girl from Haiti among the other boarders at a girls' school in Paris. King's description of this scene shows both her sophistication and her good will, for she recognizes that the little black girl is "typically negroid" but accepts the fact that the girl "was unconscious, as were her companions, of any difference in color that separated her from them."[25]

In contrast to those quadroons who lived during a period of "unwholesome notoriety,"[26] as King decorously phrased it in *New Orleans: The Place and the People,* she describes the Sisters of the Holy Family of New Orleans, founded by three young women of the quadroon caste. Only through such a vocation, King intimates, could these women be proof against the unhealthy atmosphere of New Orleans, where "race, time, and circumstance" conspired against them. "In their renunciation," she writes, "they at least, of their race, found the road to social equality. No white woman could do more; none have done better."[27]

King's discussion of the heroine of her first story, however, helps explain why scholars like Merrill Skaggs continue to dismiss King's work—apparently, in some cases, unread. The patronizing diction in King's defense of the credibility of Marcélite, the selfless hairdresser in "Monsieur Motte" and a quadroon character drawn from life,[28] conveys the unconsidered racist assumptions King made despite her relative sophistication. King wrote: "Great instances of devotion were found among even the worst treated slaves; I love to dwell on this [devotion], what I would call, holy passion of the Negro women, for it serves to cancel those other grosser ones [passions], with which they are really victimised by their blood."[29] King's implication about the hypersexuality of the Negro woman is as repellent as it is familiar even in our own day. Put off by such remarks, we tend to forget that during the period in which King wrote, few if any authors were free of unexamined racist attitudes.[30]

"Madrilène" and "Bonne Maman"

While the work of reevaluating Grace King's career goes on, readers of King's stories—*Monsieur Motte* (1888), *Tales of a Time and Place* (1892), and *Balcony Stories* (1893)—will be struck by the accuracy, depth, and impartiality of her portraits of women trapped in unfulfilling roles. Closer examination of the four King stories that deal at length with quadroon women characters, moreover, proves that critical assumptions about a benighted consistency in Grace King's racial views are ill-founded. King's concern with the faithful depiction of women characters in these stories overrides her racial ambivalence to a remarkable degree. We hardly need to know the racial identities of the women in these stories, for their oppression seems inextricably bound up in the conventional restrictions imposed upon all women.

In "Monsieur Motte" and "The Little Convent Girl," Grace King presents realistic women characters on both sides of the color line who still claim our sympathy. In "Bonne Maman" and "Madrilène; or, The Festival of the Dead," King draws contrasting pictures of quadroon prostitutes that refute Skaggs's contention that King indiscriminately detested quadroon women or even, for that matter, quadroon prostitutes. While all four of these stories are significantly different and are only a minor part of King's total canon, "Monsieur Motte" and "The Little Convent Girl" are among the best of King's works. Together with "Bonne Maman" and "Madrilène; or, The Festival of the Dead," which exhibit King's racial prejudices, they suggest the range of King's abilities and the depth of her concern with the blighting effect of female education and the traditional roles allotted to women.

Several striking similarities appear in these stories. First, in each story King depicts social environments that restrict the development of her women characters. The strict limits of acceptable "feminine" behavior— whether that behavior is the product of the brothel, the convent, or the finishing school—are portrayed in ways that show the psychologically debilitating nature of the standards imposed upon women. Second, male characters stand on the periphery in these stories. King's minimization of male characters, of course, might be seen as her exploitation of the convention of women's fiction that allowed woman to rule the hearth. However, King's women characters in these four stories are trapped in a domestic horror that cannot be softened by the solaces of domesticity. For this reason, the isolation of King's women characters gives a rare view of the thwarted lives of women. Third, the voice of a woman narrator is distinct in each of these stories. King's subtly ironic treatment of the pious attitudes and artifacts of the "true" woman's "calling" suggests the need for transcendent goals for women, not encompassed by woman's chores of cooking, cleaning, knitting, or caring for her flowers or the "little sufferers" in the household.[31] Fourth, in the woman-centered fictional world of these stories, a world nevertheless controlled by patriarchal assumptions about proper conduct for all women, the plot lines are remarkably similar: ingenue characters grope toward an understanding of their individual identities. The growth of these ingenues is blocked or facilitated by older quadroon women who represent the possible racial and the certain sexual limitations that the ingenues are seeking to escape. For this reason these older women cannot help the young girls free themselves from the penalties attached to being women.

Because the identity crisis is a feature of all these stories, King's plots might be seen in simple terms as replications or inversions of the Cinderella pattern, sans Prince Charming, with the older half-caste women in them acting in subordinate roles as evil stepmothers or as fairy godmothers to the young girls in the process of awakening. The distinctive personalities of the older half-caste women and of the young girls in these four stories, however, suggest King's effort to go beyond traditional stereotypes by presenting women limited in range, but not in aspiration, by social convention. Although these stories are undeniably infected by the racism of the author, they present a convincing picture of white and black women struggling for a sense of place and identity in a dissolving social order.

Because "Madrilène; or, The Festival of the Dead" gives a candid view of the quadroon of the demimonde and exposes the racial hatred that on occasion animates women who are black, white, or racially mixed, this story is probably the one to which Skaggs alludes in imputing a "steady detestation" of the half-caste woman to Grace King. "Madrilène" does perhaps reveal King's conventional racial views at their worst. However, these views are filtered through the consciousness of King's demented protagonist so that it cannot be determined whether or to what extent King shares them. The repellent story of the white slavery of Marie Madeleine suggests the enslavement of both white and black women. And while the predatory, profit-seeking Madame Laïs is a convincing social type, her portrait, as we will see, is only one in King's gallery of quadroon and octoroon women characters.

At the opening of "Madrilène," *la Toussaint,* the joyous but macabre religious festival, enlivens the scene and prepares for the introduction of Marie, whose morbid concern with death and race is symbolized by her refuge in the all-white cemetery. Marie's misfortune is emphasized by her name, Marie Madeleine, and by the fact that only the caretaker of the white cemetery rejects the corruption of Marie's name to Madrilène. Taught to read and to aspire to a freer life by this caretaker, Marie has "learned her alphabet from the tombstones."[32] This fact and the colors of death pervading "Madrilène" linger hauntingly to remind the reader of Marie's living death. Even her resurrection to a white identity at the end of the story, which occurs, of course, on *la Toussaint,* fails to dispel the nightmarish vision of Marie's confinement presented in the story.

The cemetery in "Madrilène" is described in detail and comes to be seen as a symbol of the vanity of human aspirations to eternally immutable social roles. It reveals the decline of the founders of the city, who had designed it as "a fit repository for the mortal remains of aristocracy and wealth, with handsome monuments, broad avenues, gentle vistas, and pleasing perspectives" (p. 129). Ironically, the view from the cemetery reveals how far the city's founding fathers failed in their design, for the encroaching houses that block the view are "accustomed to look at worse things in life than death" (p. 119).

For a moment, however, ongoing street life breaks through the gloom of the cemetery. The noises, crowds, colors, and smells of a population getting ready for All Saints' Day divert attention. Streetside vendors reminiscent of Cable's *marchandes* in *The Grandissimes* move slowly or doze in the late autumn heat. Even violence fails to disturb commerce. When a fight flares up between Marie and a young quadroon boy and is taken over by the boy's mother, who accuses Marie of trying to "pass herself off for white" (p. 140), business goes on as usual, and only one spectator pursues the question raised by the fight. Significantly, that individual is a "stranger" (p. 141); he is presumably unaccustomed to the sight of very light-skinned black children, for he eventually rescues Marie from the brothel where she has been kept for fifteen years. The fact that the stranger, alone, is seen as "not 'that kind of a man'" (p. 160) suggests that the prevalence of corruption in New Orleans is the source of Marie's problem.

Contrasts between the life of the street and the cemetery's symbols of mortality and sin reinforce the picture of the tenuous nature of life here. Further contrasts enter the scene in the depiction of Madame Laïs's oppressive but thriving establishment with its lively trade of "yellow men" coming "through the back gate to visit" Palmyre, Antoinette, Philomène, or Athalie (p. 145). White men, later identified by Madame Laïs (in the elliptical manner employed earlier by Cable) as "friends who will protect me! General——, Collector——, Major——, Colonel——, Dr.——, Judge——, Senator——, Mr.——," enter through the front door (p. 173).

The complicity of the white male aristocracy of New Orleans in keeping Madame Laïs in business is underscored by King's deft description of Madame's establishment. Because it reveals much more about the practice of King's day in such establishments than the descriptions by her New Orleans contemporaries, King's picture of Madame Laïs's establishment is valuable in itself. It is also startlingly detailed and objective, considering King's patrician background and the genteel assumption of the day that a lady could not know and in any case should not speak of such things.

King's presentation of the *chambres garnies* (furnished rooms) run by Madame Laïs is remarkable for its suggestiveness. The lavish attention showered on the male tenant at Madame Laïs's may seem to be innocent servility. King's subtle management of detail, however, reveals that Madame's *chambres* furnish both sexual attentions and an assortment of other services. Designed for the comfort and convenience of male "guests" and financed by "respectable," but anonymous, white male benefactors, these establishments, King implies, were often run by quadroon women who had graduated from the status of paramour to proprietress. The "thin, poorly clad, miserable-looking" black child with "scrubbing-brush in hand" is the first indication of the cost to the blacks of the sumptuous appointments in the establishment King describes. This child contrasts pathetically with the "velvet carpets and damask curtains, the great bedstead with lace-trimmed dressings, the *armoire à miroir;* the lavabo, with its fine porcelains and linens; the biscuit statuettes and vases of paper flowers on the mantel" (p. 157).

Possessing the financial acumen and the manipulative skill required to prosper in a man's world and on a man's terms, Madame Laïs has an unerring evaluative ability; her eyes are "trained to see as other eyes have been trained to shoot, and men, not boards, have been from time immemorial their target" (p. 158). Individualizing the type she describes, King presents a convincing encounter between Madame Laïs and an anonymous prospective tenant. King distills some of the ironies present in such transactions and gives Madame, who sizes up the "client," a degree of inner consciousness appropriate to her limited character: "A scraping from skirts sharpened as well as stiffened by unstinted starch" announces Madame's descent from the secret regions of her house (p. 157). Madame has managed her entrance so that "what the stranger sees is infinitesimal in comparison with what Madame Laïs sees." "What Madame Laïs sees in a stranger decides in an instant whether she has a vacant room, the price of it, the price of laundry and personal services—serving coffee in bed mornings, attendance when ill, etc." (p. 158). At a glance Madame Laïs determines how far she and her "daughters" will go to accommodate the tenant.

If accepted by the calculating Madame, the tenant may "travel willingly year after year from one house to the other with his *chambres garnies'* hostess, who does not attach herself generally to buildings" (p. 158)—or to people either, King implies. But if the tenant, who remains a cipher in Madame's account book, "falls ill, he is nursed; and it is safe to say no one in New Orleans can nurse like Madame Laïs—the tenderness of a mother, the devotion of a slave, the delicacy of a wife, the unflinching patience of a hospital Sister, all combined!" And besides this feminine "devotion," which awaits the deathbed bequest of the rich tenant, Madame Laïs is "comely, too, and young; or at least her daughters are, or her granddaughters, or her nieces" (p. 159).

Although in Madame Laïs King ventures no further than to hint at the dominant traits of a sinister type of woman, King's portrait of the brothel keeper implies that the feminine servility prized by a patriarchal society can be seen in the behavior of all women who pamper men. Madame's servility, of course, is the sine qua non of her profession. Her treachery to her own sex and to her race, her duplicity in preventing Marie from discovering her true identity, and her alienation from herself ensure Madame Laïs's success in her enterprise. Until she is exposed at the end of the story by Marie's "rescuer," Madame Laïs thrives by following the familiar prescribed role. Her progressive dehumanization in playing that role appears in King's observation that as Madame's handsomely furnished chambers become more and more luxuriously appointed, her "petticoats are always getting stiffer" (p. 160).

Only one of Madame Laïs's victims, Marie Madeleine, refuses to serve Madame's white customers. Victim and victimizer, Marie and Madame Laïs share ascribed racial and sexual roles. Because her position in Madame's household is much like that of the starving black child who scrubs up the filth from the rooms, however, Marie sees her position entirely in racial terms. Yet that black child is never asked to perform as it is implied that Marie has been coerced to perform. Apparently unaware that her gender compounds her problems, Marie senses the hopelessness of her situation. She feels the walls of Madame's house closing around her on nights when she cannot escape to read with the cemetery caretaker: the walls of the brothel "grimaced at her, and the days came back to torment her, and the close ladened atmosphere of the room suffocated her" (p. 154). Existing in a trap within a trap, barred from full humanity by her supposed race and by her "inferior" sex, Marie's only flight is into the fantasy of becoming white, though to be white and a woman, as she discovers, is also to be denied the power to define the self freely.

Because Marie regards her race as the reason for her imprisonment, however, she is the most vocal racist in "Madrilène." Marie's racism seems to be an index of the permanent emotional damage she has suffered rather than a reflection of King's unguarded sentiments. For example, when Marie thinks of the "truths" that she has learned in the brothel, she imagines that "the most audacious, the most impudent, the most infuriated, the most drunken, the lightest of the light-colored, whatever they might say, in their secret hearts . . . never disputed that the white are born above the black. Was not God white to them? The Saviour white? The Virgin white? The saints, martyrs, angels, all white? The people they read of in books, were they not all white? And the people they saw on the stage?" (p. 151).

King's description of Marie's fixation on white superiority discloses the psychological damage sustained by those defined as racially inferior. The extremity of Marie's concern with whiteness may be regarded as dementia, since she wishes for the release of death only if resurrection will make her white: "We resurrect white, do we not, Monsieur Sacerdote?" she asks. "I would be found out otherwise. All white—white limbs, white faces, white wings, white clothes" (p. 138).

The ironic context for Marie's simple deduction about the superiority of the white race is provided by the descriptions of and allusions to Madame Laïs's prestigious, all-white, all-male clientele. Marie, however, rather feels than perceives the irony. Almost instinctively, it would seem, Marie is repelled by white men. Thus, when she flees from an attack by one of Madame Laïs's "daughters," she hides outside, fearing a party of white men whose voices she can hear. Recoiling from the mere sound of their revelry, Marie thinks chaotically: "Oh, she was afraid of men! . . . None of Madame Laïs's family were afraid of men. Afraid of ghosts and voudoos? yes; but men, no. . . . In daylight her heart would jump and start if one looked at her. What was she afraid of? What could they do to her? She did not know; only she was afraid, afraid" (p. 164).

Here, quite obviously, Marie's interior monologue may indicate that she has preserved her virginity in spite of her sordid education in Madame Laïs's *chambres garnies*. But significantly, Marie does not possess that pristine but hidden beauty essential for the sudden, eleventh-hour transformation of the heroine: She has "no perfect beauty—no pre-eminent talents—she cannot hope to clear the ditch which separates obscurity from fame."[33] Nor is there any suggestion that the middle-aged stranger who saves her will marry her and efface the emotional scars produced by her life at Madame Laïs's establishment.

At the end of her story, with her rescue from an unknown danger posed by the white men and from the known dangers of the *chambres garnies,* Marie does not respond to the discovery that she is white. At the end of "Madrilène" Marie sinks "down, down, through sightlessness, dumbness, deafness, to nullity" (p. 178). If not dead, as the implication seems to be, Marie remains a character in a nightmare of restrictions, "created to be overshadowed by the emblems of death" (p. 126), a fragmented personality that can know no "resurrection."

"Bonne Maman" provides a contrasting view of the limited options available to young women. In this story an ingenue pointedly, conventionally, but quite ironically named Claire Blanche experiences Marie Madeleine's feelings of confinement and isolation while dutifully caring for her white grandmother. The irony of Claire Blanche's name is that her yearnings are sensual rather than spiritual, for although outwardly she conforms, inwardly she struggles with the limitations of her role.

Under the tyranny of love and duty—as totally restricting in many ways as the tyranny of racial hatred depicted in "Madrilène"—Claire ministers to her invalid grandmother and helps her keep up the delusion that they have gone to France to live an aristocratic life. Like Marie Madeleine, Claire has been deprived of childhood fun, denied a proper understanding of her place in society, and isolated from contact with other people. Like Marie, Claire longs innocently for experience forbidden to her in her prescribed role. Unlike Marie, Claire imagines that the revelry and music of the quadroon houses nearby represent energy and life.

Claire's remembrance of her school days speaks of severe restriction at school as well. There, she learned that she was inadequate. Although intended to divert her grandmother, her complaints about her convent education reveal the price Claire paid in learning to be a lady and the price she pays every day in maintaining the fiction that her grandmother wants to preserve at all costs. "How I used to wish," says Claire of her schooling, "there had been just one lazy bad one like me!"[34] At her convent, she recalls, the teachers were "always scolding you because you were not some one else, always punishing you because you were what you were" (p. 70). The solution to such constitutional "badness," so evident in most little girls, seems to have been death, for it was, as Claire recalls, only the "good girls—the good, weak girls" (p. 71) who succumbed to yellow fever.

Claire dimly perceives that her race might be the source of her problem. Just as society seems to allow the half-caste woman only one role, it dictates only one for a white woman. Despite her dissatisfaction with the confinement of her situation, however, Claire maintains an illusion of respectability for her grandmother, hiding the fact that she makes do for both of them by sewing for the quadroon women of the neighborhood. Naturally, Claire denies the usefulness of the sewing she does and pretends to sew decoratively, as a lady should. She also hides the fact that she envies the quadroon women their apparent freedom.

In the past Bonne Maman's illusions about marriage shaped her future. In her old age her illusions about her past control her granddaughter's future. "It seems to me," she says plaintively, "that all the bright hopes that used to fly before me, they fly behind me now as memories" (p. 73). Too late to be of any help to her granddaughter, she understands that times have changed: "This, then, was to be the end of a life conducted on principles drawn from heroic inspirations of other times. The principles were the same, but human nature had changed since women's hearts were strong enough not to break over bullet wounds, sabre cuts, and horse-hoof mutilations, when women's hands were large enough to grasp and hold the man-abandoned tiller of the household. It had all gone wrong" (p. 85).

Recognizing that times and women have changed, vaguely sensing that even in her own glorious days things were not quite as sentiment insisted they should be, Bonne Maman faces the grim future she has prepared for Claire Blanche. "What tomb could be lonelier or uglier than this little cabin would be to Claire," she wonders. "Would the patriotic death of the girl's father, would the martyrdom of her mother, would a proud disdain of law quibbles, would the renunciation of friends and the defiance of enemies . . . solace her in her youthful, unaided life-struggle, in those conditions for which ancestral glories, refinements, and luxuries had but poorly equipped her?" (pp. 87–88).

The grandmother's dying insights, however, are no help to Claire, who yearns for life. Claire instinctively resists confinement by opening the window when she sews so that she can see the children playing and be seen by them. Controlled and static, she sits inside and experiences life vicariously, while the children play spontaneously. Through her description of these children, King shows the life forbidden to Claire at the convent and suggests the deprivation of her ladylike existence with her grandmother. The implication is that to have been a rich lady was bad enough but to be a poor but proud lady is unendurable: "The air of desertion which hung about the little closed cottages would have been oppressive had it not been for the children—a motley crowd, accusing an 'olla podrida' parentage, chattering in tongues as varied as their complexions, and restless with the competing

energies of hidden nationalities in their veins. Dressed with tropical disregard of conventionality, they were frank, impudent, irrepressible; at all
times noisy and unanimous" (p. 64).

King's description of the boisterous play of these racially mixed children, male and female, pictures the healthy young life denied to Claire
because of her socialization to be a lady. Fantasies of escape are all Claire
permits herself. One walk alone on the street, something rare for Claire
because she has made only one friend in all the time she has lived in the
cabin with her grandmother, makes her rhapsodic. Walking freely and looking into the sunset sky, she imagines that death will liberate her: "Mon
Dieu! but it's all beautiful. I wish I could walk up there [in heaven] in all
that pink and blue and gold; walk deeper and deeper in it, until it came up
all around and over me!" (p. 90). A single solitary walk produces an
awakening and suggests the sway that the tantalizing forbidden world of
her neighborhood has over Claire.

Maturing to feel a woman's passions, but without a means of expression
for them, Claire is prey to her senses. King's description of Claire's response to her environment and to the rhythms within her is sensitive and
candid. The night jasmine evokes Claire's reveries and makes her "feel faint
with its sweetness" (p. 90). She is enchanted by the "loud, coarse, passionate waltz" from beyond "the glass-protected brick wall," the wall of her
respectable prison. "When I hear music like that," King allows her to say,
"it is as if my blood would come out of my veins and dance right there
before me" (p. 91). When Betsy, the self-appointed servant of Claire and
Bonne Maman and Claire's only friend, tells Claire that the music she
responds to so passionately is not something "good" white women listen
to, Claire answers defiantly. "It doesn't cost anything to listen to music, to
know people. I don't have to work for it, like bread and meat; and, grand
Dieu, how much better it is!" (p. 93). But Claire, like the other "good"
white women, will only be drawn to wonder about the meaning of that
music. White men know the tunes too well, King implies, for "men, their
cigarettes spangling the gloom, listened in silence, casting secret, wistful
glances in the direction of the occult merry-making" (p. 94).

King is explicit about the unnaturalness of Claire's captivity: "Could, in
fact, their enemies have prepared an extremity of suffering beyond that to
which Claire was predestined by her own grandmother?" (p. 88), Bonne
Maman wonders to herself in a lucid moment. The tyranny of Bonne
Maman's love has worked as relentlessly on Claire Blanche as the tyranny of
Madame Laïs's hatred worked on Marie Madeleine to separate the girl from
knowledge about herself. King suggests that Claire's knowledge must come
from within, for she blindly and insistently responds to the only life around
her.

In what Betsy calls this "crucifying world" (p. 97), the white Claire, a product of the convent and a solicitous grandmother, grows up "in spite of tragedy, starvation, imprisonment," cut off by "short-sighted precautions from friends, from relations, even from certification of her own identity; alone, literally alone" (pp. 97–98). Only with the death of Bonne Maman, her benevolent jailer, will Claire be released. But her rescue by long-lost relatives is ambiguously treated, since these relatives will be embraced as "the successors of bonne maman" (p. 115). In the tradition of the Southern lady, whose "best preparation for life is to know nothing about it,"[35] Claire will now become the lady her grandmother has wanted her to be.

Representing the world Claire Blanche longs for but will never know and locked into that world just as Claire is confined in hers, Aza, a quadroon prostitute and the former slave of Bonne Maman, enters Claire's life upon the death of Bonne Maman. The horrifying nature of Claire and Bonne Maman's isolation is implied by Aza's sudden appearance after Bonne Maman's death, for Aza has lived in one of the neighboring houses all along, but has not been seen by the white women since her manumission. Now death opens Bonne Maman's cabin to a procession of the curious: "Death himself had unlatched the reserved green doors" (p. 103).

It is unfortunate that the description of Aza plays a small part in "Bonne Maman" because King's characterization of her contrasts with her characterization of Madame Laïs in "Madrilène." This contrast reveals King's ability to distinguish among quadroon prostitutes. Aza is scornful of white people, but pleasure-seeking. Madame Laïs, in contrast, is all business. Both women, however, are volatile and vulgar. Neither is romanticized in the role of demimondaine.

Aza's conflicting attitudes toward white people emerge when she accidentally discovers her old mistress lying in state and exposed for the first time to the prying eyes of those who must now see the white woman's shameful poverty. Like the other curiosity seekers, Aza has visited the death chamber to satisfy the "instinctive craving of morbid curiosity." Aza's discovery that the dead woman is white produces "a contemptuous smile on her voluptuous lips" (p. 104). When she learns the identity of the dead woman, however, her contempt vanishes and she collapses, "bursting into tears" and "hid[ing] her face in the darned, worn, white 'blouse volante' shroud, moaning, with long, wailing cries" (p. 106). Aza's lament appears to be a staple scene in which a grief-stricken slave cries for a lost master. King's treatment is more restrained than others, however, and Aza is a more believable character, for her devotion to Bonne Maman is mirrored by Claire's and Betsy's devotion to the cranky, self-deluding old woman. King dwells on Aza's grief sentimentally but convincingly, having prepared earlier, with Bonne Maman's reminiscences about Aza, for the loyalty Aza expresses toward the white woman. Clearly, the reader is intended to understand that the bond between the two women was a mutual one.

Because of Bonne Maman, who set her free, and because of faithful Betsy, who now reproaches Aza for her dissolute life, Aza momentarily repents. But it is not Aza's provisional repentance that makes her a sympathetic character. Because of her dominant human loyalties, Aza's pleasure-seeking is not treated with the same horror as the profit-seeking of the starched Madame Laïs. While Aza is clearly not one of the "good" women with "the innate virtue of all good women" (pp. 109–10), and although her vitality has been misdirected, she has remained, at heart, a truly good woman. Therefore, when King presents her for the last time, walking in Bonne Maman's funeral procession and wearing a black and white bead memorial inscribed "Priez pour moi" (p. 115), the implication is clear. Aza's carnal sins are, perhaps, forgivable, considering the few options she had as a quadroon woman. Her humanity appears in her attempt to save Claire Blanche from a neighborhood where sin is the only way of survival. When, in character, Aza returns to the darkness from which she came, King's concise, nonjudgmental closing is fatalistic: "The piano had already commenced its dances" (p. 115). Presumably, Claire Blanche will never dance to this music, but she has responded to its rhythms and carries the memory of that response into her restricted adulthood.

This ambiguous happy ending for Claire, like the equally ambiguous unhappy ending for Marie Madeleine in "Madrilène," implies questions about the ways in which women are misdefined and then assigned to strictly antithetical roles—the innocent and the whore. Symbolically limited to choosing between good and bad, as society defined these terms for women, between the convent, the brothel, and the cemetery, Claire and Marie yearn for experience denied them. Their "rescues" are ambiguously treated and suggest an initiation into adult roles they will fit imperfectly if at all.

"Monsieur Motte"

Both "Monsieur Motte" and "The Little Convent Girl" employ the discovery motif that structures "Madrilène" and "Bonne Maman," a motif that illuminates the confined, limited lives of all women. Significantly, "Monsieur Motte" and "The Little Convent Girl" lack the provocative view of the demimonde of "Madrilène" and "Bonne Maman." Instead of depicting denizens of the sporting houses or hostesses of the suspect *chambres garnies* of New Orleans, "Monsieur Motte" and "The Little Convent Girl" portray their women of mixed blood sympathetically. In their portrayal of women in the process of learning about themselves, these two stories show the

destruction of the woman who believes in the necessity for strict conformity to the prejudices of a patriarchal society. Although "Monsieur Motte"
is Grace King's first published story, and "The Little Convent Girl" is a
fairly short story that depends on concision and understatement for its
startling effect, both stories handle women characters perceptively. In their
realism and ironic vision, "Monsieur Motte" and "The Little Convent Girl"
seem to plead, like Cable's courageous "'Tite Poulette" and *Madame Delphine*, for justice for women.

Begun in a white heat after Richard Watson Gilder's challenge to King
to best Cable if she could, "Monsieur Motte" resembles Cable's *Madame
Delphine* in its presentation of a powerful love joining two women. Although King's recollection of her feelings at the time indicate that she
started writing the story as a defense of the South against Cable's alleged
attacks and of Southern writers against the charge that they could not or
would not write a true account of the racial situation in the South, "Monsieur Motte" is, nevertheless, uncontaminated by defensiveness or venom.
A tour de force in its moving presentation of the self-sacrifice of a quadroon
woman for a young girl she loves as a daughter, King's story reveals the
inability of one generation to prepare the next for the penalties attached to
the female role.

Charles Dudley Warner, who saw that "Monsieur Motte" was placed in
the *New Princeton Review*, wrote to King of the reception it received: "One
paper said it was a 'selection' from foreign contemporary fiction. The N. Y.
Tribune had ten lines of hearty praise. The N. Y. Post attributes it to Cable,
the Springfield Republican to Mr. Janvier. The Boston Herald . . . said it
was the sort of fiction found in the 'Revue des deux Mondes,' and that we
ought to have more of it. All of my friends, who have read it, are thoroughly entranced with it, think it very strong, vigorous, pathetic, and
wonderful in giving pictures with a few strokes of the pen."[36] Other reviewers of "Monsieur Motte" noted that King had solved the problem of
dialect—the obsession of many local-colorists to the chagrin of many of
their readers—by sprinkling her prose with French phrases that captured
the feel of the Creole patois without making her Creoles sound like illiterate
Americans.[37]

Robert Bush suggests that in this first story King "was establishing
herself as realist rather than romantic" by using her own experience as a day
student in the late 1860s at the Institut St. Louis, a private school for girls.
King's stay at the school, Bush tells us, gave her the arch, ineffectual
Madame Lareveillère, headmistress of the Institut St. Denis in "Monsieur
Motte," and the self-reliant, self-sacrificing Marcélite, the school's hairdresser and central character of the story.[38]

The simplicity of King's realistic description of everyday life at St. Denis prepares for an understanding of the transcendent love between Marcélite and Marie Modeste, who believes that Monsieur Motte, a nonexistent wealthy uncle invented for her by Marcélite, will take her home with him after her graduation from St. Denis in two more days. The sense that Monsieur Motte is a colossal improbability is strengthened by the meticulous realism of King's description of St. Denis and by the emotional credibility of her character, Marcélite.

Before the crisis assured by Marie's graduation, the contrast between Madame Lareveillère and Marcélite foreshadows the limitations Marie must face as a woman, whether she turns out to be Marcélite's own natural daughter, as the shallowness of Marcélite's deception seems to imply, or a white girl. Against the contrast provided by the hairdresser and the headmistress, King sets Marie Modeste, who must eventually choose between them. Although neither woman is held up by King as an acceptable model for seventeen-year-old Marie, Marcélite's suffering on Marie's behalf and Madame Lareveillère's superficial maternal gestures are juxtaposed to imply the superiority of the quadroon to the aristocratic white lady. Thus, despite the fact that both women are seen sustaining false roles prescribed by their society and being cheated of the satisfaction of spontaneous, close, human relationships, the reader inevitably identifies with Marcélite. King's subtle irony falls on Madame Lareveillère, who seems to have accommodated herself selfishly to the grand role she must play. King's sympathy rests with Marcélite, whose love for Marie seems to justify her invention of Monsieur Motte.

The opening of "Monsieur Motte" presents a picture of Marie's classmates at St. Denis walking in lockstep, "their elbows scraping against the rugged bricks of the wall as they held their books up to the openings of their sun-bonnets."[39] About to become a part of the St. Denis tradition, as their mothers and grandmothers were before them, these girls with their delicate Southern complexions are beginning to experience the futility of their education. In the frenzy of preparation for final examinations, on which hinge the distribution of school prizes coveted all year, the girls anxiously memorize "disjointed fragments" from "l'Histoire de France" (p. 12). Their study is haphazard but desperate because the prizes will be all they will have to show for their finishing-school education.

All the last-minute cramming by the "panic-stricken contestants," who believe that the examination for distribution of prizes will be "conducted with such rigidity and impartiality," is worthless (p. 12). What this graduating class of 1874 does not know, as their mothers before them presumably did not, is that the competition is rigged. The headmistress, Madame Lareveillère, has a list "whose columns carried decimals instead of good and bad marks for lessons," and her "calculations" about the awarding of the gilt-edged prize books—pretty manuals of feminine etiquette, perhaps—depend upon "an equation which sets good and bad scholars against good and bad pay" (p. 45).

Madame Lareveillère's pupils believe in and dread the examination. They want vaguely to escape "the desert of education" (p. 69) at St. Denis. The younger girls do escape "full speed" when the bell rings. However, none of the students seem to perceive, as King does, that the natural scene in the schoolyard offers "a mocking contrast to the scene of doubt, hesitation, and excitement on the other side of the closed door" in the classroom, "a contrast advantageous to the uneducated happiness of the insects and flowers" (p. 15).

Indoctrinated and confined, Madame Lareveillère's crème de la crème of the young Creole women of New Orleans shares a "grace of ease, the gift of generations; a self-composure and polish, dating from the cradle" (pp. 22–23). King captures the constrained artificiality of these cultivated girls by picturing their walk, for "of course they did not romp, but promenaded arm in arm, measuring their steps with dainty particularity; moving the whole body with rhythmic regularity, displaying and acquiring at the same time a sinuosity of motion. Their hair hung in plaits so far below their waists that it threatened to grow into a measuring-tape for their whole length" (p. 23).

Such artificiality infects the relationships of the girls themselves, who carry on conversations with each other in "sweet, low voices, with interrupting embraces and apostrophic tendernesses." All apparently alike down to the minutiae of costume, uniforms designed as "buttresses against the ardent sun," the girls are merely adopting the role allotted them "from the cradle" (p. 22).

These girls are taught the controlled forms of superficial social intercourse that channel their friendships. However, they are starved for emotional contact, and the tradition of the best friend, strong at St. Denis, provides intimacy of a generalized sort. "Every class-book when opened would direct you to a certain page on which was to be found the name of *'celle que j'aime,'* or *'celle que j'adore,'* or *'mon amie chérie,'* or *'ma toute dévouée'*" (pp. 58–59). Nevertheless, the girls' deeper emotional needs are often sacrificed to appearances, for when "uncontrollable tears" signal an individual crisis, no one takes note. Instead, "tacitly employed convenient conventional excuses" cover the outburst (p. 41).

Into this description of the deprived emotional atmosphere of St. Denis, King introduces Marcélite, a vulgar, vital contrast to the mannerly, ordered, identical young ladies. The young ladies are afraid of everything, even failing to win a prize in their examination on French history, but Marcélite appears impudent and fearless. She engages Jeanne, the white *femme de ménage* (housekeeper) of the school, in a battle over whether Jeanne will violate precedent by opening the great gate of the school to admit her with her large basket. Because the basket contains Marie Modeste's costume for the graduation ceremony, Marcélite is insistent. Her insistence reflects the urgency of her mission, but it also reflects Marcélite's desire to pique Jeanne and to break the rules. The quarrel between Marcélite and Jeanne has gone on for years, "a quarrel involving complex questions of the privileges of order and the distinctions of race . . . [and] continued, year by year, with no interruptions of courtesy or mitigation by truce" (p. 17).

King's amused sympathies seem to be with Marcélite when she wins this engagement and delivers a final taunt to Jeanne in retreat. King captures Marcélite's portrait as she sits in the arbor of the school and communes with herself in Creole. Marcélite appears with "the green leaves . . . a harmonious frame for the dark-brown face, red and yellow *tignon,* and the large gold ear-rings hanging beneath two glossy *coques* of black wool. Her features were regular and handsome according to the African type, with a strong, sensuous expression, subdued but not obliterated" (p. 19).

The foliage is an appropriate "frame" for Marcélite, who is attired neatly but whose portliness is unconfined. Marcélite's serenity and the tenseness of the girls in their classroom are effectively juxtaposed. She is shown to be part of the natural scene itself and seems to be capable of expressing real emotion in a way that the girls are not. Her "soft black eyes" show "in their voluptuous depths intelligence and strength and protecting tenderness" (p. 19).

Marcélite's apparent warmth explains why the girls drop their superficial roles when she dresses their hair and why she deserves to be called "the general *chargée d'affaires, confidente,* messenger, and adviser of teachers and scholars" (p. 19). "In truth," King adds, "Marcélite was as indispensable as a lightning-rod to the boarding-school, conducted as it was under the austere discipline of the old régime" (pp. 19–20).

Intuitive, discreet, and adept at styling ladies' elaborate coiffures, Marcélite has an excellent local reputation. "In the *Quartier Créole,* there was hardly a man, woman, or child who did not call her by name: Marcélite Gaulois" (p. 20). But despite the fact that Marcélite lives and does business in other parts of the city, where she is also known and respected, her life and her heart are at St. Denis. Here, ironically, at a finishing school that teaches the denial of the basic emotions Marcélite personifies, Marcélite has left Marie Modeste to learn to be a white lady.

Initially, King allows the supposition that Marie must be Marcélite's real daughter. Monsieur Motte's thirteen-year neglect of his niece has been stressed in the jokes of the other students, and Marcélite's evasion of Marie's questions about him seems inexplicable and ominous. Thus, when

Marcélite speaks with Marie in the girls' dormitory, the hairdresser's anguish seems just below the surface. Marcélite's suffering emerges in this scene and continues to dominate King's characterization of her throughout the rest of the story. It is Marcélite's noble suffering and her tragic, misguided participation in Marie's imprisonment at St. Denis that raises Marcélite from the stereotype of the devoted slave.

Marcélite has brought Marie an exquisite graduation dress as part of the fantasy she has created that Marie's life will offer fewer restrictions than she herself has known. In this scene in the dormitory, Marcélite courts Marie, hoping to see a sign of the love she feels is slipping from her. Later, in the sequel to "Monsieur Motte," King will show Marcélite, again frozen by Marie's "apathetic *white* silence" and longing "for one moment of equality and confidence!" (p. 150). But for the moment, Marcélite's obsessive concern with the proper attire for Marie recalls King's observation that there was nothing the quadroon mother would not do to pass her daughter off as white and so gain entrance for her into white society.

Marcélite helps Marie with the graduation slippers she pretends are from *le vieux,* the fictitious uncle of the title. The intensity as well as the misguided nature of Marcélite's love for Marie appear in a long passage that describes Marcélite patiently laboring with Marie to help her into the white satin boot:

> She knelt on the floor and stripped off one shoe and stocking. When the white foot on its fragile ankle lay in her dark palm, her passion broke out afresh. She kissed it over and over again; she nestled it in her bosom; she talked baby-talk to it in creole; she pulled on the fine stocking as if every wrinkle were an offence, and slackness an unpardonable crime. How they both labored over the boot,— straining, pulling, smoothing the satin, coaxing, urging, drawing the foot! What patience on both sides! What precaution that the glossy white should meet with no defilement! Finally the button-holes were caught over the buttons, and to all intents and purposes a beautiful, symmetrical, solidified satin foot lay before them. (pp. 33–34)

The pulling, urging, straining—the sheer effort conveyed by this long emotion-fraught passage might be interpreted in many ways. The self-abasement of Marcélite, the tension apparent in such a minor act as the trying on of a new high-button shoe, and the parallel between Marie's perfect fit, achieved with great strain, and Cinderella's much easier fit, are all obvious. Taken in the context of King's depiction of the rigidity of female education at St. Denis, however, this passage indicates the tremendous effort required for the lady to look the part. The sacrifice of the natural shape and size of Marie's foot for the appearance achieved by "a beautiful, symmetrical, solidified satin foot" in white suggests the cost in comfort, time, and mobility to Marie herself. Marcélite's sacrifice to the appearance required for Marie to be a lady forces still further sacrifices on Marie. Ironically, the efforts of both women in keeping up appearances make their communication increasingly difficult.

King's attitude toward the way women sacrifice themselves for the illusions demanded of them reappears in her tongue-in-cheek description of the young students on the night before the graduation ceremonies. While recognizing the silliness of the picture they make, King seems to adopt a balanced view of the girls' concern with beauty. This concern makes them look "like so many blanched porcupines," for their hair is "done up in white paper *papillotes.*" "This," King remarks, "was one of the first of those innumerable degrees of preparation by which they expected to transform themselves into houris of loveliness by concert-time." The girls' commitment to their transformation makes them undergo the physical pain of twisting each curl "to the utmost limit of endurance; and on occasions when tightness of curl is regulated by tightness of twist, endurance may safely be said to have no limits." "As a woman's first duty is to be beautiful," or so the St. Denis girls think, they must make the small sacrifice of comfort necessary (p. 61).[40]

Madame Lareveillère, the model of feminine propriety and a fashion plate to the girls at St. Denis, sacrifices her life to the appearances that Marcélite believes are real. Although self-deluding, Madame senses from time to time the fragility of her illusions. She wages a constant "campaign" against "that uglifying process by which women are coaxed into resignation to old age and death" (p. 46), but she is beset by "a vague suspicion" that *"dans son intérieur"* she is beginning "to grow the least, little, tiny bit old." She has begun to think furtively of cosmetic miracles, confident that in Paris "the last word had not yet been said by the artists of hair-dyes and cosmetics" (p. 47).

Madame Lareveillère's dependence on Marcélite's art to maintain her illusion of youth is complete. When Marcélite fails to meet her appointments before the graduation ceremonies at St. Denis, the headmistress is left looking "in the glass at her gray, spare locks" and looking "on her toilette at her beautiful brown curls and plaits." Having literally and figuratively, but only momentarily, awakened to her inability to take care of herself, Madame thinks, "How terrible it is not to be able to comb one's own hair!" (p. 67). To meet the emergency, Madame Lareveillère fashions a makeshift, probably ridiculous, lace fichu into what she thinks is a "presentable substitute for curls and puffs" (p. 68).

Forced from time to time into compromising admissions to herself, Madame Lareveillère nevertheless manages to cover up in other ways and cows her staff and her students. When she appears before the girls, King writes, the headmistress "put off her natural manner, and assumed the conventional disguise supposed to be more fitting her high position." Like her charges, she has adopted one of the few roles provided for women: "Her stately tread and severe mien," King adds, "could hardly have been distinguished from those of her predecessor, the aristocratic old *refugée* from the Island of St. Domingo" (p. 57).

King's look into the dark inner sanctum of the headmistress exposes the self Madame Lareveillère hides from her associates. Overdecoration to a ridiculous degree suggests Madame Lareveillère's efforts to assert her importance and her underlying insecurity. The windows in Madame's room are "made to exclude the light" (p. 49), but there, fully revealed to the reader, are the trivial appointments of Madame's bureau "with its laces and ribbons, its cushions, essence-bottles, jewel-cases, *videpoches,* and little galleried étagères full of gay reflections for the mirror underneath" (p. 50); the overstated opulence of her four-posted mahogany bedstead "with its rigging of mosquito-netting and cords and tassels" looking "like some huge vessel that by accident had lodged in this small harbor" and, nevertheless, "so stupendous, so immeasurable, so gloomily, grandly, majestically imposing" that "little girls sent on occasional messages to Madame felt a tremor of awe at the sight of it, and understood instinctively . . . that here, indeed, was one of those *lits de justice* which caused such dismay in the pages of their French history" (pp. 49–50); and the clutter of Madame's prie-dieu with its "reliquaries, triply consecrated beads, palms, and crucifixes, pictures of sainted martyrs and martyresses (who contradicted the fallacious coincidence of homeliness and virtue), statuettes, prayer-books, pendent flasks of holy water, and an ecclesiastical flask of still holier liquid, impregnated with miraculous promises" (p. 50). Reminiscent of the trivial appointments of Belinda's chamber in Pope's *The Rape of the Lock,* all of the paraphernalia of Madame Lareveillère's quarters suggest Madame's slavish dependence on form and her sterile, uneasy devotion to her confined role.

Paid to direct the education of two hundred young girls, King's headmistress exemplifies the superficiality and inflexibility of the system. Even Madame Lareveillère can be seen to suffer from that system. Her pretension to sophistication only covers her disquieting uncertainty about the world. Although she has been married and widowed and her refrain is "Ah, *les hommes!*" (p. 93), "I know men" (p. 55), "Oh, I know them, like *a b c*" (p. 56), "They are not like us. Oh, I know them well. They are all *égoïstes*" (p. 84), Madame Lareveillère's fustian is undermined by doubt. What she knows about men is that she knows nothing. "I do not know," she finally admits, just after professing to know it all (p. 56).

Unable to comb out her own hair and only half believing herself an expert on *les hommes,* Madame finds that her role requires isolation even from other women. Although it might be assumed that many women would find working with young girls emotionally satisfying, Madame is shown to have formed no real attachments to the girls. Therefore, when Marie Modeste is about to graduate after spending thirteen years as a year-round boarding pupil at St. Denis, Madame muses, "I used to forget her entirely; but now she is going away, I know I shall miss her, yes, very much" (p. 53). Madame's sentiment, of course, would amaze Marie, since Marie's life, like Madame's, has been one of isolation.

The toll that Madame Lareveillère's charade takes on her students and on herself is evident. King emphasizes the pathos and the dishonesty of Madame's pose by introducing her sunset romance, "a *statu quo* affection of fifteen years or more" (p. 88), with Monsieur Goupilleau, a notary, who discreetly visits her only at night. Presumably because Monsieur Goupilleau is of the middle class, the aristocratic Madame Lareveillère will not acknowledge her love for him. She is trapped by her fear of what people will think, but clings to him as "a subterranean passage for friendship" which may offer "a retreat into matrimony" (p. 87).

The headmistress's role, which demands confinement and deception, affects the lives of everyone negatively. However, Madame Lareveillère maintains her prescribed role as the model for her students' behavior until the failure of Monsieur Motte to appear upon Marie's graduation. Madame's inability to handle this emergency, her mystification by the discovery that the school's ledgers contain no address for Monsieur Motte, receives indulgent, but pointedly ironic, treatment. When Madame Joubert, a more competent member of the faculty at St. Denis, suggests that all they need is a directory to look up Monsieur Motte's address, Madame replies, "A what?" . . . "But what is that,—a directory?" (p. 91). *"Quelle bonne idée!"* Madame says when she is told what any city dweller might be expected to know. "If I had only known that! I shall buy one." Madame Joubert must expand her definition of *directory* when Madame starts to send Jeanne to purchase one. "Pardon, Madame," Madame Joubert says tactfully, "I think it would be quicker to send to Bâle's, the *pharmacien* at the corner, and borrow one" (p. 92).

In contrast to Madame Lareveillère, Marcélite is streetwise. But she, too, is lost in an illusion of her own making. In her role as a hairdresser, she manufactures the impression of beauty so necessary to women like Madame Lareveillère. Without Marcélite's skill at creating their "crowning glories," the young girls are reduced to looking, as one of them moans about herself with unintentional irony, like a *"nègre"* (p. 72). Madame Lareveillère and her staff are also dependent on Marcélite for their ladylike appearances; on the one occasion when she fails them, Madame Joubert must go forth *"à la sauvagesse"* (p. 73).

Marcélite, however, does not recognize what an essential part she has in maintaining the cultivated beauty of the white lady. Because Marcélite cannot see Madame Lareveillère, St. Denis, or Marie objectively, she sacrifices both Marie and herself to her image of the white lady. Marcélite's sacrifice, embodied in Monsieur Motte, fully reveals the fixed nature of the roles that both the quadroon woman and the white woman were constrained to play. For without the face-saving fiction of an aristocratic uncle, Marcélite could not transcend her role as a quadroon to manage Marie's life. Nor could Marie accept Marcélite's support without the pretense and remain a lady. In effect, Monsieur Motte joins but separates Marie and Marcélite; he is the invisible patriarch who justifies but controls their interaction.

In the first carefully developed scene between Marie and Marcélite, lack of real communication emphasizes the distance that their fixed roles maintain despite their need for human closeness. Tragically, both women want the intimacy their roles prohibit, but neither dares to speak honestly. Hoping for a response from Marie, Marcélite watches her with "desperate, passionate, caressing eyes" (p. 33). The unveiling of Marie's graduation dress is a pretext for Marcélite to show Marie how much she loves her. Although Marcélite would like to be able to claim full credit for the expensive frock for which she has worked and paid in full, she can only suggest pathetically that her contribution was to improve the design with the addition of the blue bows. "That was my taste," she says. "I went back and made Madame Treize put them on" (p. 31).

The desired embrace does not come. Instead, Marie, who doesn't really care wholeheartedly for graduation finery, asks, "And the shoes, Marcélite?" (p. 31). Prompted, Marcélite, who has always been one step ahead in thinking of her *"bébé's"* needs, produces the shoes. "When did Marcélite ever forget anything you wanted?" she says, betraying herself. The shoes Marcélite has bought are again beyond all expectations. Marie cannot fail to respond to them, since she had only imagined black leather. The "radiant expression" (p. 32) fades from Marcélite's face, however, when Marie ignores her and wonders effusively how she can ever thank Monsieur Motte.

In this masterfully handled brief exchange between Marie and Marcélite, King creates an impression of the cruel limitations typical of their interaction. The racism and sexism that infect their relationship demand the mediation of a Monsieur Motte to prevent both women from confronting the ironies and similarities of their constrained roles. To all the women in the closed female world of St. Denis, of course, Monsieur Motte is symbolic fact. For beyond their tiny world looms a larger world governed by power-ful white men who profit from the class and caste prejudices instilled in women. Exercising remote control of the dealings of women with each other through token women like Madame Lareveillère, these men deter-mine which girls will be awarded the prizes. In inventing Monsieur Motte, therefore, Marcélite casts a traditional script, paradoxically and to her own cost strengthening the reality of patriarchal power. Her pretty lies to Marie sustain the false interaction that denies her the closeness she craves.

Despite the impression this exchange creates of the static nature of Marie and Marcélite's interaction, it is obvious that their intimacy will end with the end of Marie's childhood dependency. Like all young girls in the passage from childhood to adulthood, Marie wants to ask questions about what being a woman means. But Marie is now more aware than ever of the restrictions imposed by her status as a white lady and cannot phrase the questions to Marcélite, whom she now sees as an inferior. When Marie wonders whether Marcélite experienced "this longing . . . this emotion . . . blushes . . . tremors" (p. 29) and recognizes that Marcélite has "stopped at the boundary where the mother ceases to be a physical and becomes a psychical necessity" (p. 30), she demonstrates her misperception of the only mother she has ever known. Marcélite has not at this point become insuffi-cient for Marie's emotional needs; in learning to be a lady, Marie has learned to be contemptuous of Marcélite.

Although she assumed that a graduation dress would cure the vague discontent she senses in Marie, Marcélite slowly awakens to the acute prob-lems that have been building for thirteen years. She confronts the inev-itability of separation from Marie. Marie's insistence on knowing whether her uncle will attend the graduation exercises where she will receive the prize for French history—obviously further testimony to the money Mar-célite has lavished on Marie's education, since the prize is reserved by Madame Lareveillère for the girl whose parents have been "kindest" to the school—pushes Marcélite from discomfort to panic.

From the corner where she arranges Marie's clothes in an armoire with her back turned and her face hidden from Marie's view, Marcélite attempts to evade Marie's questions with familiar ploys. Understatement in this dialogue suggests the intensity of the turmoil Marcélite experiences. She is isolated by the armoire, where she performs her role as a menial. Obviously trying to avoid lying but realizing that now even the tried-and-true for-mulas are not enough, Marcélite pretends to be upset over the condition of Marie's clothes: "There is no better subject on which to exercise crude eloquence than the delinquencies of laundresses" (p. 36).

Trying to remember her mother and failing, Marie reminds Marcélite of her limited role and of the fact that even this limited role is about to end. "It *is* hard, Marcélite, it is very hard not even to be able to recollect a mother" (p. 37). Marcélite's torment at this familiar wound is intensified by the threat posed by Marie's longing for her uncle. "To-morrow evening! . . . only to-morrow evening more!" Marie sighs. Marcélite's anguish is movingly suggested in King's restrained observation: "The depravity of the washerwoman must have got beyond even Marcélite's powers of description, for she had stopped talking, but held her head inside the shelf" (pp. 37–38).

Until this moment Marcélite had stifled her need to be acknowledged and loved and her knowledge that someday her lie would be discovered. Now she undergoes a tragic change. King describes the scene through Marcélite's distorting vision. As Marcélite flagellates herself with "nigger, nigger, nigger" (p. 42), she confronts her "place," the role she, along with everyone else, assumes that she, as a Negro, must play, but a role too small for the person she has become.

In Marcélite's eyes the world of St. Denis holds everything forbidden to her as a quadroon. Under the spell of illusion, Marcélite regards Madame Lareveillère as her superior. King, however, implies Marcélite's misperception of herself, Madame Lareveillère, and St. Denis in an ironic presentation of the interview that follows Marcélite's meeting with Marie. Again, Marcélite's self-evaluation and her view of the headmistress are distorted, for Madame Lareveillère is in the act of fixing the allocation of the graduation prizes by consultation with her account book when Marcélite intrudes to speak to her.

In Madame's room Marcélite's concern is not really treated with respect, for Madame is self-importantly, superficially engaged. Not perceiving Marcélite's obvious agitation, the headmistress promises her that Marie "will be handsome, too, some day, when she does not have to study so hard, and can enjoy the diversions of society a little. By the time she is twenty you will see she will be *une belle femme.*" Then, entirely forgetting Marcélite's presence, Madame adds, "Ah, Monsieur Motte, you will be satisfied." Then "the little pen commenced scratching away again, and this time registered the deed of prize of French history to *l'élève,* Marie Modeste Motte" (p. 53).

Her last hope of reprieve exhausted, Marcélite seeks refuge outside among the poisonous, pink oleanders. Then, as day breaks, Marcélite vanishes in "the direction of the river, where the morning breeze was just beginning to ripple the waters and drive away the fog" (p. 60). The buildup to Marcélite's disappearance, the credibility of King's presentation of Marcélite's suffering, and the closural images surrounding her in preceding passages may lead the reader to assume that Marcélite has committed suicide. Symbolically, at least, Marcélite's flight does suggest the destruction of her personality, for when she reappears she has been transformed from the self-assured, admirable woman who vanquished Jeanne to an abject, "panting, tottering, bedraggled wretch" (p. 94).

King makes it clear that the "pure disinterestedness of Marcélite's devotion" explains her behavior here and elsewhere in the story. In a letter to Charles Dudley Warner, dated September 17, 1885, King remarked that a friend had suggested that she might make Marcélite's devotion more plausible if she had Marie save Marcélite from the auction block. King resisted the suggestion, feeling "this was gross and untrue to my conception."[41] Thus, Marcélite's flight from discovery is motivated by her fear that her admission that she has supported Marie all along will damage Marie's reputation as a white lady. In an impassioned outburst that brings together the shattering conscious and unconscious ironies of the story, Marcélite cries, "Oh, my God! I knew it would kill her! . . . To be supported by a nigger!"[42] Waiting for Marie's revulsion, feeling she deserves it, Marcélite explains, "I wanted you to go to the finest school with ladies" (p. 97).

In the climax of "Monsieur Motte," as first published in the *New Princeton Review,* January 1886, Marcélite's assumed role as Monsieur Motte ends. Already, the inadequacy of her role as an inferior is obvious, for the strength she manifested in loving and giving has vanished with the fiction that made it possible. Forced back into her ascribed role, an impotent role in which her noble qualities cannot find expression, Marcélite realizes that her "brave personation was over. As Marcélite, there was nothing to accomplish except the part of a faithful servant. As Monsieur Motte, what could she not do?" For the first time in her life, Marcélite begins "to reproach God, and vaguely to rebel against the shadow on her skin as casting the shadow on her life" (p. 106).

Because their lives are fatally interwoven, the shadow on Marcélite's life also darkens Marie's life. Both women, as King unfolds their characters and their relationship, are hemmed in by racism and sexism. Marie finds her role, which is prescribed by sexism, too limiting. Even Madame Lareveillère admits this fact, though her matter-of-fact unconcern reveals her inability to empathize. Marie "has been a *pensionnaire* at the Institut St. Denis for thirteen years, and she has never been anywhere except to church; she has seen no one without a chaperon; she has received no letter that has not passed through Madame Joubert's hands" (p. 91).

The unnaturalness of Marie's seclusion at St. Denis is indicated by her unhealthy, tubercular appearance. "Her black eyes were oversized for her face, oversized and overweighted with expression; and most of the time, as to-day, they were accompanied by half-moon shadows which stretched half-way down her cheek" (p. 27). Marie's unhealthy appearance serves to indict the treatment of girls of her generation, who were stunted both intellectually and physically in the process of socialization to become ideal women with the flushed cheeks, dilated eyes, and wasp waists associated with female beauty but symptomatic of tuberculosis as well.[43] This un-healthy state of affairs was encouraged by girls' schools like St. Denis, where meager bread-and-butter lunches were the rule for growing girls.

Marie's thin, sad lips, the first visible sign that she is, in fact, a white girl, are "encircled with a shadow, faint, almost imperceptible, as was the timid suggestion of nascent passion which it gave to [them]" (p. 29). Like Claire Blanche's sensuality, Marie's nascent passion sets her apart. Marie, like Claire Blanche and Marie Madeleine, yearns for experiences forbidden her. Thus, although "romances and poetry had been kept from her like wine and spices," Marie's development answers an inner rhythm denied by her edu-cation. In spite of Marie's unnatural confinement as a white young lady, "the flowers bloomed, and music had chords, and moonlight rays, and were the bars of the school never so strong, and the rules never so rigid, they could not prevent her heart from going out toward the rays, nor from listening to the music, nor from inhaling the breath of the flowers" (p. 28).

The pathos of Marie's situation cannot be perceived by Marcélite, of course, for she has a huge emotional and financial investment in providing Marie with the best education available to young women. In fact, the extreme nature of Marie's seclusion at St. Denis is Marcélite's responsibility. But this seclusion isolates Marie from her peers and perhaps allows her to develop self-reliance that the other girls do not have. Unconsciously, Marie may sense the shallowness of friendships fostered at the school and model herself on Marcélite, incorporating Marcélite's self-assurance and self-suffi-ciency. Marie rejects some of the forms to which the other girls adhere mindlessly. She resists curling her hair. Her reward for this bit of self-assertion is that she alone looks attractive when Marcélite fails to appear to comb out the other students' hair. Therefore, when her uncle does not come for her and Marie is left "standing so by the piano a long while, her gold crown on her head, her prizes in her arms, and a light shawl she had thoughtfully provided to wear home," she is able to find another identity (p. 77).

By herself in the dormitory, where she has been "the only boarder" (p. 38) summer after summer, Marie begins to put her life into perspective and to grow up. Significantly, she does not see any distinction between her confined school life and that of other women. The final disappointment on graduation night merges with all the other disappointments: "While the contents of her previous life were poured out with never-ending detail, and as they lay there, before and all around her, she saw for the first time how bare, how denuded, of pleasure and comfort it had been. . . . She saw it now, and she felt a woman's indignation and pity over it. . . . She leaned her head against the side of her bed and wept, not for herself, but for all women and all orphans" (pp. 78–79).

Marie's sympathy for the suffering of women reemerges in the denouement of "Monsieur Motte." Believing that Marcélite is her real mother, Marie prepares to leave with her. When Madame Lareveillère offers to be Marie's "mother" after learning that she is white, Marie is apathetic toward the headmistress's effusions. Here, Marie's lack of response seems appropriate, for Madame Lareveillère's unexpected maternal awakening, King implies, is self-interested. Madame has discovered in Marie's need for a mother a convenient excuse to betroth herself to the déclassé Monsieur Goupilleau: "If it were only a question of duty," she thinks aloud to herself in the sequel to "Monsieur Motte," "there was nothing a woman could not do for duty, or religion; that made marriage so much more reasonable, so much less ridiculous, *enfin;* but love!" (p. 132).

In *Monsieur Motte,* the continuation of Marie and Marcélite's story published in 1888, King's cast remains in character. Madame Lareveillère, still concerned with what her friends will think, still a woman capable only of superficial concern for others, marries Monsieur Goupilleau, her notary. Without the power to direct Marie's life, Marcélite becomes a shadow of her former self. Having inherited a passion for living from Marcélite, Marie Modeste becomes King's central character.

In this sequel to the earlier story, King's concern with the manner in which the female proprieties dehumanize women continues to appear in the interplay of her characters. Marie is developed as the contrast to Madame Lareveillère, who marries "for duty," since Marie marries unabashedly for love, refusing to sign the prenuptial contract drawn up by her fiancé's wealthy stepmother. In "The Southern Heroine in the Fiction of Representative Southern Women Writers, 1850–1960," Marie Fletcher tells us that Marie Modeste's impolitic treatment of her future mother-in-law is consistent with "the emerging of a more independent heroine—one who chooses her own husband, even in opposition to family, and one who marries into the middle class, usually for love rather than for property."[44] The marriage contract that Marie's prospective mother-in-law demands is conventional in that, as a friend remarks, marriage contracts "are all against the women, the poor women!" (p. 312). Marie, however, showing the new spirit of independence, refuses to accept it: "I give nothing, I will take nothing,—nothing! . . . I give nothing but love! I want nothing but love!" (p. 318). More unconventional are Marie's passion and the unrestrained way the engaged couple embrace and kiss before the wedding.

King emphasizes Marie's departure from convention by contrasting her behavior with that of Madame Lareveillère, who requires an excuse to condescend to love a social inferior like her notary. Marie disdains to conceal her passion. When Madame intrudes on Marie embracing her fiancé, Charles, Madame must rethink her plans for Marie's betrothal: "She had planned it otherwise, and far better,—this scene,—with a minute particularity for detail which only an outsider and a schemer in futurity can command. The young man would come to her first, of course, with his avowal, as etiquette prescribes. She would go to Marie herself, and delicately, as only a woman can, she would draw aside the veil from the unconscious heart and show the young girl the dormant figure of her love there,—love whose existence she did not dream of. . . . But the event always fools the prepared" (pp. 264–65).

Marie is obviously way ahead of Madame. However, King also raises questions about the wisdom of Marie's joyful acceptance of "woman's vocation" (p. 289). In presenting a frivolous discussion among Marie's former classmates, King shows the limited alternatives available to the young lady. The girls gossip about a friend whose mother precipitated an announcement of engagement for her daughter "to cut off retreat from the gentleman" (p. 284). "I will never get married, I'm sure," complains one of Marie's friends. The girls are indistinguishable in King's dialogue at this point. "Nor I either; I never had any luck," responds another. "If I do not get married, I do not want to live." "Nor I, *chérie*, candidly." "Not to get married, is to confess one's self simply a—a *Gorgon*." "But it's a woman's vocation! What must she do else?" "There is always the convent." "The convent! bah! The convent does n't fool any one" (pp. 284–85).

With such limited choices, it is perhaps inevitable that for the debutantes love is the whole focus of desire and expectation. In the face of a depressing future reality suggested by the sad fate of Odile, who threatened to kill herself or enter a convent if frustrated in her matrimonial plans but found ennui and neglect in her marriage, these would-be wives persistently encourage each other's hopes of finding the right man. Odile serves as an example only to those who are already married. "Poor Odile! but she would marry him; she was warned enough! . . . And that is what is called having a husband!" says Tante Pauline (p. 204).

Although Marie Modeste is better fitted to find the marital happiness she seeks than Odile and her unmarried girlfriends, King treats Marie's decision to marry ambivalently. The description of Marie's appearance on her wedding day is strangely macabre. For Marie appears as a "bride or corpse" already "on that road which [the other girls] could travel as yet only in imagination" (p. 282). Whether Marie's journey will bring happiness or the death of her hard-won self is unclear. However, King obviously hopes that Marie will transform the "vocation of wife." In Marie's self-assertion concerning the terms of her marriage and in her final recognition that

Marcélite deserves to be honored as her foster mother, Marie moves from the conventional code of St. Denis to an identity responsive to true human emotion. King's final words reveal that even racial prejudice must fall under the influence of love and gratitude, for about Marie Modeste's wedding ceremony she writes: "It was not Madame Goupilleau, but Marcélite, who walked behind the bride that night to the altar, for so Marie Modeste had commanded. It was not to Madame Goupilleau, but to Marcélite, that the bride turned for her first blessing after the ceremony. . . . It was not from Madame Goupilleau, but from Marcélite, that Charles Montyon received his bride" (p. 326).

"The Little Convent Girl"

While the triumph of love in *Monsieur Motte* makes it the happiest of Grace King's stories that deal with woman's place and the color line and the only one of these stories to present any escape for the heroine, it is Marie's unconventional rejection of racism that allows for the happy ending. Marie's refusal to accept the dictates of propriety indict sexism and racism. In "The Little Convent Girl," a story Anne Goodwyn Jones finds "a nearly perfect allegory" of the submerged identities of Southern women authors, the unnamed heroine's total acceptance of a racist, sexist view of life results in tragedy.[45] Awakening to the fact that she is racially mixed, the little convent girl commits suicide. Her inability to cope with this unsettling discovery or with any of the basic demands of life outside the convent speaks of her cruel, stunting education to become a lady. It is clear that this little girl's education has succeeded where Marie Modeste's has failed. Upholding a rigid standard of feminine decorum, the little convent girl is faced with the plight of the white lady living among slaves. Winthrop D. Jordan's description of closed options afforded the white lady fits King's character: "Her choices were to withdraw from the world or to create an unreal one of her own. She withdrew from the colored race and, perhaps not entirely because of prevailing notions about health, scrupulously shielded her face from the darkening effects of the tropic sun. A tanned skin implied an affinity which she had to deny."[46]

The debilitating nature of the role the little convent girl attempts to play is evident. Social convention, religion, and convent education appear to have warped the girl's personality, for from the beginning of King's narrative the girl withdraws from life. She attempts to deny the attraction that the forbidden world has for her. And she must be told how to do everything or be given permission to do those few things she is able to do. Pointedly, King remarks, "She could not do anything of herself; she had to be initiated into everything by some one else."[47]

Described in poignant detail, the eighteen-year-old girl is helped to board the steamboat in Cincinnati by nuns and sets out on a journey down the Mississippi to meet a mother she cannot remember. The raconteur who narrates the story, perhaps we are intended to assume, is one of the other female passengers on the downriver trip with the little girl. This narrator tells the story in a relaxed, colloquial tone that contrasts markedly with the tension evident in the little convent girl. The narrator's tone implies that she is a woman of some sophistication who has often made the trip that so awes the girl.

Although the girl is regarded by the captain, the pilot, and all the males aboard as "the beau-ideal of the little convent girl" (p. 144), King's raconteur views their attitude toward the girl with worldly-wise detachment. The narrator, perhaps, is well aware that their reverence for the girl's innocence is proof of their own licentiousness. But she sympathizes with the girl, since she imagines that this male ideal was achieved at the convent by breaking the girl's spirit and teaching her to despise herself and her emotions. Thus, the narrator dwells on the scene in which the sisters say farewell to the little convent girl by only shaking her hand: "Good-bys have really no significance for sisters" (p. 143), she says in an aside.

The fact that the girl's father immured her for twelve years in a convent where such formality was the rule, that he prevented her from having any contact with her mother all those years, and that he maintained a disagreement with her mother after taking control of the girl suggest that even with her father the girl had found little human warmth. Upon her father's death, the girl seeks out what she has been lacking. She asks to go to her mother. Even after her father's death, however, matters must be arranged with strict formality by others. A letter from the Mother Superior "had arranged it all with the mother of the girl" (p. 149). A formal letter is sent to the girl's mother, and a facsimile of that letter is given to the captain of the steamboat by the nuns, who part with the girl so coldly.

Apprehensive about the end of her journey and panic-stricken about every minor event along the way, the little convent girl behaves like a catatonic. Even after being shown around the boat, she still waits to be taken from place to place. "Unless the captain or the clerk remembered to fetch her out in front, she would sit all day in the cabin, in the same place, crocheting lace, her spool of thread and box of patterns in her lap, on the handkerchief spread to save her new dress" (pp. 147–48). This kind of helplessness reveals a pathetic lack of some kind to the woman watching, but procures a flurry of chivalrous activity from the captain and the pilot, who are charmed by this paragon of feminine frailty and less perceptive about the abnormality of the girl's compulsive femininity than the woman who tells the girl's story. The narrator's ironic voice implies a richer reality "to be seen and heard, but only by those who are 'fine' and 'sensitive,' not limited by the perceptual expectations of the male world, that colors be bright, and sounds loud."[48]

The narrator also recognizes that the extra pains that the men aboard take for the little convent girl are a departure from their usual practice. When the girl recoils from the bawdy language of the deckhands, for example, and refuses to venture back on deck anymore, the captain redoubles his assurance that the language will cease. Swearing changes to sarcasm as the mate alters his four-letter commands and politely requests "the colored gentlemen not to hurry themselves—on no account whatever; to take their time about shoving out the plank; to send the rope ashore by post-office—write him when it got there; begging them not to strain their backs; calling them mister, colonel, major, general, prince, and your royal highness" (pp. 152–53).

Under the silent influence of this good little girl, the men's behavior changes superficially, and the captain feels "stuck as fast aground in mid-stream" as his steamboat had been the moment before, when he lost control of his vocabulary in a perilous instant and then saw "the little black figure hurrying through the chaos on the deck" (p. 153). The waiters feel the necessity to "importun[e]" (p. 148) the girl to try the delicious food on the boat. The clerk tries to make her laugh. And the pilot singles her out for company in the pilothouse and explains everything about the journey "as exquisitely and respectfully as if she had been the River Commission." "It was a miracle," King's storyteller says tongue in cheek, "that the pilot ever got her up into the pilot-house." His treatment of the little convent girl accords with the captain's, for he treats her as if "there could be no tenderer consideration in life for him than her comfort" (p. 154).

Truly, the little convent girl is an ideal to the men aboard the steamboat—she is presumed white. Under her chaste, white influence they are transformed into the finest Southern gentlemen. In her perfect performance of her role, the little convent girl is seen sympathetically and perceptively by the narrator, whose ironic view and seemingly gratuitous comments imply that she, too, has experienced and not quite overcome the effects of rigid female education.

The narrator's description of the girl's clothing reveals her understanding of restrictive dress. She describes the hard-edged rigidity of the girl's mourning costume as though she laments its function in restraining natural impulse and energy. Noting first the girl's "stiff new bombazine dress [with] crape collar and cuffs" and her black straw hat "trimmed with stiff new crape," the narrator focuses her irony on the "tight and fast" coiffing of the girl's hair, which "had a strong inclination to curl" but had had that "taken out of it as austerely as the noise out of her footfalls." Indeed, remarks the narrator, the girl "walked with such soft, easy, carefully calculated steps that one naturally felt the penalties that must have secured them—penalties dictated by a black code of deportment" (p. 144).

In the emotion-tinged description above, the verb "felt" and the phrase "penalties dictated by a black code of deportment" seem to suggest both the narrator's identification with the little convent girl and her bilingual sophistication in linking the system of education that has ensured the girl's neurosis to the infamous *Code Noir* that Harriet Beecher Stowe and George Washington Cable deplored. Here, the narrator's descriptive legerdemain is especially impressive, for it allows her to condemn subtly but absolutely the system that produced the girl. Were it not for the separation afforded by the narrator and the contrary evidence of King's other works in which ingenues suffer from the severe restrictions imposed upon women, the reader might justly suspect the author herself of anti-Catholicism despite her urbanity. Certainly, in her description of the effects on the girl of her system of education, there can be detected some hostility and some familiarity. But although the little convent girl displays the austerity of the convent system, Marie Motte also displayed the effects of the "austere discipline" of her secular school. Here, "austerity" is perhaps a matter of degree, for Marie's experience at St. Denis was ameliorated by her constant contact with Marcélite. In contrast, the little convent girl appears to be the ne plus ultra of a young girl robbed of her individuality by religion, convention, and sexism.

"Never leaning back—oh, no! always straight and stiff, as if the conventual back board were there within call" (p. 148), the girl attempts to withstand the disordered world outside the convent walls by maintaining her adherence to the convent rules. She is terrified. On Friday she fasts; she refuses to eat anything but convent fare; she always remembers to pray and genuflect before eating; she observes the devotional hours in spite of the absence of church bells. Terror explains her rigidity. For when, in the ordinary course of life on the river, the boat stops to take on freight, the ensuing clamor always alarms her. "Every time she thought it was shipwreck, death, judgment, purgatory; and her sins! her sins!" (p. 149).

After the captain begins "fetching her" out to watch the noisy, daily landings, however, the little convent girl becomes mesmerized by the scene. No longer frightened, but eager to watch the ritual, "she would stay all day just where the captain put her, going inside only for her meals. She forgot herself at times so much that she would draw her chair a little closer to the railing, and put up her veil, actually, to see better" (pp. 150–51). Although the girl so "forgets herself" and everyone has begun to "feel a personal interest in her," the girl's "shyness" preserves her privacy (p. 151).

Seen through the eyes of the little convent girl and through the eyes of the more sophisticated woman who watches the girl and the scene, steamboat landings were "worth seeing" (p. 151). Landings seem chancy and eventful even though they happen again and again. Loadings are almost as interesting, with "rolling of barrels, and shouldering of sacks, and singing of Jim Crow songs, and pacing of Jim Crow steps; and black skins glistening through torn shirts, and white teeth gleaming through red lips, and laughing, and talking and—bewildering! entrancing!" "Surely," the narrator speculates, "the little convent girl in her convent walls never dreamed of so much unpunished noise and movement in the world!" (pp. 151–52). At this point, the reader might be led to conjecture that the little convent girl is watching blacks for the first time.

In watching, the little convent girl is brought up short by the swearing of the men. "The first time she heard the mate—it must have been like the first time woman ever heard man—curse and swear, she turned pale, and ran quickly, quickly into the saloon, and—came out again? No, indeed!" the narrator remarks almost audibly, "not with all the soul she had to save, and all the other sins on her conscience" (p. 152). Although the narrator only hints at what "sins" the girl imagines she could have committed, the description of the girl's response to river life implies that the girl feels that any emotion or response is inherently sinful. Thus, when the little convent girl stays up in the pilothouse listening to the pilot talk about astronomy until after her nine o'clock bedtime, "she appeared almost intoxicated at the wild pleasure" but "was immediately overwhelmed at the wickedness of it, and observed much more rigidity of conduct thereafter" (p. 155).

This pattern of "wild pleasure" and repentance is terminated by the "immanence of arrival into port." Joining in the "panic of preparation" (p. 156), the little convent girl compulsively packs and repacks her suitcase. Suspense is heightened for all the passengers by delays, but especially for the little convent girl, who fears that her mother, whom she cannot remember, will now reject her as her father once did. This fear is emphasized by the description of the girl's toilet: "Her hair was brushed and plaited and smoothed over and over again until the very last glimmer of a curl disappeared. Her dress was whisked, as if for microscopic inspection; her face was washed; and her finger-nails were scrubbed with the hard convent nailbrush, until the disciplined little tips ached with a pristine soreness" (pp. 156–57).

In this description, as in the earlier description of the girl's hair with its inclination to curl and the girl's mouth with its "pathetic little forced expression" (p. 147), the narrator prepares for her final disclosure. The description's functional foreshadowing should not, however, be interpreted as an indication of the narrator's racist attitudes toward the girl. Since she also describes the girl blushing and blanching just as a white girl would do in similar circumstances (violating a racist pseudoscientific belief that mulattoes could not blush or blanch no matter how light they were), the narrator's observations seem less biased than might be expected.

The similarity between the little convent girl's anxious preparations to meet her mother and Marie Modeste's preparations to meet Monsieur Motte is striking. The different reactions of the girls to shocking discoveries can be explained by the difference in the severity of their training. Although Marie initially believes that she is Marcélite's daughter, she is prepared to cope with her new identity. The little convent girl, however, has been shown incapable of coping with the smallest change in her rigid, convent-imposed schedule. Marie's ability to resist, in some measure, the strictures of St. Denis life and her experience of the strong maternal love of Marcélite help explain why Marie has the ability to survive her disillusionment, whereas the little convent girl—also a "good little girl"—cannot survive.

Because she has the carefully edited view of life of the woman on the pedestal, the little convent girl cannot respond when she goes down the gangplank to meet the mother she has journeyed to see. Perhaps she does not even perceive immediately that all is not as it should be. But the captain and her fellow travelers, who are all interested in partaking of what they assume will be a heartwarming reunion, respond for her. The electrifying irony of the captain's lame parting, "Be a good little girl," closes the girl's story thematically. Her tragedy is that she has no other role and the only alternative is unthinkable. The whistles of surprise and the audible or inaudible exclamations of the word "Colored!" by her fellow travelers, of course, receive no response from the girl, who does not "turn her eyes to the right or left, or once (what all passengers do) look backward at the boat" (p. 158).

When, a month later, the girl's mulatto mother returns with the girl to the steamboat, she tells the captain that she brings the girl back because "she don't go nowhere, she don't do nothing but make her crochet and her prayers, so I thought I would bring her for a little visit of 'How d' ye do' to you." The captain, however, does not perceive any real change in the girl herself, for the behavior her mother describes is consistent with the girl's behavior on the steamboat journeying to New Orleans. The narrator, in contrast to the captain, senses something amiss in the situation. Once more she seems to imply that the captain is not discerning enough: "There was, perhaps, some inflection in the woman's voice that might have made known, or at least awakened, the suspicion of some latent hope or intention, had the captain's ear been fine enough to detect it. There might have been something in the little convent girl's face, had his eye been more sensitive—a trifle paler, maybe, the lips a little tighter drawn, the blue ribbon a shade faded. He may have noticed that, but—" (p. 160).

Superficially, however, the little convent girl responds as she has been programmed to respond at the convent. The captain views her passivity uncritically, not recognizing the cost of such passive feminine behavior to the girl. Because neither the captain nor the girl's mother comprehends the little convent girl's self-hatred, neither recognizes the danger when the girl slips away as her mother releases her hand to shake hands with the captain. "No one was looking," the narrator observes, "no one saw more than a flutter of white petticoats, a show of white stockings, as the little convent girl went under the water. . . . her body was never found" (p. 161).

Tragically, the convent girl, who had so closely guarded her wayward petticoats in ascending the stairs to the pilothouse at the beginning of the story, abandons propriety only in the flash of white stocking glimpsed upon her suicide. But even at this moment, her abandon is strictly conventional. Following the course of despairing nineteenth-century heroines before and after her, the little convent girl yields to the impulse to end it all. At this instant of unconscious self-revelation, the girl remains pathetically dependent on others to present her with the opening she needs: Her mother ventures back to the steamboat in an attempt to cheer the girl up; only one moment of inattention on the mother's part permits the girl's leap to freedom.

Examining the literary convention the convent girl's suicide reflects, Emily Toth sees the drowning of other heroines in straitened circumstances as "indictments"—"dramatic translations of the themes discussed by feminist critics" of the eighteenth and nineteenth centuries.[49] Certainly, the white heroine's suicide is a well-established convention in nineteenth-century fiction. However, suicides also became commonplace in fiction dealing with miscegenation. Cable's Honoré Grandissime, f. m. c. (free man of color), drowns himself in despair. Sherwood Bonner's Zoe in "A Volcanic Interlude" (1880) dies of heart failure when she learns the awful secret from which her white, dandy father has been shielding her. In *An Imperative Duty* (1892) William Dean Howells allows Rhoda, his racially mixed heroine, to survive the discovery of her black ancestry. The aunt who breaks this bit of bad news, however, takes an "accidental" overdose and dies. So the reader assumes that Marcélite Gaulois of King's "Monsieur Motte" has drowned herself simply because she walks despondently toward a river. King counts on this assumption in "The Little Convent Girl," exploiting both conventions to suggest the girl's kinship with other women caught in no-exit situations.

Both the girl's death and the concrete description King provides to show the girl's deformed image of herself reinforce the indictment the story makes of the proscriptive, passive virtues taught to women at some of the best schools in the nineteenth century: piety, domesticity, docility, and prudery.[50] Because she possesses these virtues to a pathological degree, the little girl is revered by the male characters in King's story as a "beau-ideal." But these virtues prevent her from surviving the disillusionment life has in store for her. If she differs from King's other ingenues, that difference lies primarily in her total conformity to her role and her dependence on that role and the responses it elicits for her will to live.

"The Little Convent Girl" distills King's earlier treatments of young girls thwarted by patriarchal assumptions about women. King's portrayal of Marie Modeste, Marie Madeleine, Claire Blanche, and most tragically the little convent girl, who is destroyed by the dehumanizing role foisted on her, are fictional embodiments of Charlotte Perkins Gilman's observation that "each woman born ... has had to live over again in her own person the same process of restriction, repression, denial; the smothering 'no' which crushed down all her human desires to create, to discover, to learn, to express, to advance."[51]

Under this "smothering no," Grace King's women characters enact the relative powerlessness of women. Because they are defined by their sex, by their race, and by their class, King's women of mixed blood also reveal her bitter awareness of sexism in the post–Civil War South. Women of suspect race, as King knew, were in double jeopardy in this society. Deeply conscious of the limitations white women faced, King seized the provocative stereotype of the tragic octoroon and transformed it, showing the limitations placed on all women in a man's world where the breadth of nose, shape of lip, thickness and color of hair, tautness of skin determined a woman's chances of happiness.

In creating realistic characters out of stereotype, King's conscious concern was, perhaps, the plight of the white girl who typically aborted her journey to adulthood.[52] But as Helen Taylor recognizes, King "wrote of her own frustrations, feelings of violation and helplessness, and resentment of patriarchal attitudes and regimes women had endured in the South by analogy with the oppression of other groups—notably black slaves and then freedmen";[53] and her art and human sympathies led her beyond racial chauvinism to a position far closer to George Washington Cable's than has until recently been allowed. Although she still languishes in the shadow of Cable, recent reexaminations of King's work have brought to light the wide range of her achievement in fiction writing, literary criticism, historical narrative, biography, and autobiography. As Robert Bush reminds us, King's "career, as much as that of anyone of her generation, was an announcement that women of the South could successfully compete with men in the intellectual world."[54]

In King's fiction, the reader may miss the romantic vision of Cable, but revel in King's meticulous rendering of commonplace detail. King's literary treatment of women whose lives were darkened and whose chances were diminished by race, sex, and class prejudice amplifies Cable's plea for justice; and the subtle variations King plays on the theme of the tragic octoroon resonate with her deep, if largely unconscious, understanding of the way in which oppression shapes human life.

CHAPTER FOUR

· Kate Chopin ·

FROM STEREOTYPE TO SEXUAL REALISM

Chopin's Revelations

Although Kate Chopin did not share George Cable's and Grace King's intense concern with race, and although dark women characters are frequently peripheral or ambiguously identified in her fiction, close examination of these women characters deepens our appreciation of Chopin's achievement as a sexual realist. For in "Désirée's Baby," "La Belle Zoraïde," "At the 'Cadian Ball," "The Storm," and *The Awakening*, Chopin depicts the destructive symbiosis of power and powerlessness, measuring the distance between romantic views of marriage and motherhood and the reality of the sexual lives of women on both sides of the color line.[1] Those attempting to solve the riddle posed by the white women Chopin portrays, however, have neglected to examine this symbiosis and with it the dark women characters through whom she first tested and transgressed the Victorian proprieties in her fiction.

This neglect is perhaps defensible in light of the arresting ambivalence of Chopin's depictions of white women who merely drowse on the verge of awakening to their own sexual possibilities. Per Seyersted, Chopin's biographer, observed this ambivalence: "Mrs. Chopin concentrated on the feminine and the emancipated females, and the fact that she often created these two opposites in pairs, exemplifying—in the course of a few weeks—first the one and then the other, would suggest that she was keeping up a running dialogue with herself on woman's lot."[2]

Joan Zlotnick and others have located ambivalence in the way Chopin "undercuts with irony the dreams and ambitions of her [white] heroines."[3] The focus of much study, of course, has been the baffling treatment of Edna Pontellier in *The Awakening*, the culmination of Chopin's literary dialogue concerning women's lot and the only white woman character to succumb to the sexual temptation many of her other white women characters respond to but resist.[4] Edna's singularity and significance among Chopin's heroines has further obscured the racially shaded gallery of women characters who preceded her, anticipating and preparing for her violation of sexual taboos and defining the dimensions of her solitary despair as a privileged white woman in *The Awakening*. An examination of the novel that takes into account the dark women characters in "Désirée's Baby," "La Belle Zoraïde," "At the 'Cadian Ball," and "The Storm" illuminates Chopin's evolving perspective as she probed the facts of life half concealed by the genteel stereotype of the tragic octoroon, discovering therein the tragic alienation of women from each other, from full self-knowledge, and from self-expression in a society made by and for white men.

Chopin was, of course, familiar with the stereotyped octoroons of other authors. In a diary entry of May 12, 1894, she disparaged the rendering, by her neighbor Mrs. Hull, of a story "upon the theme which Cable has used effectively. A girl with negro blood who is loved by a white man. Possessing a noble character she effaces herself and he knows her no more—she dies of consumption." Succinctly, Chopin added that Mrs. Hull's story "is in the conventional groove." She concluded: "I have no objection to a commonplace theme if it be handled artistically or with originality."[5]

Emily Toth discusses Chopin's appropriation of the stereotype of the tragic octoroon and finds that her use of this character "relies to a degree on the conventions used by such writers as Grace King and George W. Cable," but that "in 'Désirée's Baby' [the story most clearly patterned on the tragic-octoroon formula] she makes stronger connections between the social situations of blacks and [white] women." Surveying Chopin's characters, Toth asserts that her "most skillful use of blacks in fiction is closer to George W. Cable's: a critique of Southern social mores through the conventional figure of the tragic octoroon."[6]

Chopin's black characters, as Toth and others have noted, are usually carefully drawn and realistic. Her detached observations reveal both the extent to which oppressed people are shaped by the stereotypes applied to them and the extent to which they may use these stereotypes to dupe their oppressors. In "In Sabine" (1894), for example, Chopin produced a remarkably unconventional picture of race relations by telling the story of a white woman's escape from her brutal husband with the collusion of a black man. Pouring out the distressing details of her married life to a visitor who finally helps her escape, 'Tite Reine, the heroine in this story, confesses that once when her drunken husband attempted to strangle her, she was freed by their slave, Uncle Mortimer, who threatened the white man with an axe. Uncle Mortimer's enigmatic manner as he breaks the bad news of 'Tite Reine's flight to the man he had once challenged suggests that the weak have finally outfoxed the strong. Beyond this, Chopin's image of Uncle Mortimer saving 'Tite Reine from her putative protector issues a bold, if tacit, denial of the chivalrous claims of white men and their rationalization of lynch law as a means of dealing with the brute "nigger." In this story Chopin clearly anticipates the dawning racial awareness of white women of her generation that found expression in the campaign against lynching in the 1890s.[7]

While Chopin's unorthodox pictures of black characters suggest the range of her sympathies, her concerns are only incidentally race and Southern mores in those stories that deal with the situation of racially mixed women. Even in a minor sketch, "A Little Free-Mulatto," Chopin shows the absolute power of males over females. Aurelia, the little mulatto girl, is bereft of playmates because of her father's unyielding pride. In Chopin's other stories of the color or class line, male power is also a deplorable fact of life. In "A Horse Story," one of her unpublished works, Chopin presents Herminia, a "'Cadian girl of the old Bayou Derbanne settlement."[8] When this 'Cadian girl transgresses the class and caste distinctions that mark her inferior place in Creole society by dropping in on a planter's house party, she is made to feel the intruder she surely is. Her assumption of equality seems to depend upon an earlier indication of favor from Mr. Prospère, the planter, but now he merely gives her a hasty, and perhaps embarrassed, "Hello! Herminia!" (p. 17). Herminia is mortified by this tepid greeting and forgets her scheme to ask for a ride home with Mr. Prospère, even though she has allowed her horse to wander off. Chivalry obviously does not extend to Herminia, who now recognizes her place in Mr. Prospère's world and marries Solistan, a 'Cadian suitor. In gaining Herminia, Solistan gets the woman and the last word. "But who knows!" he opines, "maybe it is all fo' the best" (p. 20). The fact that he is speaking about the death of the runaway horse does not disguise the ironic applicability of his remark to Herminia, who attempted to break the bounds of caste and class only to be tied to Solistan for life.

The significance of the Aurelias and Herminias in Chopin's canon may be inferred from the relative audacity of her treatment of sex in stories that deal with such women. Moreover, stories that feature both stereotypically "dark" women such as these and "white" women such as Clarisse ("At the 'Cadian Ball") and Edna (*The Awakening*) exploit an iconographic convention that assimilates the presumed sexual ardency of the black woman to the sexuality of the white woman by juxtaposing them.[9] Thus, although Chopin makes free with the racist assumptions prevalent in her day to depict realistically those women already stigmatized by imputations of hypersexuality, she creates women characters on both sides of the chasm of color who are motivated by romantic dreams but react in similar ways to sexual urges. Stressing the similarity of her women characters, Chopin exploits the blurred racial categories of the milieu she describes. Because her treatment of race and ethnicity is sometimes negligent and sometimes purposeful, many readers have been baffled by those stories that present the complex and ambiguous racial categories of nineteenth-century Louisiana. Even *The Awakening* has caused confusion on this score. In *The Oxford Companion to American Literature,* for example, James D. Hart calls the novel an "objective account of mixed marriage and adultery."[10] If Hart means by this that Edna Pontellier crossed the color line by marrying a Creole, he is obviously mistaken, but the mistake is an understandable one. The same sort of error occurs in Susan Cahill's introduction to Chopin's "The Story of an Hour," where she remarks that Chopin presented "miscegenation" and adultery in *The Awakening* and published nothing thereafter.[11]

The racial scene in Chopin's Natchitoches parish was complex and might have taxed the powers of the most sociologically minded writer of fiction. However, Chopin was unusually nonchalant about observing racial distinctions that were crucial to her Cane River neighbors but less significant to a woman with a St. Louis origin. Chopin's father was Irish; although her mother's family were aristocratic St. Louis Creoles, she had no personal contact with the complex racial milieu of the Louisiana Creole until she married Oscar Chopin and went with him to Louisiana, where she lived fourteen years before returning to St. Louis a widow with six children.

In *The Folk of Southern Fiction,* Merrill Maguire Skaggs notes Chopin's lack of concern about distinguishing between Creoles and Cajuns (Acadians) in her fiction and observes that "the difference between Creoles and Acadians is so much assumed in Kate Chopin's stories that the uninitiated sometimes have difficulty knowing which group a character belongs to. For practical purposes the reader must simply assume that the rich are Creoles; the poor, Acadians, unless they are otherwise identified."[12]

Skaggs's practical injunction is a useful guide. However, the issue is more complicated than such a guide might lead one to think, for racial and class biases infect the terms *Cajun* and *Creole,* and individuals of both groups are frequently vehement in their insistence on their own racial purity. Although Chopin seldom draws attention to the question of race in depicting Cajuns and Creoles, she often shows the downward and upward mobility of these two groups. Yet the seemingly crucial distinction of race may on occasion be inferred from Chopin's characterizations. In cases where racial distinctions seem essential to a reading of a particular story, such inferences become the subject of critical dispute. Thus, in his biography Seyersted identifies "Ozème's Holiday" (1896) as one of Chopin's best tales, "particularly because of [its] excellence in character delineation," but denies the assertion of some critics that Ozème is a free mulatto.[13] Whatever Ozème's racial status, however, his desultory holiday among the Creoles, Cajuns, free mulattoes, and Negroes of Cane River demonstrates his total disregard for the distinctions that are so important in a racist society.

In her careless handling of the question of race in "Ozème's Holiday," Chopin was being more faithful to the real complexity of the racial situation of the Cane River region than an attempt at a more careful handling would have permitted. However, Chopin's relative lack of concern with racial distinctions throws her emphasis on the racial characteristics of some of her heroines into sharp relief. On occasion, Chopin took pains to raise questions of race. In "A Rude Awakening" (1893), for example, the racial identity of the heroine Lolotte is undisclosed until the end of the story, when Lolotte, who has disappeared, is rediscovered recuperating in a hospital by Aunt Minty, who says: "An' dah you is! . . . settin' down, lookin' jis' like w'ite folks!" Lolotte's answer, "Ain't I always was w'ite folks, Aunt Mint?" is the only direct indication in the story of her race.[14]

In this story the question of Lolotte's racial identity is held in abeyance in order to reinforce the negative picture Chopin draws of Lolotte's shiftless father and the marginal life he allows his family to live. In "At the 'Cadian Ball" Chopin raises the question of race again by drawing attention to the hot-blooded vivacity of the "Spanish vixen" Calixta. Chopin's blurred image of Calixta as she appears to an infatuated suitor named Bobinôt suggests the stereotyped imagery frequently associated with racially and therefore sexually stigmatized women: "Her eyes,—Bobinôt thought of her eyes, and weakened,—the bluest, the drowsiest, most tantalizing that ever looked into a man's; he thought of her flaxen hair that kinked worse than a mulatto's close to her head; that broad, smiling mouth and tiptilted nose, that full figure; that voice like a rich contralto song, with cadences in it that must have been taught by Satan, for there was no one else to teach her tricks on that 'Cadian prairie" ("At the 'Cadian Ball," 1:219). Moreover, Calixta has also been touched by the breath of desire. The Cajun onlookers, "stirred by recollections" of their own experiences with women of her kind, murmur, "Bon chien tient de race" (A good dog is true to its breed) (1:219). Clearly, Calixta's tricks have a profound effect on those around her, and all who know her attribute her powers to what they assume is her exotic racial endowment.

Although Chopin's use of racist imagery here and elsewhere confirms her conventionality to a degree, her critiques of other authors and her descriptions of her own methods reveal her conscious hostility toward received truths of all kinds. Her ability to suggest the sexual politics that required the passion of women like Calixta and the prudery of her white women characters lifts her characterizations of these women from the region of cliché to the realm of social criticism. Chopin's criticism of the works of other writers proves her awareness of the interdependence of aesthetic and experiential validity in fiction. Commenting that the controversial *Jude the Obscure*, which had begun as a serial in *Harper's* in 1894, was a "detestably bad" novel, "unpardonably dull; and immoral, chiefly because it is not true," Chopin charged Hardy with failing to involve the reader because his "characters are so plainly constructed with the intention of illustrating the purposes of the author, that they do not for a moment convey any impression of reality" ("As You Like It," 2:714). In fairness to Hardy it must be noted that his manuscript had been Americanized by Henry Mills Alden at *Harper's*, who blue-penciled portions of it, explaining that "our rule is that the MAGAZINE must contain nothing which could not be read aloud in any family circle."[15]

Chopin's literary awakening began as a reaction against such dicta in her excitement about Maupassant's rejection of the standardized plots, stereotyped characters, and heavy-handed didacticism demanded by genteel editors and readers. Recalling her initial reaction to Maupassant's works in "Confidences," Chopin wrote: "Here was life, not fiction; for where were the plots, the old fashioned mechanism and stage trapping that in a vague, unthinking way I had fancied were essential to the art of story making. Here was a man who had escaped from tradition and authority, who had entered into himself and looked out upon life through his own being and with his own eyes; and who, in a direct and simple way, told us what he saw" (2:700–701).

Although her point of departure for a story was often, at least initially, a Maupassant title or situation, Chopin's fiction was neither simple nor direct. Acknowledging that she thought that the value of fiction lay in its depiction of life's "subtle, complex, true meaning, stripped of the veil with which ethical and conventional standards have draped it" ("The Western Association of Writers," 2:691), Chopin attempted to capture this complex meaning. In doing so, she took greater risks with her material than Maupassant had taken. Deploring the conventionality of the American fiction of her day, Chopin broached vital issues Victorian readers refused to discuss.

Chopin's first novel, *At Fault* (1890), for example, was the first American novel to present a nonmoralizing view of divorce, an issue of growing concern that had virtually been ignored by fiction. Although the American divorce rate surged after the Civil War, almost quadrupling by 1900, genteel authors passed over this topic despite all its rich possibilities for their fiction. Even such exceptions as Howells and James refused to sanction divorce in *A Modern Instance* (1882) and *The Portrait of a Lady* (1882). Chopin, in contrast, shows the folly of attempting to live according to inflexible views of the sanctity of marriage. In *At Fault*, Chopin presents Thérèse Lafirme, a rich Creole widow, who commands the man she loves to remarry his alcoholic wife in order to reform her. Thérèse's grand gesture, however, is futile, for Fanny (the wife) goes on drinking. Only Fanny's convenient drowning saves Thérèse and her married lover from the "exacting and ignorant rule of . . . moral conventionalities" (2:777).

Chopin's attack on the "moral conventionalities" about marriage, motherhood, and sex made her an exception in American literature of the turn of the century. But only in her treatments of women already stigmatized in the American racist's imagination is her treatment of sex unrestrained. Page Smith's examination of the erotophobic record of Chopin's period suggests why this is so. Smith observes that "virtually all of the women who wrote, even in the most elliptical terms, of sex and sexuality, viewed it as a blight or illness which must somehow be suppressed or cured. It was a disease peculiar to men and a few depraved women."[16]

What Smith does not note, however, is the almost total control by men of the sexual discourse of this period. This control was so effective in stifling women's voices that we are only now beginning to revise our view of the sexually "repressed" or antisexual Victorian woman by taking into account her oppression and the attempt to estrange her from her experience of sex.

However, Chopin was able to identify the tension between opposing cultural values. Her Creole great-grandmother, Madame Charleville, seems to have fostered her questioning of the domestic verities by telling her stories of married women who had gone astray for passion. Thus, from childhood Chopin had a perspective unusual for an American woman. Emily Toth notes Chopin's peculiar upbringing, which allowed her to compare the values of "the more relaxed French milieu, in which a married woman had more opportunities for self-assertion," with the values of "the American domestic cult, in which a young girl's marriage was intended to confine her to monogamy and to one sphere for life, if not beyond the grave."[17]

Chopin's avid reading of French authors also encouraged her to adopt an open-minded approach to matters that few American authors had been inclined to scrutinize. But because she was a woman of her time, Chopin recognized the need for personal reticence. She was careful even in the confidences she committed to her diary. There is also evidence that she censored her private writings, for Per Seyersted reports that her journal account of a talk with a vagabond in her store in Louisiana had been altered by the vigorous scratching out of the last two words, which suggested that it would be good to emulate the vagabond and lose oneself in the silence, mystery, and *sin* of night. Speaking of the enigmatic quality that Chopin preserved throughout her life, Seyersted finds it remarkable that she was never "to make literary use of her own childhood, for example, or to refer to her late husband. . . . Though she could be outgoing and spirited, she was also very reticent and secretive, perhaps in part because she felt a need of hiding a passionate nature."[18]

Whatever Chopin's various motives for concealment, her fiction refuted the popularly held view of the "good" woman's indifference to sex and her contentment with the narrow range of her womanly duties. For even in her most timid presentations of the charged relationship of women and men, Chopin implies that "nice girls" can have passionate natures. In "A Shameful Affair" (1893), for example, Chopin teases her readers by describing a shamefully impassioned kiss between virtual strangers—a kiss sought by her heroine, Mildred Orme, a white woman, who cannot endure the indifference of a handsome young man who works in the neighborhood of the house where she is spending a boring summer vacation.

Other authors of the period had lavished attention on the kiss, their literary code for sexual consummation. Gertrude Atherton, who dabbled in stories of the color line in *Senator North* (1900), for example, delighted her shocked fans in *Patience Sparhawk and Her Times* (1897) by presenting a soul-shattering kiss inspired, not by love, but by the "electrical forces of the universe."[19] More than a decade earlier, Henry James had electrified and confused his audience with the kiss between Isabel Archer and Caspar Goodwood at the end of *The Portrait of a Lady*. In many respects Atherton's kiss is a mere copy of James's, since her heroine also is both attracted and repelled by the possessiveness of the man who seizes her. In its final form James's description of Isabel's reaction to Caspar had revealed Caspar's control of their sexual encounter:

> He glared at her a moment through the dusk, and the next instant she felt his arms about her and his lips on her own lips. His kiss was like white lightning, a flash that spread, and spread again, and stayed; and it was extraordinarily as if, while she took it, she felt each thing in his hard manhood that had least pleased her, each aggressive fact of his face, his figure, his presence, justified of its intense identity and made one with this act of possession. So had she heard of those wrecked and under water following a train of images before they sink. But when darkness returned she was free. She never looked about her; she only darted from the spot.[20]

Kate Chopin, however, insisted on her heroine's responsibility for a passionate encounter prompted by sexual attraction rather than romantic love or external cosmic forces. Chopin's Mildred suffers more than the requisite remorse for abandoning herself to the "most delicious thing she had known in her twenty years" ("A Shameful Affair," 1:135) because she initiated the encounter. Her shame implies that despite her passion she is a "nice" girl after all, thereby making the story acceptable in genteel terms. But implicit in Mildred's insistence on the truth of her passionate experience is an assault on the double standard and the belief in white female passivity and the sanctity of sexual experience. Mildred's remorse and Chopin's restraint in treating her suggest the constraint Chopin experienced in attempting to delineate full-bodied female sexuality in a white woman character.

Like Mildred Orme, however, Chopin's other white women often play the aggressor to attract men who are accustomed to taking their "low" impulses elsewhere. Significantly, these women are frequently tempted by men with whom they could not possibly be in love. The ambivalence these women experience is typified by Edna Pontellier's reaction when Alcée Arobin, an inveterate womanizer, looks at her, and she finds that "the effrontery in his eyes repelled the old, vanishing self in her, yet drew all her awakening sensuousness" (*The Awakening*, 2:959). Similarly, Mrs. Baroda in "A Respectable Woman" (1894) initially dislikes her husband's house-guest, Gouvernail, but succumbs to the sound of his voice as she sits next to him in the moonlight: "Her mind only vaguely grasped what he was saying. Her physical being was for the moment predominant. She was not thinking of his words, only drinking in the tones of his voice. She wanted to reach out her hand in the darkness and touch him with the sensitive tips of her fingers upon the face or the lips. She wanted to draw close to him and whisper against his cheek—she did not care what—as she might have done if she had not been a respectable woman" (1:335).

Chopin seems to have been aware of the problems such stories as "A Shameful Affair," "A Respectable Woman," and "The Story of an Hour" (1894) might have caused her. "The Story of an Hour" had been turned down by Richard Watson Gilder at the *Century*. Still desiring to appease Gilder and publish her works in his prestigious magazine, Chopin reworked "A Night in Acadie" for him. After revising the story, she wrote: "I have made certain alterations which you thought the story required to give it artistic or ethical value. . . . The marriage is omitted, and the girl's character softened and tempered by her rude experience."[21] In "A Woman's Place: The Search for Identity in Kate Chopin's Female Characters," Peggy Skaggs remarks on Chopin's willingness to change one of her other heroines if necessary: "The original ending having been lost, one can only speculate on its content; but apparently it was less sentimental and edifying, more realistic and consistent with Zaïda's [the heroine's] character."[22]

Per Seyersted insists that Chopin's willingness to comply was rare; however, the ambivalence of her white heroines and her nonjudgmental stance toward them had practical as well as aesthetic value. The lack of restrictions on the depiction of women on the color line also had practical value, for in

"Désirée's Baby," "La Belle Zoraïde," "At the 'Cadian Ball," and "The Storm," Chopin treats more openly issues that she had skirted in stories about white women. In these stories she presents the sexual, racial, and class dimensions of the double standard without muting the impact of her discoveries. Although the heroines in these stories lack the psychological complexity of a Mrs. Baroda or a Mildred Orme, they experience more fully the overt weight of oppression, which Chopin's white women characters experience only as a vague malaise. Clear and economical, these stories of women on the color line set into motion the revelatory interaction between white and racially stigmatized women that finds fullest expression in *The Awakening*.

"Désirée's Baby"

"Désirée's Baby" (1893) is a story of peripeteia and doom. Held in a narrative balance through images of dark and light, power and powerlessness, lust and love, it moves with relentless intensity to a foregone, tragic conclusion: Désirée, the apotheosis of white wifehood and motherhood in Victorian terms, finds that the son she has borne her slaveholding husband, Armand, is a mulatto. When she beseeches Armand to explain how this can be so, he accuses her of not being white. Crushed by Armand's rejection of her, Désirée disappears with her infant into the bayou; only later does Armand discover in a letter written by his mother to his father that he himself "belongs to the race that is cursed with the brand of slavery" (1:245).

Although inadvertent miscegenation provides the plot line for "Désirée's Baby," race becomes only one more counter in the conflict that follows inevitably from the rigid categories Armand Aubigny seeks to impose on experience. Armand's power to impose a false dichotomy on all aspects of his experience is ultimately self-destructive because the world Chopin portrays admits of love that defies the rigid polarities of "black" and "white" in the case of Armand's parents' love for each other, Désirée's love for the baby, and Madame Valmondé's love for Désirée even after she perceives the color of Désirée's child. The shadowy and enigmatic presence of La Blanche on the Aubigny plantation reveals Armand's power over women but also his powerlessness to make the world conform to reductive racial categories. The irony of Armand's insistence on a dualistic view is stressed by the fact that his world is filled with mixed racial types like La Blanche and that he himself is mixed. In marrying Désirée, so visibly white, and in fathering a baby also apparently white, at least for three months, Armand may have assuaged his secret subconscious racial fears. A dark-skinned aristocrat who may vaguely remember his racially mixed mother (he was eight years old when he left Paris, where his parents lived together), Armand is the only racially obsessed character in Chopin's story. Therefore, Armand's ability to define and dismiss Désirée on the basis of an arbitrary conception of racial distinctions has its penalties for him as well as for her.

The inequitable nature of these penalties, however, only becomes clear when we stop to look at the consequences of permuting the possible variations of the roles that color might play in the story. We see that if Armand is white and Désirée is white, he may hold her against her will and maintain illicit relationships with other women on the side or cast her out on any pretext and without appeal. The presumption of her infidelity would be sufficient to end the marriage, whereas the proof of his infidelity would be insufficient. If he is white and she is black, he may cast her out or relegate her to the status of La Blanche and make a house slave of their son. If Armand is black, Désirée may be vindicated by the discovery that she is not responsible for the racial characteristics of their child, but she will be forever stigmatized socially by the fact that she has been possessed by a black man and has borne his son. Désirée is clearly in a powerless position. The unresolved ambiguity about her racial identity—for we know no more about her actual origins at the end of the story than at the beginning—suggests the fact of her powerlessness: It does not really matter whether she is white or black, since her very life depends on the whims, social class, and race of her husband.

The most exquisite irony of the story, since it reflects the full extent of Désirée's powerlessness, is her name. Because she is female, Désirée's life depends upon being desired, but her life begins and ends with the antithesis of desire, abandonment. The irony of Désirée's situation is further intensified by her trust in men who betray her. When she is found by Monsieur Valmondé, who becomes her adoptive father, she awakens crying for the "Dada" (1:240) who has abandoned her. Later, she trusts in Armand to interpret reality for her when she discovers that their baby has Negroid features, and he rejects her. Thus, even when Désirée is desired, that desire is conditional. Armand's hubris, the result of male privilege buttressed by family pride and a sense of racial superiority, makes unconditional love for Désirée impossible.

In Chopin's compressed prose, the years between Désirée's discovery by Monsieur Valmondé and her marriage to Armand Aubigny flash by, but Désirée remains the same "beautiful and gentle, affectionate and sincere" (1:240) girl that she was as a toddler. The negotiations of Valmondé and Aubigny for Désirée's marriage signal the transfer of power from father to husband, not a rite of passage to adulthood. Thus, when Madame Valmondé looks forward to visiting Désirée and her baby at L'Abri, her new home, Madame thinks with amusement that "it seemed but yesterday that

Désirée was little more than a baby herself" (1:240). When Madame Valmondé greets Désirée, she finds her lying among soft white muslin and laces with her infant beside her, passive and inert, changed but unchanging.

The fact that Désirée is a foundling makes possible Armand's conclusion that Désirée must be racially "tainted"; after all, *he* has a name that is "one of the oldest and proudest in Louisiana" (1:241). Chopin's reference to the "prevailing belief . . . that [Désirée] had been purposely left" (1:240) adds another dimension, perhaps suggesting something about the "prevailing" attitude toward girl children. In a conventional observation about Armand's joy at the birth of a son, Désirée herself attributes this prejudice to Armand: "Oh, Armand is the proudest father in the parish, I believe, chiefly because it is a boy, to bear his name; though he says not,—that he would have loved a girl as well. But I know it is n't true. I know he says that to please me" (1:242).

Our sense of the conventionality of Désirée's happy admission adds to the poignance of the scene between Désirée and Madame Valmondé, for Madame Valmondé perceives but cannot tell Désirée that her infant is a mulatto. Finally happy because she has managed at last to completely please her husband, Désirée confides in her foster mother the details of Armand's transformation since the baby's birth. Obviously more important to Armand than Désirée suspects, the birth of a "white" son has dispelled those occasional frowns that marriage to Désirée had not fully obliterated. Désirée assures Madame Valmondé, despite Madame's premonitions, that everything is perfect now that the baby has come. Yet, despite Armand's joy, Désirée is desperate to please him. Chopin suggests the difficulty of doing so and emphasizes the isolation of Désirée in the home "which for many years had not known the gentle presence of a mistress." Such a place is no place for a woman or a slave: "Young Aubigny's rule was a strict one, too, and under it his negroes had forgotten how to be gay, as they had been during the old master's easy-going and indulgent lifetime" (1:241).

This is not to say, of course, that L'Abri "shelters" no women, for Désirée has a mulatto nurse named Zandrine for her baby, and La Blanche lives somewhere on the plantation in a cabin with her quadroon sons, one of whom has been given to Désirée to serve the new baby. La Blanche's palpable absence hints at the reality that will shatter Désirée's romantic illusions. Significantly, Désirée becomes conscious of La Blanche only at the moment she awakens to the truth of her own situation. Therefore, La Blanche's importance is as clear as her origins are hazy. The possibility that she may be Désirée's predecessor, sent to the slave quarters for having given birth to a mulatto son, is implied by the dark parallel Armand draws when he compares the two women. La Blanche's existence reveals the distance between Désirée's romantic illusions about marriage and her experience of a marriage that requires social hypocrisy and the innocence of its victim.

In Désirée's happy prattle to Madame Valmondé about Armand's pleasure at the birth of a son, the necessity for Désirée's self-deception about Armand's character is striking. Désirée can recognize neither the possible implications of Armand's transformation nor the fact that conditional transformations are always subject to reversal when conditions change. Accepting Armand Aubigny's "imperious and exacting nature" (1:242) as the ground of her being, Désirée must find a way to be happy, even if that way means lying to herself and attempting to justify her husband's behavior to her mother. Désirée's reason for pleasure and a temporary sense of power over her husband is his sudden kindness to his slaves. As Désirée whispers to her mother about Armand's behavior since the birth of his son, she betrays the situation: "And mamma," . . . "he has n't punished one of them—not one of them—since baby is born. Even Négrillon, who pretended to have burnt his leg that he might rest from work—he only laughed, and said Négrillon was a great scamp. Oh, mamma, I 'm so happy; it frightens me" (1:242).

Désirée's sense of foreboding emphasizes her sensitivity to the powerlessness of her position. She must watch for Armand's moods to shift as they have before when he "frowned" and "she trembled, but loved him" (1:242). Recognizing Désirée's helplessness and her own, Madame Valmondé does not tell Désirée her discovery about the baby, just as she did not express her concerns about Désirée's marriage.

Because the antithetical characterizations of Désirée and Armand evoke other tragic pairings in romantic fiction, we can see that they too are trapped by sexist conventions that govern marriage as well as by racist notions that seal their fateful interaction. Bound together by all that divides them, they are victims of Armand's disastrous urges, his presumption of his right to impose his will on slaves and women. Both suffer from a fatal lack of self-knowledge. Neither can afford the luxury of seeing the world as it is. Perhaps in the uncritical adoption of the rigid roles they play, Armand and Désirée find the only secure identities available to them. These identities, Chopin implies, offer no real security at all.

Although, on reflection, we perceive the similarities between Armand and Désirée, our sympathies are engaged by Désirée. The imagery that surrounds her as she takes that last walk to the bayou is reminiscent of depictions of saints and martyrs, for Désirée is enveloped in a nimbus of light playing in golden gleams on her hair. Her tender feet and diaphanous white gown are torn by the stubble. Armand, on the other hand, is described as being possessed by "the very spirit of Satan" (1:242), and this description is reinforced by his penultimate gesture in burning all of Désirée's effects in a pyre with the help of his slave minions.

If this traditional contrast were the story's only claim on our imagination, we might resist its calculated design and dismiss it. The subtlety of the story and its extraordinary imaginative power, however, are evident. Despite the obvious patterns that set up the contrast between Désirée and Armand and prepare for the role reversal at the end, "Désirée's Baby" cannot be dismissed. Its power lies in its brevity and its lack of authorial moralizing, in its unexpected inversion of a familiar stereotype, and in the series of interlocking functional ambiguities that Chopin deploys to emphasize the meaning of Désirée's tragedy. Building to a climax from Désirée's moment of discovery to Armand's moment of discovery, these ambiguities reveal in horrifying detail the extent of Armand's power.

Désirée is, of course, the last to perceive the racial characteristics that become more pronounced as the baby's features develop. A mother's love does not depend upon race, Chopin seems to suggest, for Madame Valmondé, believing as she must that Désirée is racially mixed, tells her in a letter to come "back to your mother who loves you" (1:243) when Désirée asks for assurance that she is not contaminated by black blood. But in spite of her unwillingness to admit that she is in peril, Désirée has noticed Armand's coldness and is distraught by behavior "which she dared not ask him to explain" (1:242). Her whole world is shaken. Disorientation and inability to perceive reality replace self-assurance. Looking aimlessly from one of La Blanche's quadroon boys to her own child, Désirée sees for the first time the resemblance between the two half-naked children: " 'Ah!' it was a cry that she could not help; which she was not conscious of having uttered. The blood turned like ice in her veins, and a clammy moisture gathered upon her face" (1:242).

Does Désirée recognize a racial resemblance, a family resemblance, or both? Whatever Désirée knows or suspects, she seeks Armand for an explanation: "Look at our child. What does it mean? tell me," Désirée asks. In answering, Armand springs to the attack: " 'It means,' he answered lightly, 'that the child is not white; it means that you are not white.' " Armand's simple deduction and his laconic coldness sting Désirée: "A quick conception of all that this accusation meant for her nerved her with unwonted courage to deny it. 'It is a lie, it is not true, I am white! Look at my hair, it is brown; and my eyes are gray, Armand, you know they are gray. And my skin is fair,' seizing his wrist. 'Look at my hand; whiter than yours, Armand,' she laughed hysterically. 'As white as La Blanche's,' he returned cruelly; and went away leaving her alone with their child" (1:243).

Whatever Désirée knows, she knows that she is no longer desired. Her question, which Armand answers incorrectly, brings into focus a series of unanswerable questions that linger in the reader's mind long after the story is finished: Does Désirée know that she is adopted? What is her origin? What is her race? Does Désirée come to believe that she is racially mixed? Does she look at Armand and see that he is racially mixed? When she looks at the quadroon child and her own child and then at Armand's dark face, does she see that Armand could be the father of both children? Does Armand suspect his racial "taint" subconsciously? What is La Blanche's origin? Has Armand had a sexual relationship with La Blanche, and, if so, did that relationship continue after his marriage to Désirée, as might be suggested by Désirée's remark that Armand can hear their baby crying "as far away as La Blanche's cabin" (1:241)?

In confronting these questions, the reader must come to see the one indisputable fact—Désirée's total powerlessness—the result of the life-and-death power of the husband in her society. For whatever is actually the case about Désirée's understanding or Armand's conscious guilt, Armand has the ability to make Désirée pay for *his* transgressions, as La Blanche, we may infer, has also paid. The only recourse for Désirée is to a heavenly Father, and His good will toward women is suspect, since Madame Valmondé's prayers for Désirée and Madame Aubigny's prayers for Armand have been answered with tragedy. This final awareness leaves the reader little satisfaction other than the aesthetic satisfaction of seeing a complex view of experience validated.

"La Belle Zoraïde"

In "La Belle Zoraïde" (1894), Chopin demonstrates that the "separate spheres" maintained at such cost by Armand Aubigny are cultural constructs. The tragedy of la belle Zoraïde, like the tragedy of Désirée, lies in perversion of human relationships by conventional codes. In depicting the shared powerlessness of Madame Delisle, who hears, and la belle Zoraïde, who lives the tragic story, Chopin casts light on the function of the story for a white audience titillated and at the same time terrified by the traditional tale and its variations.

"La Belle Zoraïde" frames one story with another. The heroines of these stories are Madame Delisle, a true Southern "lady," and la belle Zoraïde, a tragic octoroon whose fatal love for le beau Mézor, a virile savage, precipitates the tragic tale told to Madame Delisle. Taken together, the characterizations of these two women reflect and comment on each other, demonstrating that neither lady nor tragic octoroon can be free, since one is forced to live vicariously through tales of romance, and the other is forced to escape the realities of her lot by going mad.

"La Belle Zoraïde" opens with a scene that reveals the sensuous, symbiotic relationship of Madame Delisle and the devoted, old black slave, Manna-Loulou, who provides her mistress with stories of real experience. The character of Madame Delisle, also the heroine of an earlier story, "A Lady of Bayou St. John" (1893), remains consistent in "La Belle Zoraïde," where we view once more her indolence, her restriction to a fantasy life, and her dependence on Manna-Loulou, who still calls her by her baby name and tells her a new bedtime story every night.

Chopin emphasizes Madame Delisle's vital interest in the bits of real experience in the stories. In "A Lady of Bayou St. John," we discover that when Madame Delisle had her only opportunity to break with convention and become an independent woman by running away from her life as the child wife of a Confederate officer, she pulled back into the safety of her ladyhood. Like Mildred Orme of "A Shameful Affair" and Chopin's other "nice" white women, Madame Delisle awakens briefly to the possibility of sexual fulfillment but retreats from it. Madame Delisle's dependence on fantasies of love provides her only raison d'être. "Ah! I have memories, memories to crowd and fill my life, if I live a hundred years!" (1:301), she exclaims. Madame Delisle's parasitical need for the memories of others as well as her own, however, appears in "La Belle Zoraïde," for Manna-Loulou knows that "Madame would hear none but those [stories] which were true" (1:304).

The limits of the women's experience in the world they inhabit are established by the implicit connections between Madame's culturally sanctioned death-in-life, which must feed off the real lives of others in order to be supportable, and Zoraïde's culturally enforced suffering. The attack on racism and sexism in "La Belle Zoraïde" inheres in Manna-Loulou's narration, her expectation of Madame's total sympathy with Zoraïde, and her presumption that Zoraïde's passion for Mézor is something Madame can understand. Manna-Loulou's overt denial and apology for Zoraïde, who loves at all costs, however, tacitly exempts Madame Delisle from passion: "You know how the negroes are, Ma'zélle Titite," she says in what may be a reproach to Madame Delisle for her rejection of her own chance at love. "There is no mistress, no master, no king nor priest who can hinder them from loving when they will" (1:305). But the story Manna-Loulou chooses to tell implies her awareness that whites envy the passion forbidden them and would control it or appropriate it if they could.

The story of la belle Zoraïde suggests that given the will to power and the means to impose that will, a woman can behave just like a man. For Madame Delarivière, Zoraïde's mistress and "godmother," uses her power to bend Zoraïde to her will. Raised to be as close an approximation of the "lady" as is possible considering her race, Zoraïde is crushed because she refuses to marry the man her mistress has chosen for her. Despite, and perhaps also to spite, Madame Delarivière, Zoraïde has failed to internalize her white godmother's racist values. Zoraïde rejects M'sieur Ambroise with "his shining whiskers like a white man's, and his small eyes, that were cruel and false as a snake's" for the beautiful Mézor. Mézor, who bears obvious resemblance to Cable's Bras-Coupé, is "as straight as a cypress-tree and as proud looking as a king. His body, bare to the waist, was like a column of ebony and it glistened like oil" (1:304).

Zoraïde's preference for Mézor is understandable, but Madame Delarivière is indifferent to passion and intoxicated by power. When Zoraïde confesses her love for Mézor, Madame is revolted by the idea that Zoraïde should marry a black man, one whose darkness places him beneath her. Zoraïde seizes on the irony of her situation as a mulatto and asks, "Am I white, nénaine?" But Madame, missing the implication of Zoraïde's question, since power seldom coexists with subtlety, replies, "You white! *Malheureuse!* You deserve to have the lash laid upon you like any other slave; you have proven yourself no better than the worst." Zoraïde's response points out indirectly the hypocrisy of her godmother's paternalism, which has only been an excuse for the exercise of arbitrary power in managing Zoraïde's life: "I am not white. . . . Doctor Langlé gives me his slave to marry, but he would not give me his son. Then, since I am not white, let me have from out of my own race the one whom my heart has chosen" (1:305).

In this contest between intelligence and power, power initially wins, for Zoraïde seems to comply. A few months pass and Zoraïde makes another confession, a confession of her disobedience and of the impossibility of her obedience to Madame's command to cease loving Mézor.

Her failure to control Zoraïde leaves Madame "so actually pained, so wounded" that "there was no place left in her heart for anger" (1:305–6), Manna-Loulou says, and perhaps she speaks ironically, since Madame Delarivière finds a new way to impose her will on Zoraïde by persuading Doctor Langlé to sell Mézor. When Zoraïde gives birth to a daughter by Mézor, Madame sends the baby away and tells Zoraïde that the infant has died. The monstrous insensitivity of Madame appears in her assumption that now she will enjoy Zoraïde's renewed affection and "have her young waiting-maid again at her side free, happy, and beautiful as of old" (1:306).

Having erased the last trace of Zoraïde's resistance, Madame appeals to her once more to marry M'sieur Ambroise. This time Zoraïde "seemed to consent, or rather submit, to the approaching marriage as though nothing mattered any longer in this world" (1:306–7). But Zoraïde's look of "strange and vacuous happiness" (1:307), as she clutches a bundle of rags and croons to her little one, has taken her beyond Madame Delarivière's reach. Even Madame's remorse and the return of Zoraïde's beautiful little daughter cannot bring Zoraïde back from the safety of her dementia.

This pathetic story is highly significant in Chopin's canon. Zoraïde's passion for Mézor is Chopin's first depiction of the sexual imperative in woman's life, the first story in which she risked breaking with genteel conventions about female sexuality.[23] The distance provided by the frame and the racial identity of the heroine probably made this breakthrough in Chopin's writing easier. Furthermore, "La Belle Zoraïde" is an unconventional story in several other respects: First, Zoraïde's love for Mézor, who is blacker than she, violates the racist notion that only white blood could beautify the African. Mézor is beautiful and princely, not in spite of his blackness, but because of it. In her bold departure from racist standards of beauty, Chopin not only shows Mézor's grandeur but also suggests Ambroise's repulsive sycophancy in adopting white values. Second, Zoraïde's physical desire for Mézor anticipates his response to her. Chopin makes this abundantly clear. Zoraïde sees Mézor dancing the Bamboula and is attracted to his glistening, almost naked, "splendid body swaying and quivering through the figures of the dance," and from this moment "poor Zoraïde's heart grew sick in her bosom with love for le beau Mézor" (1:304). Third, Manna-Loulou's description of Zoraïde's "anguish of maternity" (1:306) anticipates Edna Pontellier's observation after the vigil in Adèle Ratignolle's labor room that parturition is "torture" (*The Awakening*, 2:995). This insistence on the real experience of women bearing children is a far cry from the sentimental nineteenth-century depiction of childbirth as woman's crowning achievement. And fourth, Zoraïde's rejection of her little daughter calls into question the sentimental nineteenth-century notion about the redemptive powers of the child.

The ending of "La Belle Zoraïde," however, returns us to the world of convention, where Madame Delisle says exactly what a lady might be expected to say about the tragedy of Mézor, Zoraïde, and their daughter: "La pauv' piti! Mieux li mouri!" (1:308). Madame Delisle's failure to empathize with Zoraïde except in a conventional lament for the infant who would grow up without a slave father and slave mother shows that she has missed the point of Zoraïde's story. The Lady of Bayou St. John cannot and will not see the connection between Zoraïde's escape into madness and her own escape into a world of fantasy where tragic love stories offer a safe sigh, a false sense of her own good fortune, and the encouragement to maintain her withdrawal from a world that is full of anguish for women.

Chopin's vision, however, is superior to Madame Delisle's. Taking the measure of those sometimes intimate and sometimes antagonistic relationships of women separated by race from true communion and creative purpose, Chopin nevertheless depicts the possibility of love that defies racism. The insufficiency of this love to bring about change is apparent in the implication that Manna-Loulou will go on telling her stories to Madame

Delisle, who will never, it is to be assumed, fully understand them or her own desperate need for them to fill her life. The lady will go on ritualistically and unthinkingly, as we are told in "A Lady of Bayou St. John," "once a year" having "a solemn high mass said for the repose of [the] soul" (1:302) of the husband she never really loved.

"At the 'Cadian Ball" and "The Storm"

Chopin's commitment to sexual realism grew during the four years between the publication of "La Belle Zoraïde" and the composition of "The Storm," written in 1898 and published for the first time in *The Complete Works* in 1969. Even today, "The Storm" is a startling story, perhaps the most extraordinary one in Chopin's canon. The implicit criticism of bourgeois marriage made by "The Storm" was foreshadowed in an earlier and tamer companion piece, "At the 'Cadian Ball" (1892).

In both "At the 'Cadian Ball" and "The Storm," however, Chopin hedges her criticism by imputing passion to a woman already degraded in the popular imagination, exploiting rather than challenging conventional prejudices. For Calixta, Chopin's heroine, as is repeatedly emphasized, enjoys an easy sexuality denied to white women. Exempt from the normative controls of relaxed 'Cadian society because of her presumed racial difference, Calixta experiences her sexuality fully, finally consummating an adulterous passion, unscathed and unrepentant.

Chopin encourages many assumptions about Calixta's origins and character. In "At the 'Cadian Ball" Chopin alludes to Calixta's activities on a visit to her uncle in Assumption, a place-name that has ambiguous, symbolic suggestiveness, since all kinds of assumptions are made about Calixta after this visit—the chief being that Alcée Laballière, a young planter, has possessed her. The 'Cadian (Cajun) community's gossip about Calixta and their leniency toward her are predicated on the fact that she is not considered to be truly one of them: "Calixta's slender foot had never touched Cuban soil; but her mother's had, and the Spanish was in her blood all the same. For that reason the prairie people forgave her much that they would not have overlooked in their own daughters or sisters" (1:219).

The 'Cadian men are much more tolerant than their wives, since the men remember sowing their wild oats with the Calixtas of their own day. But "the women did not always approve of Calixta" (1:224). The disapproval can be explained on two counts: jealousy (for Calixta is witty, beautiful, spirited, and self-centered) and moral indignation, for Calixta swears "roundly in fine 'Cadian French and with true Spanish spirit" and fights with another young woman over a lover "on the church steps after mass one Sunday" (1:219).

The racial tinge given Calixta's portrait is reemphasized by fragments of description that, like the cluster of dark and fiery images surrounding Armand Aubigny, point to her deviance. Alcée Laballière, the scion of a neighboring plantation family, meets her for a "fling" (1:222) after being repulsed by Miss Clarisse, his cousin. At the 'Cadian ball where Calixta is the acknowledged "belle" (1:223), Alcée expects to cut loose if only temporarily from the constraints of Clarisse and the effete society she represents. Alcée's attitude toward Clarisse's friends appears in his disgust with his mother's visitors from town: "He would have liked to sweep the place of those visitors, often. Of the men, above all, with their ways and their manners; their swaying of fans like women, and dandling about hammocks" (1:220).

At the 'Cadian ball Alcée seeks out Calixta in order to ask her to go to Assumption again. Clarisse, however, has overheard Alcée's plan and drags him home on the pretext of a family emergency. To Clarisse, Alcée's possible defection *is* a family emergency. Clarisse, despite her coldness, must act, and Alcée must go with her. Calixta is rejected at her moment of triumph. With infuriating civil condescension that suggests the syrupy sweetness of Clarisse's cultivated voice, Clarisse acknowledges Calixta before dragging Alcée away: "Ah, c'est vous, Calixta? Comment ça va, mon enfant?" Clearly, Clarisse has too much class to pull hair as Calixta has done, but Clarisse also has ways to mortify her rivals. Alcée follows Clarisse "without a word, without a glance back. . . . He had forgotten he was leaving her [Calixta] there." Calixta responds by turning a face "that was almost ugly after the night's dissipation" (1:226) to Bobinôt, a suitor of her own class, who has come forward to comfort her; and she promises to marry him.

Although Calixta's dismay and Clarisse's desperation make their motives suspect, both Bobinôt and Alcée are overjoyed at their respective good fortunes. Chopin emphasizes the parallel between Alcée and Bobinôt in describing Alcée's joy: "He thought the face of the Universe was changed— just like Bobinôt." Ironically, nothing has really changed since everything is back to normal. The story ends with the ritual discharge of pistol shots in the wee hours of the morning, announcing that *"le bal est fini"* (1:227).

The good fortune of Alcée and Bobinôt is an illusion that "The Storm" will expose. But there is abundant evidence in "At the 'Cadian Ball" as well that the forthcoming marriages of Alcée and Clarisse, Bobinôt and Calixta, have not been made in heaven. In establishing parallels throughout the story between Alcée and Bobinôt, Clarisse and Calixta, Chopin portrays the power of sex, race, and class to seal relationships of individuals programmed by social expectations to be mates, although they are not made for each other. In the realistically peopled world of "At the 'Cadian Ball," all of the characters must make do with the unsatisfactory options available to them. Because these options depend upon the conventions governing sex, class, and race, these characters stand to lose the real sexual and emotional joy of marriage.

In "At the 'Cadian Ball," Chopin shows that romantic love is a reflection and reinforcement of class and race bias. The thematic concern with the limitations of romantic love appears in the implicit cross-references of character types across the division of class. The real situations of the characters are ironic commentaries on their romantic aspirations. Both Clarisse and Calixta, for example, appear to be dependent on the largesse of their relatives. Calixta, we learn, cannot dress as fashionably as her 'Cadian rivals because her aunts and uncles have not furnished her with a dress "nearly so handsome or well made as Fronie's" (1:223).

Clarisse's existence also appears to be marginal, although at a higher level of pretense, for she "built more air-castles than enough" (1:220) with her godmother in dreaming about how they would spend the money Alcée was sure to clear on his venture in planting rice. Moreover, both Calixta and Clarisse recoil from physical contact with the men who worship them. When Alcée comes home tired and dirty from work in the fields and seizes Clarisse and pants "a volley of hot, blistering love-words into her face," she fends him off. Chopin does not emphasize Clarisse's sexual innocence but rather her dislike of Alcée's technique, since "no man had ever spoken love to her like that" (1:220). "'Par exemple!' she muttered disdainfully, as she turned from him, deftly adjusting the careful toilet that he had so brutally disarranged" (1:221). Likewise, Calixta teases Bobinôt but refuses to let him come near her. At the moment of their rebound betrothal, Calixta holds "out her hand in the business-like manner of a man who clinches a bargain" (1:226) but refuses to kiss Bobinôt: "'I don' want to kiss you, Bobinôt,' she said, turning away again, 'not to-day. Some other time. Bonté divine! ent you satisfy, yet!'" (1:227).

Like Clarisse and Calixta, Alcée and Bobinôt are analogues. Both men are farmers who spend their days in the fields. Alcée is a farmer on a larger scale, but he works as hard as Bobinôt: "It was an every-day affair for him to come in from the field well-nigh exhausted, and wet to the waist" (1:220). Bobinôt is "big, brown, good-natured" (1:219)—in fine, something of a rube—but Alcée is also strong, physical, and uncultivated. Alcée is much more aggressive than Bobinôt, but Alcée has the class privilege to throw his weight around. Both men want a woman who will be a real challenge and therefore a real triumph. And both men are passionately and possessively enamored of these women they will win on questionable terms.

Alcée's jealousy toward Clarisse's attentions to her city friends may be inferred from his hostility to male city visitors and his fantasy of pitching them over the levee into the river, "if it had n't meant murder" (1:220). Bobinôt's jealousy appears in his determination to go to the ball when he hears that Alcée Laballière will be there.

All this jealousy and passion are directed toward "unattainable" women who are desired and idealized because it is presumed that they are unlike or superior to other women. The irony here, of course, is that Clarisse and Calixta are depicted as being essentially similar, since they are both beautiful, manipulative, and cold to the men who adore them, but stirred by romantic fantasies of cavaliers with more prestige. Thus, Alcée, who can have charming Calixta, idolizes Clarisse because she received tribute from the city friends he despises. Alcée's unconscious choice of the word *worth* in picturing Clarisse is revealing: "She was worth going a good deal farther than that to see. Dainty as a lily; hardy as a sunflower; slim, tall, graceful, like one of the reeds that grew in the marsh. Cold and kind and cruel by turn, and everything that was aggravating" (1:220). Bobinôt, as we have seen, also directs his passion toward the unobtainable and not toward "Ozéina, who would marry him tomorrow; or Fronie, or any one of a dozen others, rather than that little Spanish vixen" (1:219).

Thus, Alcée's and Bobinôt's illusions of love's realization, like Clarisse's desperation and Calixta's humiliation, are part of the pattern that Chopin has drawn with devastating if amusing precision. Whether or not she perceives the effects of her sex, social class, and race on her chances for happiness, in a real sense Calixta is no freer than Désirée or Zoraïde. The covert and largely unconscious workings of sexism and racism in Alcée have made Calixta, who is so real in her passion, "like a myth" and have made Clarisse, who has feigned passion for reasons of expediency, "the one, only, great reality" (1:227) in Alcée's world.

Making a connection between Calixta and other rejected dark women of American literature, Robert Arner anticipates the action of "The Storm." Arner writes that "in spurning the full-bodied, full-blooded female Calixta in favor of the more pallid and virginal Clarisse, Alcée Laballière joins the ranks of other American heroes—in Cooper's, Poe's, Hawthorne's, Melville's, James', Hemingway's, and Faulkner's fiction—who have made the same choice." In this interpretation of "At the 'Cadian Ball," Arner acknowledges his debt to Leslie Fiedler, but he does not recognize that "At the 'Cadian Ball" can be read as an implicit critique of both the literary tradition that he and Fiedler describe and the economically determined prejudice it reflects. Slighting the complexity of the story, Arner writes that "Calixta gets what she deserves for her vixenishness. Had she been a 'good' girl, she might have married the prosperous and socially prominent planter, but as it is she must settle for the poorer and less esteemed Bobinôt."[24]

In the world of Calixta and Clarisse, Bobinôt and Alcée, however, no one gets what she or he deserves or needs. In "The Storm," a story that Chopin wrote while awaiting publication of *The Awakening* and that she never attempted to publish, we see the kinds of accommodations that must be made to make marriage supportable. Chopin makes her point about marriage in "The Storm" by showing the joyous possibilities of sexual communion rather than by belaboring the inadequacies of conjugal love in bourgeois society. The explicit, yet nonjudgmental, treatment of sex in this story makes it unique in American literature of the nineteenth century. Bypassing the oblique metaphors other writers had used to let their readers know that something had happened while the hero and heroine were off-stage, Chopin directly depicts a gratifying sexual experience.

In "The Storm" Chopin is obviously indebted to French masters and to the French attitude toward adultery characterized chauvinistically by Mark Twain when he noted that "the two great branches of Fr[ench] thought [are] Science &—&—adultery" and defined the Frenchman's home as a place "where another man's wife is."[25] But while Chopin's debt to the French, especially to Maupassant, is great, in "The Storm" we see how much further she had gone in delivering the subject of passion from domination by a male point of view. In this story Chopin portrays a woman's subjective experience of sex and a woman's active involvement and pleasure in lovemaking, in defiance of the genteel literary restrictions of her day. The audacity of Chopin's description diverts attention from the stormy, over-blown prose with which she renders the sexual act.

The plot of "The Storm" provides the frame for the human passion that the storm symbolizes and reflects. Calixta' has now been married for five years to Bobinôt and is the mother of four-year-old Bibi; Alcée Laballière, married for five years to Clarisse, is the father of more than one baby. They meet before a torrential rain. Clarisse is away visiting her old friends and acquaintances, happy to be free from the demands of marriage, since "intimate conjugal life was something which she was more than willing to forego for a while" (2:596). Bobinôt is minding Bibi, waiting for the on-coming storm to pass before he returns home to Calixta.

Alcée seeks shelter at Calixta's house, and the storm without soon becomes a sexual storm within. For the first time, both Alcée and Calixta experience unalloyed, physical pleasure. Their marriages have made them only more responsive to each other. In a fragment of description that resumes the action where Clarisse interrupted them at the 'Cadian ball, Alcée is still as powerfully attracted to Calixta as she is to him: "He pushed her hair back from her face that was warm and steaming. Her lips were as red and moist as pomegranate seed. Her white neck and a glimpse of her full, firm bosom disturbed him powerfully. As she glanced up at him the fear in her liquid blue eyes had given place to a drowsy gleam that unconsciously betrayed a sensuous desire. He looked down into her eyes and there was nothing for him to do but to gather her lips in a kiss. It reminded him of Assumption" (2:594).

In the description of the lovemaking that follows, Chopin shows the need of both individuals for this release. But with the end of the storm, the encounter between Calixta and Alcée ends. Alcée rides away and writes a "loving" letter to his wife, telling her that "he was willing to bear the separation a while longer—realizing that [her] health and pleasure were the first things to be considered." After this interlude Calixta forbears scolding Bobinôt for dirtying the floor with his muddy boots. Feasting on the canned shrimp that Bobinôt has brought Calixta as a present, the 'Cadian family members relax and enjoy themselves, laughing "so loud that anyone might have heard them as far away as Laballière's" (2:596).

The last line of the story takes all that has happened in stride: "So the storm passed and every one was happy" (2:596). The implicit suggestion that everyone will be happier for the encounter of Calixta and Alcée is, perhaps, given a twist by Alcée's consent to Clarisse's extended absence. The omission of the "ever after" in the last line leaves open the future of Calixta and Alcée, Bobinôt and Clarisse, and casts an ironic reflection on the Victorian notion of "holy" love.

The sacramental language of "The Storm" and Calixta's stereotypical lush, dark beauty provide the matrix for Chopin's description of the physical act. The allusion to Assumption reestablishes the basis for Calixta and Alcée's involvement. But in this story the reference to Assumption, a religious holiday celebrating the Assumption of the Virgin into heavenly bliss as well as a place-name, suggests the secularization of religious experience and the elevation of sexual experience to the status of a religious sacrament. In Chopin's description of Calixta and Alcée's passion, man and woman participate in one of the mysteries of nature. The essence of this mystery as Chopin describes it is a revelation of oneness of man, woman, and nature in an experience that precludes moral judgments:

> They did not heed the crashing torrents, and the roar of the elements made her laugh as she lay in his arms. She was a revelation in that dim, mysterious chamber; as white as the couch she lay upon. Her firm, elastic flesh that was knowing for the first time its birthright, was like a creamy lily that the sun invites to contribute its breath and perfume to the undying life of the world.
>
> The generous abundance of her passion, without guile or trickery, was like a white flame which penetrated and found response in depths of his own sensuous nature that had never yet been reached.
>
> When he touched her breasts they gave themselves up in quivering

ecstasy, inviting his lips. Her mouth was a fountain of delight. And when he possessed her, they seemed to swoon together at the very borderland of life's mystery.

He stayed cushioned upon her, breathless, dazed, enervated, with his heart beating like a hammer upon her. With one hand she clasped his head, her lips lightly touching his forehead. The other hand stroked with a soothing rhythm his muscular shoulders.

The growl of the thunder was distant and passing away.

(2:594–95)

What is especially significant about Chopin's perception here is the loss of the sense of the boundaries of self in this profound mystery. In this sexual experience, these boundaries, maintained in part by arbitrary distinctions based on class, race, and sex, disappear temporarily. Pleasure is asserted not merely as a possibility but as a right for a woman. Open to ecstasy in a way that Clarisse is not, Calixta teaches Alcée that guile and trickery are not an integral part of woman's response in lovemaking. For an orgasmic moment, class antagonism is dispelled. But only for a moment, since Calixta and Alcée must return to a world where a woman of Calixta's kind and a man of Alcée's class can have a secret rendezvous but can never marry.

An awareness of this fact, no doubt, leaves many readers of "The Storm" with a bad aftertaste. Having read many trash depictions of the brief tempestuous love of dark women and white men, the reader may with good reason resent what seems a stereotypical presentation of another easy, racially mixed heroine. The claim that Calixta can experience sexual passion hardly seems a courageous one, since the sensuality of women like Calixta is one of the chief features of the stereotype used to malign them.

Yet "The Storm" is a remarkable story that suggests more about the limitations of bourgeois marriage than about the antithetical sexual natures of white women and dark women. It is obvious that marriage is only viable for Chopin's characters through the release afforded by separate vacations and illicit sexual episodes. As Simone de Beauvoir has written:

The constraint of "conjugal love" leads . . . to all kinds of repressions and lies. And first of all it prevents the couple from really knowing each other. Daily intimacy creates neither understanding nor sympathy. The husband respects his wife too much to take an interest in the phenomena of her psychic life: that would be to recognize in her a secret autonomy that could prove disturbing, dangerous; does she really find pleasure in the marriage bed? Does she truly love her husband? Is she actually happy to obey him? He prefers not to ask; to him these questions even seem shocking.[26]

These are the very questions Chopin poses implicitly in "The Storm," for the joyous passion shared by Calixta and Alcée calls into question both the "constraint of conjugal love" and the literary evasions that had denied depiction of woman's passion a place in American literature.

The Awakening

The questions implicit in the "happy" adultery of Calixta and Alcée, the "happy" ignorance of Bobinôt, and the "happy" absence of Clarisse had already been raised by *The Awakening* in its presentation of Edna Pontellier's solitary rebellion against bourgeois marriage and motherhood and against the paralyzing aimlessness and alienation she experiences as a privileged white woman. These questions, however, were ignored by Chopin's contemporaries, who deplored the amorality of her novel's treatment of white womanhood. W. M. Reedy, the publisher of the *Mirror* and responsible for introducing some of Maupassant's racier pieces to America, for example, could not sanction *The Awakening,* since it allowed a "real American lady" to "disrupt the sacred institutions of marriage and American womanhood" without repentance.[27]

More than three quarters of a century later, the critical dispute about Chopin's motives continues to divert attention from consideration of the novel's full array of female characters and its rich social texture. Most interpretations of the novel have been directed by the disagreements between those who affirm Edna's heroic "decision" to take her own life, thereby transcending the insurmountable obstacles to her personal freedom and fulfillment as a woman, and those who assert the neurotic nature of the "impulse" that leads her to drown herself. The novel bears these contradictory interpretations. For Chopin's ambivalent narrative voice "encourages its readers to project their own fantasies into the novel and to see Edna as they wish to see her."[28]

Edna's awareness that she is a "devilishly wicked specimen of the sex" (2:966), by conventional standards, contrasts with the lack of awareness of Calixta, Zoraïde, and Désirée. Because of her self-conscious struggle to define herself and to maintain her integrity, Edna attains greater stature than Flaubert's Emma Bovary, to whom she has often been compared. Chopin's debt to *Madame Bovary* is less than has been suggested by those who analogize Edna Pontellier's situation and Emma Bovary's. Significantly, Emma is surrounded by male characters, whereas Edna is surrounded by a gallery of female types, white, black, and racially mixed.

At the turn of the century, Edna stands alone, for while male authors such as Stephen Crane, Hamlin Garland, and Theodore Dreiser broached the subject of women's sexuality, they permitted sexual passion only to lower-class women and generally maintained a point of view detached from their characters' sexual experience. Edna is unique because her creator was female and because Edna is a white, upper-class wife and mother. Crane's Maggie (*Maggie: A Girl of the Streets* [1893]), Garland's Rose (*Rose of Dutcher's Coolly* [1895]), and Dreiser's Carrie (*Sister Carrie* [1900]) manifest passion, but only Edna gains an independent sense of herself as a sexual being; and she defies race, class, and gender conventions regarding woman's sexual nature as she moves by fits and starts to a partial understanding of the obstacles to her personal freedom and fulfillment.

The chief obstacle to freedom of expression for Edna, as Chopin dramatizes her plight, is the social status and class perspective that destroy Edna's potential for empathy. It is therefore not until the penultimate episode and Edna's rending recollection of her own participation in childbirth that she can generalize her experience of the delusive and disabling effects of white female privilege. Edna's lack of empathy is so profound that some readers of the novel recoil from her. However, Chopin shows this lack to be in part the product of a domestic routine that deadens Edna's ability to feel, except as she and other privileged white women have been programmed to feel. Such a routine eliminates the possibility of subversive thoughts or vital connections with the experience of other women. Bound by her sex, class, and race to a narrow existence, Edna is defined by those assumptions about women she seeks vainly to escape. Presuming to speak for all women but clearly wishing to be regarded as the exception, Edna remarks, "We women learn so little of life on the whole" (2:990). This negative view of those with whom she shares a stigmatized status retards the intellectual and emotional development she requires to survive.

The novel repeatedly stresses Edna's inability to know herself or those around her. From first to last she relies on "obstructed" (2:896) vision, and despite her "natural aptitude" (2:891) as an artist, she never draws a convincing likeness; nor does her perceptual field encompass the richly textured and gregarious Creole society she inhabits. In contrast to George Cable's Frowenfeld, Edna, a Protestant Kentuckian, fails to understand the racial realities of Creole society or to recognize the dangers posed by Creole difference. Instead she is the "solitary soul" of Chopin's original title. As Margaret Culley notes, "the word *alone* resounds like a refrain in the text, occurring some two dozen times." The key scenes in the novel are Edna's epiphanies. Edna's contemplation of her existence begins and ends, says Culley, in the "'abyss of solitude' which is the sea."[29] Striving for individual transcendence, Edna discovers the bounds of her prison, coterminous with those confining other women. But because her thinking, including a negative view of her own sex, is grounded in convention, her solitary insights are unfocused, dissolving until her final awakening in a mist of genuine feeling, suffused with romantic illusions about a completely conventional lover.

Edna's illusions about love merge with her misperceptions of the women surrounding her, leaving her to face her final awakening alone. She fails to know her friends, Madame Ratignolle, a Creole "mother-woman" who lives only for and through her growing family, and Mademoiselle Reisz, a "liberated" woman who sacrifices every social and personal amenity for her art, but who can only perform music written by male composers. She also fails to note the dark women who predominate in her society. Although her "white solipsism"[30] resembles that of others of her class, her failure to see the women on the margins of her social world ultimately proves fatal, since they direct attention to the illusions animating her belief in transcendent passion. Because they disclose the division of oppression that determines women's life chances in the novel, Edna's blindness to them must be seen as disabling. Thus, although she defies the prescriptions that define the white woman's purity and the dark woman's passion, she finally fails to achieve more than the partial, objectifying vision of woman's nature afforded by convention.

At Grand Isle, where her story opens, the seductive murmurings of the sea and the seeming openness of Adèle Ratignolle allow Edna the "first breath of freedom" (2:899); she begins to question the conventional restraint she has been taught from her girlhood in Kentucky. Confused and entranced by Creole custom, Edna is out of her element among the Creoles, whose relaxed acceptance of the facts of life is epitomized by Adèle's freely relating "the harrowing story of one of her *accouchements,* withholding no intimate detail," to a male friend; by Robert Lebrun's seeking out a new married woman for his romantic devotion each summer and choosing a female audience for his "droll" stories; and by the other guests' casual discussion of a novel that she had "felt moved to read . . . in secret and solitude" (2:889–90).

Initially shocked by the apparent liberty of the Creoles she knows, Edna eventually recognizes her need for experience incompatible with what she assumes is the "lofty," "inborn and unmistakable" (2:889) chastity of Creole ladies. Because they are so sweeping, Edna's generalizations about Creole women seem less astute than Adèle's observations about Edna. Adèle detects the danger to Edna in the promiscuous flirtation of Robert Lebrun and warns him that Edna "is not one of us; she is not like us. She might make the unfortunate blunder of taking you seriously" (2:900).

Edna does make this blunder and others. Unaccustomed to "an outward and spoken expression of affection, either in herself or in others," Edna cannot handle her own emotions and initially shrinks from them. She "had had an occasional girl friend, but whether accidentally or not, they seemed to have been all of one type—the self-contained. She never realized that the reserve of her own character had much, perhaps everything, to do with this" (2:897).

Edna feels the sympathetic receptivity of Adèle and begins "to loosen a little the mantle of reserve that had always enveloped her" (2:893). For the moment, Adèle's maternal warmth dispels Edna's inhibitions and allows her, in relating the infatuations of her adolescence, to confess the passionate nature she has so closely guarded. Adèle's soothing *"Pauvre chérie"* (2:897) confirms the limitations of her maternal character. But in her infantile intoxication "with the sound of her own voice" (2:899), Edna emerges from a self incapable of shared communication. Edna's inability to comprehend her friend's situation is also apparent in her failure to capture Adèle's likeness on drawing paper, though Adèle is a tempting and obvious subject. When Adèle expresses disappointment in finding that the portrait Edna paints does not look like her, Edna draws a broad smudge of paint across the surface of the portrait and crumples it in her hands.

Clearly, Edna does not understand Adèle, but she is powerfully attracted to Adèle as the personification of romance. The "embodiment of every womanly grace and charm," Adèle can only be described by clichés that "picture the bygone heroine of romance and the fair lady of our dreams" (2:888). Nor does Edna understand Mademoiselle Reisz, although Mademoiselle's music unleashes her dormant passions. After she has performed, Mademoiselle perceives Edna's agitation, pats her upon the shoulder, and tells her, "You are the only one worth playing for. Those others? Bah!" (2:907). However, Mademoiselle senses the destructiveness of Edna's illusions and weaves fragments of Wagner's *Liebestod* into the Chopin piece she plays for her.[31]

Twice Mademoiselle attempts to warn Edna of the price of reckless disregard for convention. To Edna's assertion that she is becoming an artist, Mademoiselle replies, "You have pretensions, Madame." When Edna asks whether such a life is possible for her, Mademoiselle observes that "to succeed, the artist must possess the courageous soul. . . . The soul that dares and defies" (2:946). Later Edna reports that Mademoiselle has felt her shoulder blades "to see if my wings were strong" and warned her that "the bird that would soar above the level plain of tradition and prejudice must have strong wings. It is a sad spectacle to see the weaklings bruised, exhausted, fluttering back to earth" (2:966).

Although both Madame Ratignolle and Mademoiselle Reisz perceive more about Edna than she about them, Edna pursues the freedom that they have already relinquished in order to be true to the roles they play. Thus, although contact with these women fosters Edna's discovery of her passionate nature, neither woman ventures to swim, while Edna practices and finally masters the art, wanting "to swim far out, where no woman had swum before" (2:908).

Both Madame and Mademoiselle have given up their own identities in conforming to antithetical but equally acceptable female roles. Both wear proof of the static nature of these roles. Adèle, in billowing white, insists on carrying the delicate, unfunctional needlework that she is making for her little ones wherever she goes with Edna. Mademoiselle Reisz, in dingy black, will not be seen without tattered, artificial violets in her false hair.

Edna feels the seductive charm of Adèle Ratignolle's role but views ironically Adèle's exploitation of her "condition" to gain attention. "Fault-less" yet "sensuous" (2:890–91), Adèle is a reflection of Creole culture and of the demands placed on women who would be perfect wives and mothers. Like the other "mother-women" at Grand Isle, Adèle finds that the accomplished performance of her role allows her a great deal of personal power; but this power has its price, for her role is her only means of self-expression. Characteristically blind to any other adaptation than her own, Adèle cannot understand Edna's assertion that "she would never sacrifice herself for her children, or for any one" (2:929).

Edna senses the inferiority of Adèle's musical skill to Mademoiselle Reisz's artistic power. Adèle, who announces that she is keeping up her music "on account of the children . . . because she and her husband both considered it a means of brightening the home and making it attractive" (2:904), plays piano well enough. One favorite piece evokes for Edna a highly stylized image that she calls "Solitude": a naked man standing beside a desolate rock on the seashore, watching a distant bird winging its flight away from him. The personal reality for Edna of this image of solitude does not disguise its derivative nature. As James H. Justus notes, the figure synthesizes the sentimental features of nineteenth-century calendar art epit-omized by "September Morn" and the posters of Maxfield Parrish.[32] Al-though Justus locates the origin of the image in romantic iconography, he fails to see that it has a significance in the novel that goes beyond its personal reality for Edna in that it suggests her programming by her cul-ture, a programming she shares with other women encouraged to visualize themselves as men in order to attain vicarious individuality and to adopt a negative view of the potential of women as well. Edna's later perception that her passionate directness must appear to Robert "unwomanly" (2:990) suggests her pride in what she assumes are her unconventional and un-feminine modes of thought and feeling.

Edna's sentimental response to Adèle's performance prepares for her emotional response to Mademoiselle's music. When she hears Mademoi-selle play at Grand Isle, Edna listens receptively, waiting for the familiar pictures to appear, but sees "no pictures of solitude, of hope, of longing, or of despair. But the very passions themselves were aroused within her soul, swaying it, lashing it, as the waves daily beat upon her splendid body. She trembled, she was choking, and the tears blinded her" (2:906).

Although Mademoiselle Reisz's music becomes the objective correlative of passion for Edna, Mademoiselle's life is limited, for just as Adèle must give up everything for her children, Mademoiselle sacrifices everything for her art. Although the simple categories represented by "mother" and "artist" (i.e., "nonmother") have been the traditional categories with which white women have been forced to define themselves, Edna refuses to define herself in these terms, failing to recognize that another reality may exist for her friends beneath their conforming masks.

The habit of reserve fostered by her childhood leaves Edna at a loss with her friends. Class consciousness isolates her from women on the margins of her social world. But the ubiquitous presence of dark women cushions everyday life for women of Edna's class. Although they are objectified or invisible to Edna, they appear at critical junctures in the story, encoding both the social and the psychological reality of female oppression. Without questioning the social order that puts them at her disposal, Edna uses the services of dark women in her household and experiences only vague curiosity about those she meets or those of whom she hears. However, the quotidian presence of dark menials or rivals repeatedly illuminates the precariousness of Edna's status as an object of male desire, possession, and protection.

Once more, Edna's inadequacy as an artist reveals her flawed perceptions. Edna's inability to produce convincing likenesses or to imagine more than clichéd images reappears when she paints the quadroon and the maid of her household. When her children tire of posing, she commands the servants to pose: "The quadroon sat for hours before Edna's palette, patient as a savage, while the house-maid took charge of the children, and the drawing-room went undusted" (2:939). When Edna tires of the fit of her earlier inspiration with the quadroon, the housemaid serves a turn as model. The mannered, objectified treatment Edna accords the maid appears in her discovery that the woman's back and shoulders are "molded on classic lines" (2:940). Her inability to see except as guided by convention is again clear.

In describing Edna's interaction with her servants, Chopin clearly sees more than Edna does, for she examines the racial order of Edna's society tongue in cheek. Wealthy Creoles, we learn, have a facade of aesthetic sophistication, but they distrust the darker races, like the provincials they truly are. So when Robert's plans to leave for Mexico become a topic at the dinner table at Grand Isle, several of the diners chime in with stories about the Mexicans. The most alarmed, Adèle Ratignolle hopes "that Robert would exercise extreme caution in dealing with the Mexicans, who, she considered, were a treacherous people, unscrupulous and revengeful. She trusted she did them no injustice in thus condemning them as a race." Victor, however, feels that the Mexicans, especially Mexican women, are an innocuously happy, childlike people, for he regales Monsieur Farival with a "droll story" of his meetings with "a Mexican girl who served chocolate one winter in a restaurant in Dauphine Street" (2:924).

While Edna's friends and acquaintances have a keen interest in foreigners they do not know, they have no curiosity about the servants in their own homes. Chopin, however, endows these invisible but essential dark women—for the servants are female—with an inner consciousness at variance with their forced conformity to the roles they play. While these women perform their parts with "fictitious animation" (2:935), Chopin suggests the facts of their experience obliquely, describing the appropriation of their energy by privileged whites. Thus, Victor Lebrun begins "droll" stories of his conquests across the color line twice in Edna's hearing.[33] Exemplifying white male power at its most defensive, he also berates his mother's maid for her laxity, explaining to Edna "that the black woman's offensive conduct was all due to imperfect training, as he was not there to take her in hand" (2:942). Marginal themselves in wealthy Creole society, since they only keep the resort at Grand Isle, the Lebruns jealously maintain their racial ascendancy. Chopin pokes fun at their pretensions, describing Victor claiming as "his achievement" (2:905) a frozen dessert concocted by two black women in the kitchen and Madame Lebrun enlisting a black girl to push the treadle of her sewing machine. "The Creole woman does not take any chances which may be avoided of imperiling her health" (2:901), Chopin notes in a sly aside.

Chopin laces the text with reminders of Edna's inadequacy as an observer of these social realities. While posing her captive models with uncalculated disregard for their individuality, Edna sings the romantic little air, *"Ah! si tu savais!"* ("Ah! if you knew [what your eyes tell me]!") (2:940, 974). Failing fatally to know herself or these women, Edna parrots the words that confess the answering passion of her own dark eyes; but the ironic connection between the lyrics of this refrain and the flashing eyes of her dark rivals in the novel translates a message she fails to hear. Though haunted by this refrain, Edna refuses to admit its truth until the end of the novel, when she confronts the ephemeral nature of passion.

The refrain and Chopin's description of Edna's eyes, however, link Edna with the dark women Robert and Victor Lebrun and Alcée Arobin know and discuss.[34] Robert serenades Edna with the refrain on their return from Chênière Caminada. Edna picks up the melody as she paints the dark women in her household. At the party to celebrate her separation from

Léonce, Victor echoes the refrain once more. When Edna places her hand over his mouth to still his taunting voice, he kisses her soft palm. The "pleasing sting" (2:974) of this kiss prepares for Edna's passionate response to Alcée Arobin's "gentle, seductive entreaties" (2:976). Edna, however, resists accepting what her body tells her, just as she resists hearing Victor's rendition of the melody. This resistance is played out against her misperceptions of Robert and of women with flashing eyes whom Robert, Victor, and Alcée know.

For just as Robert and Victor Lebrun share a surname that reinscribes their dark proclivities and a melody that murmurs the same message, they also share Mariequita, whose dark presence at crucial junctures in the story underscores her unacknowledged importance in Edna's world. In the Chênière Caminada episode that juxtaposes the limiting facts of life and the romantic fantasies Edna and Robert weave for each other, the presentation of Mariequita making "eyes" at Robert introduces what will become an insistent reminder of Edna's blindness. For to Edna, Mariequita appears stereotypically dark and carefree, bringing up the rear of the expedition burdened by a basket of shrimps. Unable to understand Mariequita's amused banter in Spanish to Robert about the lovers in the boat, Edna looks at Mariequita's feet and notices only "the sand and slime between her brown toes" (2:914). Here, Edna's view of Mariequita divides and anatomizes her, anticipating the partial vision of her own body she achieves in the following scene when she awakens to her sensuality as though newborn and looks "at her round arms as she held them straight up and rubbed them one after the other, observing closely, as if it were something she saw for the first time, the fine, firm quality and texture of her flesh" (2:918).

Unlike Mariequita, whose "ugly brown toes" (2:914) have been buffeted by the elements, Edna's "fine" arms have been shielded. A badge of class, Edna's white skin requires protection. In a parallel scene at the beginning of the novel, Léonce Pontellier looks at her "as one looks at a valuable piece of personal property which has suffered some damage," reproaching her for allowing her skin to tan. In response, Edna examines her "fine" flesh as an objet d'art: "She held up her hands, strong, shapely hands, and surveyed them critically, drawing up her lawn sleeves above the wrists. Looking at them reminded her of her rings, which she had given to her husband before leaving for the beach. She silently reached out to him, and he, understanding, took the rings from his vest pocket and dropped them into her open palm" (2:882).

From vague dissatisfaction with the tacit understanding signaled in this exchange of rings, however, Edna progresses by degrees to open revolt against the terms of marriage, motherhood, and sex as she experiences them. She is not whole until the end of the novel, when she emerges "naked in the open air, at the mercy of the sun, the breeze that beat upon her, and the waves that invited her." At this moment, Edna, like Mariequita, stands barefoot in the sand: "The foamy wavelets curled up to her white feet, and coiled like serpents about her ankles" (2:1000).

Three scenes from the novel illustrate the unequal power of husband and wife in patriarchal marriage and depict Edna's faltering attempts to take possession of the self she begins to discover at Chênière Caminada. They culminate in Edna's confrontation with one of the dark women in her household, who reminds her of her place as wife. Edna's confrontation with this woman, the most direct of a series of confrontations with dark women who shadow her throughout the novel, anticipates later confrontations that confirm Edna's place as a mother and as a sexual being in a society where only men and dark women are sexual beings. In this society Edna's chief function is to evidence wasted effort in caring for her children, seeing to the meals, acting as a willing but undemanding sexual partner for her husband, and discharging her husband's social obligations in a creditable manner. The parameters of her privilege are as rigidly defined as those of the menials and rivals she fails to see.

In the first scene, Léonce takes Edna to task for her "habitual neglect" of the children. He has returned late from a gambling evening at Klein's hotel and demands her attention, although she is sleeping. The real issue, however, is revealed by Léonce's chagrin that Edna, "the sole object of his existence, evinced so little interest in things which concerned him, and valued so little his conversation." When she continues to be unresponsive, Léonce informs her that Raoul has a high fever. Since it is "a mother's place to look after children" (2:885), Léonce leaves Edna to attend Raoul and finishes his bedtime cigar in peace. Thoroughly awake, Edna springs out of bed to see to Raoul, who, she knows, is quite well. Edna's acceptance of Léonce's devaluation of her as a mother appears in her inability to express her anger at Léonce's behavior and in the fact that "she could not have told why she was crying. Such experiences as the foregoing were not uncommon in her married life. They seemed never before to have weighed much against the abundance of her husband's kindness and a uniform devotion which had come to be tacit and self-understood" (2:886).

In the second scene, Edna resists Léonce's sexual importunities. Having settled into a hammock outside to contemplate the significance of her first swim, Edna refuses Léonce's request, his entreaty, and finally his command to come to bed. Still unable to formulate a rationale for resistance, Edna nevertheless recognizes that she has made a significant break with her past, a break that will make subsequent breaks inevitable. Just as she once walked the "daily treadmill of the life" that had been portioned out to her as Léonce's wife, in resistance Edna becomes once more the object of forces she little understands. At the moment of her most intense self-assertion, she is at the mercy of uncontrollable emotion: "She could not at that moment have done other than denied and resisted. She wondered if her husband had ever spoken to her like that before, and if she had submitted to his command. Of course she had; she remembered that she had. But she could not realize why or how she should have yielded, feeling as she then did" (2:912).

The intensity of Edna's emotion and her conviction fade when Léonce intrudes on her vigil with a glass of wine and a cigar. "Like one who awakens gradually out of a dream, a delicious, grotesque, impossible dream, to feel again the realities pressing into her soul" (2:912), Edna finally asks, "Are you coming in, Léonce?" Léonce's smug reply testifies to his sense of his victory: "Yes, dear. . . . Just as soon as I have finished my cigar" (2:913).

In the third scene, following the return to New Orleans from the summer freedom of Grand Isle, Léonce wins again. Edna's resistance emerges to the social rituals she has "religiously followed since her marriage, six years before," when she fails to be at home on her Tuesday reception day to receive the wives of Léonce's business acquaintances. At dinner Léonce defends "les convenances" (2:932) against such assaults and vents his anger at Edna for failing to manage the cook so that he could "procure at least one meal a day which a man could eat and retain his self-respect" (2:933). Edna, however, lacks contrition, although "on a few previous occasions she had been completely deprived of any desire to finish her dinner. Sometimes she had gone into the kitchen to administer a tardy rebuke to the cook. Once she went to her room and studied the cookbook during an entire evening, finally writing out a menu for the week, which left her harassed with a feeling that, after all, she had accomplished no good that was worth the name" (2:934).

Notwithstanding her growing consciousness of the triviality of her functions as Léonce's wife, Edna's resistance is futile, for when she takes off her wedding ring and flings it to the carpet, her small boot heel cannot make even "an indenture, not a mark upon the little glittering circlet" (2:934). When, in frustration, she throws a vase on the hearth, a maid enters to remind her of her position as Mrs. Pontellier. Submitting to this dark woman as she submitted to Léonce earlier, Edna holds "out her hand, and taking the ring, slipped it upon her finger" (2:935).

Caring for Edna as she cares for the other possessions in Léonce Pontellier's household, the maid extends the reach of Léonce's power by reenacting his gesture with Edna's wedding ring. Edna's response to the maid signals once more her blind resignation to the relationships that perpetuate her husband's power over her. For if she cannot govern herself or her servants, she lacks the capacity both for her role and for the rebellion she contemplates.

With this final scene, the revolt that began at Grand Isle has touched the whole of Edna's social world, from her diasppointed callers to the servants in her home. But the revolt has achieved nothing of substance, as her resignation at the end of this scene discloses. Edna's flickering insight into her situation compounds her problem. Her ability to conclude "that it was very foolish, very childish, to have stamped upon her wedding ring and smashed the crystal vase upon the tiles" is compromised by the "spell of her infatuation" (2:936) with Robert Lebrun, which colors her perception of the possibilities of fulfillment and leads her to await "life's delirium" (2:938). Similarly, the sharpness of her reported assertion that "a wedding is one of the most lamentable spectacles on earth" (2:948) loses conviction because she lends herself to "any passing caprice" (2:939) in an attempt to avoid coming to terms with her situation.

Although her aimless responses do not invalidate her experience, Edna repeatedly avoids confronting the implications of her actions. Thus, she emerges at the feast to celebrate her independence crowned by Léonce's gift of "a magnificent cluster of diamonds that sparkled, that almost sputtered" (2:970). Later, although beyond the point of reconciliation, she answers Léonce's letter concerning a projected family trip to Europe with "friendly evasiveness,—not with any fixed design to mislead him, only because all sense of reality had gone out of her life" (2:988).

Edna's inability to continue complying with her social role as a Victorian wife merges with her inability to focus on the implications for her of a fully realized sexuality. Adèle's chronic "condition," Mademoiselle Reisz's spinsterhood, and Léonce's repeated trips to his club, however, signal what was the Victorian woman's primary existential choice: pregnancy, celibacy, or continence in marriage, maintained at her expense by the double standard.

Edna's inability to respond in the accepted Victorian way to motherhood, "that outward and visible sign of the angelic condition of wifehood,"[35] foreshadows her ultimate awakening to the biological trap sprung by sexual desire. Initially, Edna's vague distrust of the way in which Adèle exploits her "condition" fails to penetrate the falseness of the sentimental image; Edna never notices the presence of quadroon women who maintain the illusion that Adèle serves.

Looking resigned and out of sorts, these women follow the Pontellier and Ratignolle children at Grand Isle and in New Orleans—their ill humor a silent testimony to the backbreaking job of child-care and to the ornamental nature of motherhood as Edna and Adèle know it. Relieved and also deprived of any vital connection to Etienne and Raoul, Edna is alienated from her role as mother. Adèle's contrasting delight in the role originates in her love for attention, which manifests itself when she receives her children "with the grace and majesty which queens are sometimes supposed to possess," taking her baby from its nurse "with a thousand endearments," though, "as everybody well knew, the doctor had forbidden her to lift so much as a pin!" (2:892). Although the work of servant women makes it possible for women like Edna and Adèle to wear spotless white, the pretty social fiction dark women are employed to maintain cannot easily survive the white woman's experience of childbirth. In this elemental context, the laboring woman is alone, the privileged woman perhaps more so than the woman forced daily to confront the facts of life. The doctor who may have exhorted the privileged woman to remember her delicate condition may now urge her to suffer the pains that rend her and to be still.

Chopin's depiction of Adèle's *accouchement* and of Edna's awakening to the torture it represents, however, exposes Victorian twaddle about the "apotheosis of womanhood."[36] For polite fictions break down as Edna watches her friend being transformed by travail. Adèle's face becomes "drawn and pinched, her sweet blue eyes haggard and unnatural." She becomes petulant, complaining of abandonment and neglect—though she is attended by Edna and by Josephine, an experienced black woman. Sweating and setting "her teeth hard into her under lip" (2:994), Adèle hardly embodies every womanly charm and grace as she demands a male audience for another of her grand performances.

A mute contrasting mirror of Edna's response, Josephine urges "Madame [Adèle] to have courage and patience," refusing "to take . . . too seriously . . . a situation with which she was so familiar." Edna, however, applies the memories of her own "half remembered" deliveries to Adèle's ordeal: "She recalled faintly an ecstasy of pain, the heavy odor of chloroform, a stupor which had deadened sensation, and an awakening to find a little new life to which she had given being. . . . She began to wish she had not come. . . . With an inward agony, with a flaming, outspoken revolt against the ways of Nature, she witnessed the scene of torture" (2:994–95).[37]

Although Edna has not yet registered the meaning of this revelation, she begins to reassess her experience in the light of its shattering truth. Her revolt against the ways of Nature is marked by the incoherence of her thoughts, for although she assures Doctor Mandelet that she has discovered it is "better to wake up after all, even to suffer, rather than to remain a dupe to illusions all one's life" (2:996), she, like other white heroines in Southern fiction, decides that "to-morrow would be time to think of everything" (2:997). With the echo of Adèle's parting injunction to "think of the children" (2:995) ringing in her ears, Edna rushes home to consummate her love with Robert, and "all the tearing emotion of the last few hours seemed to fall away from her like a somber, uncomfortable garment, which she had but to loosen to be rid of" (2:996).

At this critical moment in the story, Chopin's use of the uncomfortable garment as a metaphor for the facts of life Edna evades in leaving Adèle's bedside recalls its contrasting use as a metaphor for the "fictitious self" (2:939) she sheds during the course of the novel—the contrast exposing the paradoxical nature of an awakening predicated on delusion and discovery. This paradox inheres in Edna's partial vision of reality and in her relationship with Robert Lebrun, for she invests her passion with a conventional belief in romantic love. Her adolescent infatuations, however, have prepared her to respond to Robert uncritically. Her passion for the "dignified and sad-eyed cavalry officer" (2:897) who had visited her father in Kentucky, and whose face she remembers as Napoleonic, dissolves and evaporates with her passion for the fiancé of a lady on a neighboring plantation in Mississippi. Her grand passion for the face and figure of a "great tragedian," whose framed photograph she had placed on her desk and kissed surreptitiously, lingers until after her marriage. Although, and undoubtedly because, she has never seen the tragedian, her impossible passion for him persists with an "aspect of genuineness" (2:898).

In contrast to the tragedian, Robert is close and available to a degree, but his love affairs have a predictable, safe, socially imposed pattern, a pattern that involves the displacement of passion onto dark women he is reluctant to discuss. Thus, after the death of his amour of the two previous summer seasons, he *poses* as "an inconsolable, prostrating himself at the feet of Madame Ratignolle for whatever crumbs of sympathy and comfort she might be pleased to vouchsafe" (2:890). Adèle fixes the limits of Robert's role as lover in Creole society when she tells him: "If your attentions to any married women here were ever offered with any intention of being convincing, you would not be the gentleman we all know you to be, and you would be unfit to associate with the wives and daughters of the people who trust you" (2:900).

Propinquity and prohibition increase Edna's attraction to Robert and her romantic illusions about him. In attempting to merit the continued trust of Adèle and the others, however, Robert begins to avoid Edna. Edna's interest in him, of course, is heightened by his inexplicable absences: "She missed him the days when some pretext served to take him away from her, just as one misses the sun on a cloudy day without having thought much about the sun when it was shining" (2:907).

First through identification with Robert and then through solitary contemplation of him, whom she fatally misunderstands, Edna falls in love. She assumes that Robert's feelings and opinions coincide with hers. Robert's all-occasion flattery and her intense need for validation lead her on. In the excursion to Chênière Caminada, for example, her need determines her perceptions. Excluding any thought about the meaning of Mariequita's sullen glances, Edna assumes that Robert (who divides his attentions during the trip) would have preferred to stay with her. Though she has spent much of the time on the island alone sleeping, Edna fails to grant Robert an independent existence, an existence that his interaction with Mariequita and his absence from the scene during Edna's nap invite us to suppose. Edna, however, can only concede to Robert the feelings that she is discovering in herself: "It did not occur to her to think he might have grown tired of being with her the livelong day. She was not tired, and she felt that he was not" (2:921). While Robert is surely attracted to Edna as she is to him, he continues to resist the involvement she feels is so natural. Edna is the last to learn of his plans to leave for Mexico. Characteristically, she recognizes her great love for him only when she has apparently lost him. The parallel between the hopeless infatuations of Edna's youth and her infatuation with Robert is pointedly drawn, suggesting Edna's arrested development and the power of romantic illusions in her life: "For the first time she recognized anew the symptoms of infatuation which she had felt incipiently as a child, as a girl in her earliest teens, and later as a young woman. The recognition did not lessen the reality, the poignancy of the revelation by any suggestion or promise of instability. The past was nothing to her; offered no lesson which she was willing to heed" (2:927).

Edna's passion for Robert is not slaked by her passionate affair with Alcée Arobin. Her sense of "Robert's reproach" makes "itself felt by a quicker, fiercer, more overpowering love, which had awakened within her toward him" (2:967). However, when Robert returns at last, Edna is dismayed that their meeting does not come up to her romantic expectations: "A hundred times Edna had pictured Robert's return, and imagined their first meeting. It was usually at her home, whither he had sought her out at once. She always fancied him expressing or betraying in some way his love for her. And here, the reality was that they sat ten feet apart, she at the window, crushing geranium leaves in her hand and smelling them, he twirling around on the piano stool" (2:982).

In the crucial scene that follows this unsettling meeting, Edna begins to intuit the distance between her imaginary love and reality. Neither she nor Robert has been true to her conception of romantic love. She has a photograph of Alcée that she claims to have been sketching. Robert, who describes Mexico as uncongenial, has brought back a memento that suggests the congeniality of its dark women (2:981). When she learns that the memento, a finely embroidered tobacco pouch that Robert now carries, is a gift from a "generous" Vera Cruz woman, Edna's jealous suspicions are confirmed. Her questions about the women of Mexico, whom she describes as "very picturesque, with their black eyes and their lace scarfs," betray the limited range of her worldly experience. Robert's response demonstrates his contrasting worldly wisdom. Although his assertion that the woman "wasn't of the slightest importance" is presumably as genuine in its way as Edna's claim that Arobin's photograph means nothing to her, Robert's ability to generalize about women from his experience illuminates his sense of male privilege. His callous assertion that "there are some people who leave impressions not so lasting as the imprint of an oar upon the water" is underlined by his gallant insistence that it would be ungenerous for him to "admit" that the Vera Cruz woman "was of that order and kind." Edna's lack of empathy for the woman Robert has used and left allows him, in pocketing his memento, "to put away the subject with the trifle which had brought it up" (2:985).

With Arobin's untimely visit, however, the subject comes up again. Arobin is eager to exchange male small talk about the "stunning girls" (2:985) he has known in Vera Cruz. Robert's discomfort with these suggestive remarks prompts a hasty departure and a pointed request that Edna convey his regards to Mr. Pontellier when she writes. Edna's realization that Robert "had seemed nearer to her off there in Mexico" (2:987) reveals her unconscious perception of the gap that is opening between her dream lover and the real Robert.

When Edna finally declares her love, Robert's behavior widens this gap. Secure as never before in his sense of male privilege, Robert, like Léonce and Alcée before him, now smokes a cigar in Edna's presence. He has bought a whole box, he tells her. His view that Edna is Léonce's property surfaces when he responds to her declaration by confessing his own "wild, impossible" dreams of "men who had set their wives free." His perception that these dreams make him a "cur" demonstrates his adherence to the values Léonce and Alcée tacitly share. But Edna ignores the implications of Robert's shocked reaction, though he turns white at her insistence that she is "no longer one of Mr. Pontellier's possessions to dispose of or not" (2:992).

Only after reading his characteristic parting cliché—"Good-by—because I love you" (2:997)—does Edna relinquish the illusions that have served as her narcotic throughout the novel. Her realization that even her passion for Robert will eventually "melt out of her existence, leaving her alone" (2:999) forces her to recognize the primacy of her need to be herself and the impossibility of being herself in her society. Standing naked against the sky "like some new-born creature," Edna at last opens her "eyes in a familiar world that [she] had never known" (2:1000).

In this final awakening, Edna confronts the fundamental similarity between the restrictive, emotionally impoverished world of her childhood and the world of seemingly limitless possibility of New Orleans. Believing that here her love could triumph over convention, she has followed a fantasy by taking Robert and her passion for him seriously. Now she comprehends much that she had misconstrued. Her belief in the depth of her commitment to Robert and his to her has vanished as surely as her earlier belief in the "sympathy of thought and taste" (2:898) she shared with Léonce before marrying him. But her awakening to love's "illusions" and her hard-won understanding of her responsibility to her children remain bounded by sex, race, and class biases. The solitude that has made her gradual awakening possible has also limited its range and its significance.

In the ambivalent final chapter of *The Awakening*, as in the beginning, Edna is Mrs. Pontellier.[38] Intruding upon Mariequita and Victor, to whom she gives orders for a supper she never intends to eat, she betrays once again her programming as a privileged white woman. Through food, the emblem of her subjugation and her self-indulgence throughout the novel, Edna establishes her claim on Mariequita, the dark woman she needs to provide a plausible story of her accidental drowning. Mariequita will provide that story, for she believes in the mythic Edna, Victor's construct—a woman "who gave the most sumptuous dinners in America, and who had all the men in New Orleans at her feet" (2:998). Mariequita's belief in the mythic Edna reconfirms the potency and prevalence of the romantic illusions that divide women from each other. A final contrast to Edna, who detaches herself from story-making and story-hearing by committing suicide, Mariequita survives untouched by Edna's awakening. In the world of the novel, the conventions Chopin challenged remain to motivate mythmaking and to preclude for all women a full awakening to life's possibilities.

CHAPTER FIVE

· *Conclusion* ·

In their stories of women on the color line, 1870–1900, George Cable, Grace King, and Kate Chopin personified complex and contradictory human responses to what Mark Twain called "a fiction of law and custom,"[1] the fiction of racial difference. Beyond the masks of race and costumes of gender, their women characters defy categorization as racial types. They are believable, memorable, and striking; and the stories they inhabit indict the social masquerades that inscribe race, class, and gender difference, thereby fixing an individual's life chances from birth. These stories raise questions of social justice and equality that have never been answered in America, questions that lie at the heart of our national experience, questions that Americans have never been comfortable confronting.

As Southerners who grappled with these questions a century ago, Cable, King, and Chopin transcended through their best works the times that shaped and constrained them. Their contributions to the fictive dialogue on race and gender claim for them a place in a literary tradition that is only now in the process of coherent formulation. Although they were perhaps never fully conscious of the devastating reach of their realism and were unaware of the racial debacle that lay ahead for Americans, they captured in their best works a defensively racist, sexist, class society, a society shaken by civil war and possibly, it must have seemed to them, capable of reconstruction. Significantly, although they did not speak in unison, none of them, not even the patrician Grace King, who revered the aristocratic life and manners of the New Orleans past, yielded in these works to the temptation to excuse slavery with pretty romances of antebellum life, as had so many Southern writers of their generation. In refusing to valorize Southern patriarchy, they anticipated the authors of the Southern Renaissance, who after 1930 returned to the dismantling of the Southern "family romance"[2] initiated by Cable's *The Grandissimes,* King's *Monsieur Motte,* and Chopin's *The Awakening* more than fifty years before.

The history of the two decades in which Cable, King, and Chopin produced their best fiction helps us understand their exceptional achievement, their eventual silence, and their long neglect or misclassification as minor "local-color" writers. They struggled in their fiction with the great issues of their day, the Negro Question and the Woman Question. Then they were buried by the tide of history, by the emotional current of racism that crested in a frenzy of violence and Negrophobia during the period in which they wrote and that surged on after the *Plessy v. Ferguson* "separate but equal" decision (1896) with primal force in fifty years of de jure segregation in the South and de facto segregation in the North. Given the virulent racism engulfing the nation after 1900, Grace King's hope that her stories might someday "prove a pleasant record and serve to bring us all nearer together blacks and whites"[3] seems touching, but naive. The time and the place and the Southerners who believed with Cable in the responsibility of fiction to present and defend truth "even though it shake the established order of things like an earthquake"[4]; with King in the need for fiction to give a true account of the lives of "white as well as black women"[5]; or with Chopin in the obligation of fiction to portray life's "subtle, complex, true meaning, stripped of the veil with which ethical and conventional standards have draped it"[6] seem to be features of a newly discovered stratum unaccounted for by mainstream literary history, which has focused on the unity and continuity of the Great Tradition.

With regard to Cable, King, Chopin, and "the other Southerners"[7] who attacked the dominant ideology of the South, what W. E. B. Du Bois characterized as the "propaganda" of Reconstruction produced collective amnesia.[8] Moreover, in the decades flanking the turn of the century, intellectuals tended to rationalize rampant white supremacy as the United States reached its moral nadir in the virtual enslavement of ten million dark-skinned people in the Caribbean and the Pacific. The "black image in the white mind" suffered corresponding debasement.[9] In *The Strange Career of Jim Crow,* C. Vann Woodward contrasts the image of the Negro that surfaced in the works of white authors such as Cable, King, and Chopin and the one that emerged in the pages of Thomas Dixon, Jr., whose trilogy (*The Leopard's Spots: A Romance of the White Man's Burden—1865–1900* [1902]; *The Clansman: An Historical Romance of the Ku Klux Klan* [1905]; and *The Traitor: A Story of the Fall of the Invisible Empire* [1907]) "was the perfect literary accompaniment of the white-supremacy and disfranchisement campaign, at the height of which they were published."[10] It is no accident that *The Leopard's Spots,* published only four years after the United States' imperial adventure began, was subtitled *A Romance of the White Man's Burden*. Jim Crow and jingoism battened together. With Thomas Dixon in the ascendant, the literary landscape of the South was bleak for the next twenty years, so bleak in fact that H. L. Mencken mapped it satirically in his famous "The Sahara of the Bozart" (1920).

In this period authors found commitment to social justice risky. The genteel proscriptions they found so lethal to art worked hand in glove with the nation's imperialistic aims. Thus, Kate Chopin ran afoul of genteel critics by making Edna Pontellier, "a real American wife and mother," behave as only foreign, lower-class, or ethnically "tainted" women were popularly supposed to behave. In a by-now familiar complaint, Charles Chesnutt diagnosed the racial schizophrenia of American society, writing to George Cable "de plein coeur" to lament his inability to write "the kind of stuff I could write, if I were not all the time oppressed by the fear that this line or this sentiment would offend somebody's prejudices, jar on somebody's American-trained sense of propriety."[11] Chesnutt, who perceived that the black community with its "blue vein" societies mirrored the white community in a bizarre and self-destructive way, abandoned literature to return to a profitable law practice. In *The Marrow of Tradition* (1901), a fictional account of the Wilmington, North Carolina, race riot of 1898, Chesnutt depicted the benighted new age of race relations, noting that the race question had "reached a sort of *impasse,* a blind alley, of which no one could see the outlet"[12] and lamenting the growing indifference of whites to the racial issues that had once been the moral fulcrum of public debate. In light of the violence that threatened white dissenters who went as far as George Cable in pressing "the Negro Question," this turning from the question for a time, though deplorable, was perhaps understandable.

When he was awarded the NAACP's Spingarn Medal in 1928, thirty-eight years after his letter to Cable, Chesnutt looked back on his own aborted career as an author and implied that other authors at the turn of the century had reached a similar impasse, noting that his books, especially *The House behind the Cedars* (1900), which had occasioned the letter to Cable, and *The Marrow of Tradition,* "were written, from one point of view, a generation too soon," since he "was writing against the trend of public opinion on the race question at that particular time."[13]

By the time of Chesnutt's award, the trend of public opinion had changed. Vast migrations of Southern blacks into Northern industrial cities in the most virulent days of Jim Crow had altered the complexion of the country, giving Northern whites firsthand acquaintance with the demented racism so long associated in the popular mind with the South.[14] During the Harlem Renaissance, 1917–29, however, white intellectuals celebrated and patronized "the savage"; and a new generation of black and white authors resurrected, reconceived, and reclaimed the "tragic octoroon" in their fiction. Especially noteworthy was her emergence in works of black women authors such as Jessie Redmon Fauset (*There Is Confusion*, 1924; *Plum Bun*, 1929; *The Chinaberry Tree*, 1931; and *Comedy, American Style*, 1933) and Nella Larsen (*Quicksand*, 1928; and *Passing*, 1929), who portrayed the lives of light-skinned women much like themselves, women of the "talented tenth," who Du Bois hoped would help save the Negro race.[15]

In *Black Women Novelists: The Development of a Tradition, 1892–1976*, Barbara Christian calls attention to the fact that both black and white women authors of this period depicted "tragic mulattas" in their fiction and asks "if [such fiction] offered vicarious wish fulfillment, as well as amusement for those blacks who would pass if they could, and titillating drama for a largely white reading audience."[16] Whether white readers were titillated or black readers tantalized by these depictions of women caught in the color bind so long central to fiction on race, it is clear that for some of these authors, especially Fauset and Larsen, the trope of "passing" was an unmasking device, revealing both the "double consciousness" of blacks, psychologically warped by racism, and the racial duplicity of American society. Significantly, in the works of black women authors, the "passer" is usually a woman who risks all in a society where appearances tell most tragically against women. To this extent, the new treatment of the "tragic mulatta" bears a marked resemblance to that of George Cable (*Madame Delphine*, 1881), Grace King ("The Little Convent Girl," 1893), and Kate Chopin ("Désirée's Baby," 1893).

The convincing depictions by Fauset and Larsen of the circumstances that coerce their women characters into lying about "race" or denying their sensuality reveal both the sham of racial uplift and the reality of women's oppression. Thus, in *Quicksand*, a novel in which "the tragic mulattas of the abolitionist novels finally reach bitter fruition,"[17] Nella Larsen portrays Helga Crane, whose life has been distorted by the stereotyped image imposed upon her. Feeling she must deny her sensuality in order to live down the racial slurs black women suffer, Helga nevertheless perceives the death-dealing nature of the bourgeois values whites have foisted on blacks. She comes to see her school, "a show place in the black belt" (modeled on Tuskegee), as "a big knife with cruelly sharp edges ruthlessly cutting all to a pattern, the white man's pattern." Here, "teachers as well as students were subjected to the paring process, for it tolerated no innovations, no individualisms. . . . Enthusiasm, spontaneity, if not actually suppressed, were at least openly regretted as unladylike or ungentlemanly qualities."[18] However, the paring process makes its mark on Helga herself, who flees to Denmark—where she rejects a Danish suitor, saying, "I'm not for sale. Not to you. Not to any white man"[19]—and then to rural Alabama with a husband she marries to escape her sexual attraction to another man. From this moment, the irony of Helga's "choice" becomes clear. Mired and suffocating in the quicksand of respectability, she gives birth to her fifth child by the husband she does not love at the novel's end.

Although it is doubtful that Nella Larsen read Kate Chopin, it is clear that Helga Crane and Edna Pontellier are linked. For while they are unalike in almost every superficial way, the fact that they are women in a racist, sexist society defines their life chances. Thus, the biological trap Helga falls into as she sidesteps racist stereotypes joins her to Edna Pontellier, who drowns herself when she awakens to the incompatibility of her dreams with the reality of her life as a privileged woman in Creole society. Furthermore, the common, though in many ways contrasting, treatment of woman's plight by Chopin and Larsen, who are separated by race, class, and history, testifies to the longevity and power of a literary dialogue as yet incompletely documented. In this dialogue George Cable, Grace King, and Kate Chopin were insightful early participants.

NOTES

Preface

1 · Elaine Showalter, "Review Essay: Literary Criticism," *Signs* 1 (Winter 1975): 435.

2 · Adrienne Rich, "When We Dead Awaken: Writing as Re-Vision," *College English* 34 (October 1972): 18. Rich argues that women's writing must begin with a "re-vision" of the past. Sandra M. Gilbert sets Rich's essay in context, noting that "words beginning with the prefix *re-* have lately become prominent in the language of feminist humanists," who recognize that it is necessary to reinterpret, rewrite, and revise the history of "what is called Western culture" ("What Do Feminist Critics Want? A Postcard from the Volcano," in *The New Feminist Criticism: Essays on Women, Literature, and Theory,* ed. Elaine Showalter [New York: Pantheon Books, 1985], p. 32).

3 · Judith Fetterley's *The Resisting Reader: A Feminist Approach to American Fiction* (Bloomington: Indiana Univ. Press, 1978) describes the strategies that she and other feminist scholars and critics (Sandra M. Gilbert, Susan Gubar, Elaine Showalter, and Annette Kolodny, to name but a few) employ to gain access to repressed possibilities for interpretation in canonical works of literature.

4 · Recent studies demonstrate that literary and scientific theory reflects unconscious forces as well. For a discussion of this observation, see Fredric Jameson's *The Political Unconscious: Narrative as a Socially Symbolic Act* (Ithaca, N.Y.: Cornell Univ. Press, 1981) and Stephen Jay Gould's *The Mismeasure of Man* (New York: W. W. Norton, 1981). Gould writes: "Some topics are invested with enormous social importance but blessed with very little reliable information. When the ratio of data to social impact is so low, a history of scientific attitudes may be little more than an oblique record of social change. The history of scientific views on race, for example, serves as a mirror of social movements" (p. 22).

5 · Winthrop D. Jordan, *White over Black: American Attitudes toward the Negro, 1550–1812* (Chapel Hill: Univ. of North Carolina Press, 1968), p. 150. Jordan's recognition of the social expediency of American views of the black woman is echoed by

164 · NOTES

psychological research into white male attitudes toward interracial sex. In *Sexual Racism: The Emotional Barrier to an Integrated Society* (New York: Elsevier Scientific Publishing, 1976), pp. 32–34, Charles Herbert Stember cites the findings of a study by Gary I. Schulman entitled "Race, Sex, and Violence: A Laboratory Test of the Sexual Threat of the Black Male Hypothesis" (*American Journal of Sociology* 79 [March 1974]: 1260–77). This study replicates Stanley Milgram's famous experiment, which induced subjects to deliver what they believed to be ever-increasing levels of electrical shock to strangers. Schulman adapted Milgram's design, using two white males and two black male confederates. As a control, one white and one black male were used as innocent "victims." A white male who was perceived by the naive subjects to be sexually involved with a black woman was introduced along with a black male who was perceived to be sexually involved with a white woman. Although Schulman selected his naive subjects on the basis of a questionnaire designed to identify "sexually insecure" and racially bigoted white males, the experiment revealed that white males have the greatest proclivity to deliver high voltages to black men perceived to be involved with white women and the least proclivity to "punish" white men perceived to be involved with black women. Obviously, miscegenation continues to arouse intense and angry feelings even among the most "liberated" white males. It is interesting to note here, as Stember does, that many white males continue to regard the black male as a sexual threat and the black female as a sexual facility.

6 · The "dark" woman is a stock character in pornography. In *Against Our Will: Men, Women, and Rape* (New York: Bantam Books, 1976), Susan Brownmiller writes:

> The master-slave relationship is the most popular fantasy perversion in the literature of pornography. The image of a scantily clothed slave girl, always nubile, always beautiful, always docile, who sinks to her knees gracefully and dutifully before her master, who stands with or without boots, with or without whip, is commonly accepted as a scene of titillating sexuality. From the slave harems of the Oriental potentate, celebrated in poetry and dance, to the breathless descriptions of light-skinned fancy women, *de rigueur* in a particular genre of pulp historical fiction, the glorification of forced sex under slavery, institutional rape, has been a part of our cultural heritage, feeding the egos of men while subverting the egos of women—and doing irreparable damage to healthy sexuality in the process. The very words "slave girl" impart to many a vision of voluptuous sensuality redolent of perfumed gardens and soft music strummed on a lyre. Such is the legacy of male-controlled sexuality, under which we struggle. (p. 184)

7 · Alice Walker, "Coming Apart," in *The Other Woman: Stories of Two Women and a Man,* ed. Susan Koppelman (Old Westbury, N.Y.: Feminist Press, 1984).

8 · Teresa de Lauretis, *Alice Doesn't: Feminism, Semiotics, Cinema* (Bloomington: Indiana Univ. Press, 1984), p. 8.

9 · Joel Williamson, *New People: Miscegenation and Mulattoes in the United States* (New York: Free Press, 1980), p. 90.

10 · Joel Williamson, *The Crucible of Race: Black-White Relations in the American South since Emancipation* (New York: Oxford Univ. Press, 1984), p. 40. The word *miscegenation*, the most famous and enduring of the nineteenth century's designations for interracial sex, was coined by the anonymous authors of an inflammatory pamphlet entitled *Miscegenation: The Theory of the Blending of the Races, Applied to the American White Man and Negro* (1864), which purported to be the work of Radical Republicans or abolitionists. An elaborate hoax designed to discredit the Republican Party before the election of 1864, *Miscegenation* created an immediate sensation because of its advocacy of racial mixing; its title passed into the language thereafter as a noun denoting amalgamation of the races. See George M. Fredrickson's *The Black Image in the White Mind: The Debate on Afro-American Character and Destiny, 1817–1914* (New York: Harper & Row, 1971) for a discussion of the period that produced *Miscegenation* and a host of other racist diatribes.

11 · Warner Berthoff, *The Ferment of Realism: American Literature, 1884–1919* (New York: Free Press, 1965), p. 83.

12 · Adele Logan Alexander, "How I Discovered My Grandmother . . . and the Truth about Black Women and the Suffrage Movement," *Ms.* 12 (November 1983): 29.

13 · George Washington Cable, "The Freedman's Case in Equity," in *The Negro Question: A Selection of Writings on Civil Rights in the South*, ed. Arlin Turner (Garden City, N.Y.: Doubleday, 1958), p. 78.

One · Stereotyped Women on the Color Line: Texts and Contexts

1 · In elucidating romantic racialism, George M. Fredrickson writes: "The American 'ethnologic' self-image, whether described as Anglican, Anglo-Saxon, Celtic–Anglo-Saxon, or simply Caucasian, was being formulated and popularized at the very time when the slavery controversy focused interest on the Negro character." Fredrickson identifies a change in the premises of the slavery debate during the 1840s and 1850s and notes that ideas of innate and fundamental racial difference were articulated by both proslavery and antislavery advocates (*The Black Image in the White Mind: The Debate on Afro-American Character and Destiny, 1817–1914* [New York: Harper & Row, 1971], p. 100).

2 · Robin W. Winks, General Introduction to *Four Fugitive Slave Narratives*, ed. Winks et al. (Reading, Mass.: Addison-Wesley, 1969), p. vi.

3 · Quoted in Sidney Kaplan, "*The Octoroon:* Early History of the Drama of Miscegenation," *Journal of Negro Education* 20 (1951): 550.

4 · Francis P. Gaines, "The Racial Bar Sinister in American Romance," *South Atlantic Quarterly* 25 (October 1926): 396.

5 · John Greenleaf Whittier, "The Farewell of a Virginia Slave Mother to Her Daughters Sold into Southern Bondage," in *Anti-Slavery Poems: Songs of Labor and Reform* (New York: Arno Press, 1969), p. 57.

6 · Jules Zanger, "The 'Tragic Octoroon' in Pre–Civil War Fiction," *American Quarterly* 18 (Spring 1966): 64.

7 · Black women writers have also exploited this tragic story to illuminate the

suffering of black people and to assert black female virtue. In *Iola Leroy; or, Shadows Uplifted* (Philadelphia: Garrigues Bros., 1892), Frances E. W. Harper, long popularly assumed to be the first black woman novelist, tells the edifying story of a quadroon sold into slavery who survives many trials, is rescued, and lives happily ever after. Harper's vision of her heroine is rare in its optimism but clearly controlled by the conventional depiction of the ladylike qualities deemed necessary for salvation in the nineteenth century.

8 · Dion Boucicault, *The Octoroon; or, Life in Louisiana* (Miami, Fla.: Mnemosyne Publishing, 1969), pp. 16–17.

9 · Margaret Fuller, *Woman in the Nineteenth Century* (New York: W. W. Norton, 1971), pp. 33–34. (*Woman in the Nineteenth Century, and Kindred Papers Relating to the Sphere, Condition, and Duties of Woman,* with an introduction by Horace Greeley, was edited by Fuller's brother, Arthur, and was first published by J. P. Jewett in Boston, 1855.)

10 · Quoted in C. Vann Woodward, ed., *Mary Chesnut's Civil War* (New Haven: Yale Univ. Press, 1981), pp. li, 15. In *The Southern Lady: From Pedestal to Politics, 1830–1930,* Anne Firor Scott looks at the privately expressed racial attitudes of Southern "lady" diarists and conjectures that there was a connection between the perception of the oppression of women and the understanding of the brutality of slavery on the part of aristocratic Southern women ([Chicago: Univ. of Chicago Press, 1970], pp. 50–51). In analogizing slavery and marriage, Mary Chesnut and other Southern women employed the dominant trope of nineteenth-century feminist writing. Chesnut echoed John Stuart Mill, who wrote: "No slave is a slave to the same lengths, and in so full a sense of the word, as a wife is" (*The Subjection of Women* [New York: D. Appleton, 1870], p. 57). Although tropes of slavery and racial oppression continue to be used by white feminists to describe woman's plight in patriarchal society, many blacks resent and resist this appropriation of their experience. Bell Hooks indicts white feminists for drawing the analogy between "women" and "blacks," noting that this pervasive comparison deflects "attention away from the fact that black women were extremely victimized by both racism and sexism—a fact which, had it been emphasized, might have diverted public attention away from the complaints of middle and upper class white feminists" (*Ain't I a Woman? Black Women and Feminism* [Boston: South End Press, 1981], p. 141).

11 · Sterling A. Brown, "Negro Character as Seen by White Authors," in *Dark Symphony: Negro Literature in America,* ed. James A. Emanuel and Theodore L. Gross (New York: Free Press, 1968), pp. 158–59.

12 · Richard Hildreth, *The Slave; or, Memoirs of Archy Moore* (Boston: John H. Eastburn, 1836), pp. 5–6.

13 · Zanger, "The 'Tragic Octoroon,'" p. 64.

14 · William Wells Brown, *Clotel; or, The President's Daughter* (New York: Macmillan, 1970), p. 42. Subsequent reference to *Clotel* is given parenthetically in the text of the chapter. Clotel bears an octoroon daughter whom Brown pictures vividly, borrowing from Lydia Maria Child's "The Quadroons" (originally published in *The Liberty Bell,* the first abolitionist literary annual, compiled by "Friends of Freedom" and published for the Massachusetts Anti-Slavery Fair of 1842): "The iris of her large

dark eye had the melting mezzotinto, which remains the last vestige of African ancestry, and gives that plaintive expression, so often observed, and so appropriate to that docile and injured race" (p. 58).

15 · Helen Waite Papashvily, *All the Happy Endings: A Study of the Domestic Novel in America, the Women Who Wrote It, the Women Who Read It, in the Nineteenth Century* (New York: Harper & Bros., 1956), p. 71.

16 · In *Philosophy in a New Key: A Study in the Symbolism of Reason, Rite, and Art,* 3d ed. (Cambridge: Harvard Univ. Press, 1957), pp. 79–102, Susanne Langer makes the famous distinction between discursive and presentational forms in literature and explains the ability of the latter to create "virtual life." In *Uncle Tom's Cabin* Stowe "presents" the scenes of Cassy's degradation.

17 · Forrest Wilson, *Crusader in Crinoline: The Life of Harriet Beecher Stowe* (Philadelphia: J. B. Lippincott, 1941), p. 255.

18 · Of the formative reading of her childhood, Ann Douglas remarks: "But what I remember best, what was for me as for so many others, the archetypical and archetypically satisfying scene in this domestic genre, was the death of little Eva in Harriet Beecher Stowe's novel, *Uncle Tom's Cabin*" (*The Feminization of American Culture* [New York: Knopf, 1977], p. 3).

19 · George Washington Cable, quoted in Arlin Turner, *George W. Cable: A Biography* (Baton Rouge: Louisiana State Univ. Press, 1966), p. 15.

20 · Grace King, *Memories of a Southern Woman of Letters* (New York: Macmillan, 1932), p. 77.

21 · Mrs. L. H. Sigourney, *Letters to Young Ladies,* rev. ed. (London: Jackson and Walford, 1841), p. 233; Harriet Beecher Stowe, *Uncle Tom's Cabin* (New York: Washington Square Press, 1963), p. 403. (Originally serialized in *The National Era* 5, no. 23 [June 5, 1851] to 6, no. 14 [April 1, 1852], the novel was first published in book form in Boston by J. P. Jewett and Co. in 1852.)

22 · Stowe, *Uncle Tom's Cabin,* p. 333.

23 · According to Mr. Compson in Faulkner's *Absalom, Absalom!* Thomas Sutpen betrayed his lack of classical erudition, the distinguishing mark of a true Southern gentleman, when he named his mulatto daughter Clytemnestra instead of Cassandra.

24 · Stowe, *Uncle Tom's Cabin,* p. 360. Subsequent references to this work, except where context makes the reference unclear, are given parenthetically in the text.

25 · Papashvily, *All the Happy Endings,* p. 73.

26 · Stowe, quoted in Russel B. Nye, Introduction to Stowe, *Uncle Tom's Cabin,* p. xiv.

27 · Sigourney, *Letters,* p. 4. In *Daughters of the Promised Land: Women in American History,* Page Smith observes that "the nineteenth century had two major (and sometimes overlapping) ways of neutralizing woman. One was to elevate her to the angelic creature, fragile and ethereal; the other was to deify her as The Mother" ([Boston: Little, Brown, 1970], p. 210). Stowe obviously was not neutralized. Nor were many other matrons who took advantage of the power conferred by deification. Twentieth-century social phobias about "Momism" suggest that in glorifying

The Mother, nineteenth-century patriarchs unwittingly gave the moral control of their offspring to their wives.

28 · Margaret Fuller articulated the desperation of these disenfranchised white mothers. Many of the tyrannies she cites existed in reality on both sides of the color line and were therefore reasons for the enfranchisement of women. White women were as helpless to protect themselves or their children from vicious husbands as slave mothers were to protect themselves or their children from vicious masters. Fuller wrote:

> We will not speak of the innumerable instances in which profligate and idle men live upon the earnings of industrious wives; or if the wives leave them, and take with them the children, to perform the double duty of mother and father, follow from place to place, and threaten to rob them of the children, if deprived of the rights of a husband, as they call them, planting themselves in their poor lodgings, frightening them into paying tribute by taking from them the children, running into debt at the expense of these otherwise so overtasked helots. Such instances count up by scores within my own memory. I have seen the husband who had stained himself by a long course of low vice [presumably referring to the high incidence of venereal disease in men of this sort], till his wife was wearied from her heroic forgiveness, by finding that his treachery made it useless, and that if she would provide bread for herself and her children, she must be separate from his ill fame—I have known this man come to install himself in the chamber of a woman who loathed him, and say she should never take food without his company. I have known these men steal their children, whom they knew they had no means to maintain, take them into dissolute company, expose them to bodily danger, to frighten the poor woman, to whom, it seems, the fact that she alone had borne the pangs of their birth, and nourished their infancy, does not give an equal right to them. I do believe that this mode of kidnapping—and it is frequent enough in all classes of society—will be by the next age viewed as it is by Heaven now, and that the man who avails himself of the shelter of men's laws to steal from a mother her own children, or arrogate any superior right in them, save that of superior virtue, will bear the stigma he deserves, in common with him who steals grown men from their mother-land, their hopes, and their homes.

Here, Fuller is obviously carried away by the recollection of the wrongs suffered by women around her, for she follows this moving digression with an apology: "I said, we will not speak of this now; yet I *have* spoken, for the subject makes me feel too much" (*Woman in the Nineteenth Century,* pp. 31–33).

29 · William Heyward, quoted in Joel Williamson, *New People: Miscegenation and Mulattoes in the United States* (New York: Free Press, 1980), p. 92.

30 · Ibid.

31 · Henry Raymond, quoted in Kaplan, *"The Octoroon,"* p. 551.

32 · In *The Portrait of a Lady* (1882), Henry James wrote that there is "no more nutritive or suggestive truth . . . than that of the perfect dependence of the 'moral'

sense of a work of art on the amount of felt life concerned in producing it" ([New York: W. W. Norton, 1975], p. 6).

33 · Josiah Quincy, quoted in Julia Cherry Spruill, *Women's Life and Work in the Southern Colonies* (New York: W. W. Norton, 1972), p. 177.

34 · Stephen Longstreet, *Sportin' House: A History of the New Orleans Sinners and the Birth of Jazz* (Los Angeles: Sherbourne Press, 1965), p. 83.

35 · George Washington Cable, *The Grandissimes: A Story of Creole Life*, ed. Newton Arvin (New York: Sagamore Press, 1957), p. 59.

36 · James R. Frisby, Jr., "New Orleans Writers and the Negro: George Washington Cable, Grace King, Ruth McEnery Stuart, Kate Chopin, and Lafcadio Hearn, 1870–1900," Ph.D. diss., Emory University, 1972, pp. 8–23.

37 · Both Harriet Beecher Stowe and George Washington Cable were appalled by the barbaric provisions of the *Code Noir*, which mandated mutilation for several "crimes." Stowe kept a copy of the notorious *Code* on her desk throughout her work on *Uncle Tom's Cabin*.

38 · Frisby, "New Orleans Writers and the Negro," p. 12.

39 · *The Writings of Lafcadio Hearn* (Boston: Houghton Mifflin, 1922), 1:48.

40 · Grace King, *New Orleans: The Place and the People* (New York: Macmillan, 1904), pp. 336–37.

41 · Winthrop D. Jordan, *White over Black: American Attitudes toward the Negro, 1550–1812* (Chapel Hill: Univ. of North Carolina Press, 1968), p. 175.

42 · Judith R. Berzon, *Neither White nor Black: The Mulatto Character in American Fiction* (New York: New York Univ. Press, 1978), p. 11. See Virginia R. Domínguez's *White by Definition: Social Classification in Creole Louisiana* (New Brunswick, N.J.: Rutgers Univ. Press, 1986) for a fascinating discussion of the heritage of racial mixing and the difficulties of racial categorization in contemporary Louisiana.

43 · Joe Gray Taylor, *Negro Slavery in Louisiana* (Baton Rouge: Louisiana Historical Association, 1963).

Winthrop Jordan makes a distinction between the customary usage of the Americans, who employ the word *mulatto* in only very limited contexts, and the customary usage of the English in the Caribbean. Apparently, Negroes of mixed blood were preferred to Africans in the islands, especially as concubines. "Though the English in the Caribbean thought of their society in terms of white, colored, and black, they employed a complicated battery of names to distinguish persons of various racial mixtures. This terminology was borrowed from the neighboring Spanish, but words are never acquired unless they fulfill a need. While the English settlers on the continent borrowed one Spanish word to describe all mixtures of black and white, the islanders borrowed at least four—*mulatto, sambo, quadroon,* and *mestize*—to describe differing degrees." In a note Jordan explains these designations: *"Mulatto* meant one-half white; *sambo*, one-fourth white; *quadroon*, three-fourths white; and *mestize* (which did not imply Indian mixture as it did on the continent), seven-eighths white" (*White over Black*, pp. 174–75).

Grace King also discusses the elaborate terminology used to designate various degrees of negritude in Louisiana. She notes that the whites adopted the terminology, "using, as the negroes themselves did, shades of colour as expressions of mea-surement" (*New Orleans*, p. 336). To Jordan's list of Caribbean designations, King adds the fanciful *griffe* and *octoroon*, noting that such terms were graded, with "each term [meaning] one more generation's elevation, one degree's further transfigura-tion in the standard of racial perfection; white blood" (p. 333).

44 · In *Kate Chopin: A Critical Biography*, Per Seyersted asserts that Doctor Chopin, who was "mean and dictatorial to his wife," also served as a model for Edna Pontellier's domineering father in *The Awakening* ([Baton Rouge: Louisiana State Univ. Press, 1969], p. 36).

45 · George Washington Cable, *Madame Delphine*, in *Old Creole Days* (New York: Charles Scribner's Sons, 1893), pp. 5–6.

46 · King, *New Orleans*, p. 342.

47 · Ibid., p. 344.

48 · In 1837 Harriet Martineau painted a picture of this exotic society:

The Quadroon girls of New Orleans are brought up by their mothers to be what they have been; the mistresses of white gentlemen. The boys are some of them sent to France; some placed on land in the back of the State; and some are sold in the slave-market. They marry women of a somewhat darker colour than their own; the women of their own colour objecting to them, "ils sont si dégoutants!" The girls are highly educated, externally, and are, probably, as beautiful and accomplished a set of women as can be found. Every young man early selects one, and establishes her in one of those pretty and peculiar houses, whole rows of which may be seen in the Remparts [*sic*]. The connex-ion now and then lasts for life: usually for several years. In the latter case, when the time comes for the gentleman to take a white wife, the dreadful news reaches his Quadroon partner, either by a letter entitling her to call the house and furniture her own, or by the newspaper which announces his marriage. The Quadroon ladies are rarely or never known to form a second connexion. Many commit suicide: more die broken-hearted. Some men continue the connexion after marriage. Every Quadroon woman believes that her partner will prove an exception to the rule of desertion. Every white lady believes that her husband has been an exception to the rule of seduction. (*Society in America* [New York: Saunders and Otley, 1837], 2:116–17)

49 · King, *New Orleans*, p. 348. The custom of keeping a mistress to supplement a marriage of convenience has long been a Gallic custom. In *Black New Orleans, 1860– 1880*, John W. Blassingame suggests another reason that the system of concubinage became institutionalized. The population of white males and black females in New Orleans prior to the Civil War far exceeded the population of white females and black males ([Chicago: Univ. of Chicago Press, 1973], p. 14).

50 · King, *New Orleans*, p. 344.

51 · Gary B. Mills, *The Forgotten People: Cane River's Creoles of Color* (Baton Rouge: Louisiana State Univ. Press, 1977), p. 247.

52 · Blassingame, *Black New Orleans, 1860–1880*, p. 204.

53 · Edward Larocque Tinker, *Creole City: Its Past and Its People* (New York: Longmans, Green, 1953), p. 270.

54 · Williamson, *New People,* p. 98.

55 · Lafcadio Hearn, quoted in Edward Larocque Tinker, *Lafcadio Hearn's American Days* (New York: Dodd, Mead, 1924), pp. 95–96.

56 · Edmund Wilson, *Patriotic Gore: Studies in the Literature of the American Civil War* (New York: Oxford Univ. Press, 1962), pp. 562–63; Herbert Asbury, *The French Quarter: An Informal History of the New Orleans Underworld* (New York: Knopf, 1936), p. 3.

57 · Longstreet, *Sportin' House,* p. 136.

58 · Grace King to Fred Lewis Pattee, January 19, 1915, in *Grace King of New Orleans: A Selection of Her Writings,* ed. Robert Bush (Baton Rouge: Louisiana State Univ. Press, 1973), p. 398.

59 · King, *New Orleans,* p. 348.

60 · Malcolm Cowley, "Lafcadio Hearn," in *The Selected Writings of Lafcadio Hearn,* ed. Henry Goodman (New York: Citadel Press, 1949), p. 3. In *Suburban Sketches* William Dean Howells referred to men as "the newspaper sex" ([Boston: Houghton Mifflin, 1883], p. 137).

61 · Richard Watson Gilder to Grace King, September 24, 1891, in box 8, folder 47, acc. no. 1282, Grace King Papers, Grace King Collection, Louisiana and Lower Mississippi Valley Collections, LSU Libraries, Louisiana State University, Baton Rouge.

62 · Henry Mills Alden, quoted in Louis D. Rubin, Jr., *George W. Cable: The Life and Times of a Southern Heretic* (New York: Pegasus, 1969), pp. 45–46.

63 · Rubin, *George W. Cable,* p. 46.

64 · Wilson, *Patriotic Gore,* p. 579.

65 · William Dean Howells, *The Rise of Silas Lapham* (New York: Holt, Rinehart and Winston, 1949), p. 212. It is worth noting that Howells, whose support of realistic good sense in portrayal of the "commonplace" encouraged many despondent fiction writers, also could not resist the temptation of treating the unhappy woman of mixed blood in his own fiction. In *An Imperative Duty,* Howells introduced Rhoda, a heroine who is one-sixteenth black (her grandmother had been a slave in New Orleans). When Rhoda finds out that she is not completely white, she becomes hysterical. Olney, the white hero, marries her in spite of her blemished blood, but Rhoda has "hours of despondency" and "hypochondria of the soul" because of her "guilty deceit" ([New York: Harper & Bros., 1892], p. 149).

66 · King to Pattee, January 19, 1915, in *Grace King of New Orleans,* ed. Bush, p. 398.

67 · Thomas Nelson Page, quoted in King, *Memories,* p. 378.

68 · Robert Bush, Introduction to *Grace King of New Orleans,* ed. Bush, p. 24.

69 · Turner, *George W. Cable,* p. 132.

70 · Rubin, *George W. Cable,* p. 224. In *Southern Writers and the New South Movement, 1865–1913* (Chapel Hill: Univ. of North Carolina Press, 1980), Wayne Mixon writes persuasively of the strengths of *John March, Southerner,* Cable's last

attempt to write important fiction. In discussing the realistic complexity of Cable's portrait of Cornelius Leggett, a Negro and a Southern politician, Mixon says: "Cable added a touch of bitters to the saccharine brew of the literary Plantation Tradition" (p. 108).

71 · James D. Hart, "Kate Chopin," in *The Oxford Companion to American Literature*, 4th ed. (New York: Oxford Univ. Press, 1965), p. 155.

72 · Jordan, *White over Black*, p. 150.

Two · George Cable: The Stereotype Resurrected

1 · Cable, quoted in Kjell Ekström, *George Washington Cable: A Study of His Early Life and Work* (Cambridge: Harvard Univ. Press, 1950), p. 56. "'Tite Poulette" was published in *Scribner's Monthly*, October 1874 and was later included in the collection of New Orleans stories *Old Creole Days*, published by Charles Scribner's Sons in 1879. *The Grandissimes* was published serially in *Scribner's Monthly*, November 1879–October 1880; the book was first published by Scribners in 1880. *Madame Delphine* was published serially in *Scribner's Monthly*, May–July 1881; it was published as a book by Scribners in 1881 and was reissued in *Old Creole Days* in 1883.

2 · Mrs. Baskervill, quoted in William Malone Baskervill, *Southern Writers: Biographical and Critical Studies* (Nashville, Tenn.: n.p., 1903; rpt. ed., New York: Gordian Press, 1970), 2:16.

3 · W. J. Cash, *The Mind of the South* (New York: Knopf, 1941), p. 376.

4 · Lucy Leffingwell Cable Biklé, *George W. Cable: His Life and Letters* (New York: Charles Scribner's Sons, 1928), p. 47.

5 · Jay B. Hubbell, *Southern Life in Fiction* (Athens: Univ. of Georgia Press, 1960), p. 80.

6 · Jay B. Hubbell, *The South in American Literature, 1607–1900* (Durham, N.C.: Duke Univ. Press, 1954), p. 820; Van Wyck Brooks, "The Literary Life in America," in *Three Essays on America* (New York: E. P. Dutton, 1934), p. 194.

7 · Arlin Turner, "George W. Cable's Use of the Past," *Mississippi Quarterly* 30 (Fall 1977): 514.

8 · Edmund Wilson, *Patriotic Gore: Studies in the Literature of the American Civil War* (New York: Oxford Univ. Press, 1962), pp. 557, 559.

9 · Louis D. Rubin, Jr., *George W. Cable: The Life and Times of a Southern Heretic* (New York: Pegasus, 1969), p. 19; Wilson, *Patriotic Gore*, p. 564.

10 · J. Stanley Lemons, "Black Stereotypes as Reflected in Popular Culture, 1880–1920," *American Quarterly* 29 (Spring 1977): 106.

11 · Trudier Harris, *Exorcising Blackness: Historical and Literary Lynching and Burning Rituals* (Bloomington: Indiana Univ. Press, 1984), p. 7.

12 · Warner Berthoff, *The Ferment of Realism: American Literature, 1884–1919* (New York: Free Press, 1965), pp. 83, 84n.

13 · Quoted in Arlin Turner, *George W. Cable: A Biography* (Baton Rouge: Louisiana State Univ. Press, 1966), p. 326.

14 · George Washington Cable, "The Freedman's Case in Equity," in *The Negro Question: A Selection of Writings on Civil Rights in the South*, ed. Arlin Turner

(Garden City, N.Y.: Doubleday, 1958), p. 78. Turner's compilation of Cable's political writings has measurably enhanced our understanding of the relationship between
Cable's thought and his fiction. In addition to offering the scholar ready access to
works published previously but at different times and in different periodicals, it
offers the first unabridged printing of "My Politics" (completed February 1889), a
work that was rejected by Cable's editors as too personal and remained unpublished
during his lifetime.

15 · Barbara Welter noted the currency of the phrase "true womanhood" in
popular literature of the nineteenth century and observed that "authors who ad-
dressed themselves to the subject of women in the mid-nineteenth century used this
phrase as frequently as writers on religion mentioned God" ("The Cult of True
Womanhood: 1820–1860," *American Quarterly* 18 [Summer 1966]: 151n). However,
recent research has disclosed greater complexity in the social attitudes toward
women during this historical period. Nina Baym, for example, finds that in woman's
fiction "purity was so taken for granted that it was ignored, while a range of self-
assertive and aggressive behavior, including the undomestic, was seen as consistent
with 'true womanhood' " (*Woman's Fiction: A Guide to Novels by and about Women in
America, 1820–1870* [Ithaca, N.Y.: Cornell Univ. Press, 1978], p. 313).

16 · Turner, *George W. Cable*, p. 51.

17 · See Blassingame's discussion of this extraordinary story in *Black New Orleans, 1860–1880* (Chicago: Univ. of Chicago Press, 1973), pp. 19–20. See also James
Kinney, *Amalgamation! Race, Sex, and Rhetoric in the Nineteenth-Century American
Novel* (Westport, Conn.: Greenwood Press, 1985), pp. 74–76, for a summary of a
similar ploy described in Mayne Reid's *The Quadroon; or, A Lover's Adventures in
Louisiana* (1856). The hero of Reid's novel knows that the woman he loves is a
quadroon, but he offers to cut her and suck her blood so that he can swear that he
too has African blood in his veins. Edna Ferber adapted the premise of these stories,
perhaps unwittingly, in *Showboat* (1926), when she had the white male protagonist
save the "tainted" woman he loves from arrest in Mississippi by pricking her finger
and sucking her blood.

18 · Edmund Wilson's assessment of Cable's literary production of the 1890s
charts his literary decline:

> The real canon of Cable's books, the five of them that ought to be read by
> every student of American literature—*Old Creole Days, The Grandissimes,
> Strange True Stories of Louisiana, The Silent South,* and *The Negro Question*—
> were all written by 1890. Though somewhat hampered in the novels that
> immediately follow by the demands of the popular taste, the author of *The
> Grandissimes* is still trying to maintain his standing on the higher level of
> literature; but these books show Cable at a serious loss. . . . And in the interval
> between *Strong Hearts* [1899] and *Bylow Hill* [1902], he had, for the first time in
> his life [in publishing *The Cavalier*], deliberately mustered his powers for a
> full-scale exploitation of the popular taste. (*Patriotic Gore,* pp. 584–85)

19 · George Washington Cable, "The Due Restraints and Liberties of Literature" (delivered at commencement, the University of Louisiana, June 15, 1883, and

reprinted as a pamphlet in New Orleans, 1883), in *The Negro Question*, ed. Turner, p. 52.

20 · Cable, "The Freedman's Case in Equity," p. 60; George Washington Cable, "The Silent South," in *The Negro Question*, ed. Turner, p. 130.

21 · George Washington Cable, "The Negro Question," in *The Negro Question*, ed. Turner, p. 161.

22 · "Social confusion" is only one of the nineteenth century's euphemisms for miscegenation. Some other catchphrases used to indicate those interracial relationships that threatened to obliterate the color line were "amalgamation" (after the process of combining mercury with other metals to produce alloys), "social equality," "social chaos," and "social intermingling."

23 · George Washington Cable, *Gideon's Band: A Tale of the Mississippi* (New York: Charles Scribner's Sons, 1914), p. 413.

24 · George Washington Cable, *The Flower of the Chapdelaines* (New York: Charles Scribner's Sons, 1918), p. 269.

25 · Rubin, *George W. Cable*, p. 90. Cable's male critics have, if anything, exceeded him in their susceptibility to his women characters. His contemporary William Dean Howells was entranced by Cable's Creole heroine in *The Grandissimes*. Howells's assertion that "there is no more charming creation in fiction than Aurora Nancanou," however, slights the richness of Cable's characterization of Aurora, whose disillusioned statements about marriage seem to reflect her negative experience with a roué of a husband who left her and a baby daughter to face the world armed only with their charm (William Dean Howells to John Hay, March 18, 1882, in *Life in Letters of William Dean Howells*, ed. Mildred Howells [Garden City, N.Y.: Doubleday, Doran, 1928], 1:312). In *George W. Cable* (New York: Twayne, 1962) Philip Butcher responds to Cable's portrait of Olive, the nearly "tragic octoroon" in *Madame Delphine:* "The girl, as Cable describes her, would have converted any sentient male" (p. 58). Even the astute Louis D. Rubin, Jr., regards Cable's heroines as chiefly "love interest." Rubin writes: "In portraying the Nancanous, of course, Cable was creating his heroines in the accepted stereotype of the romance form, and since their chief function in *The Grandissimes*, as in most of his other fiction, is to advance the love story, they are circumscribed by the needs of the story line" (*George W. Cable*, p. 90).

26 · Bertram Wyatt-Brown, *Southern Honor: Ethics and Behavior in the Old South* (New York: Oxford Univ. Press, 1982), p. 283.

27 · Rubin, *George W. Cable*, p. 91.

28 · George Washington Cable, *The Grandissimes: A Story of Creole Life*, ed. Newton Arvin (New York: Sagamore Press, 1957), pp. 162–63. Subsequent references to *The Grandissimes*, except where context makes the reference unclear, are given parenthetically in the text of the chapter.

29 · Henry James, quoted in Larzer Ziff, *The American 1890s: Life and Times of a Lost Generation* (New York: Viking Press, 1966), p. 275. Ziff remarks on the increasing sensitivity of authors to the alienation of the sexes during the late nineteenth century. He singles out James, who noted "the growing divorce between the American woman (with her comparative leisure, culture, grace, social instincts, artistic

ambitions) and the male American immersed in the ferocity of business, with no time for any but the most sordid interests, purely commercial, professional, democratic and political. This divorce is rapidly becoming a gulf—an abyss of inequality, the like of which has never before been seen under the sun" (ibid.).

30 · George Washington Cable, "My Politics," in *The Negro Question*, ed. Turner, pp. 12–13.

31 · Ekström, *George Washington Cable*, p. 46.

32 · William Bedford Clark, "Cable and the Theme of Miscegenation in *Old Creole Days* and *The Grandissimes*," *Mississippi Quarterly* 30 (Fall 1977): 601n.

33 · Turner, *George W. Cable*, p. 60.

34 · George Washington Cable, "'Tite Poulette," in *Old Creole Days* (New York: Charles Scribner's Sons, 1893), p. 214. Subsequent page references to "'Tite Poulette" are given parenthetically in the text.

35 · Helen Waite Papashvily, *All the Happy Endings: A Study of the Domestic Novel in America, the Women Who Wrote It, the Women Who Read It, in the Nineteenth Century* (New York: Harper & Bros., 1956), pp. 176–77.

36 · Cable, *The Grandissimes*, p. 65.

37 · Cable, quoted in Biklé, *George W. Cable*, p. 158.

38 · Cable, quoted in Turner, *George W. Cable*, p. 105.

39 · Ibid., p. 105n.

40 · H. H. Boyesen, quoted in Turner, *George W. Cable*, p. 90.

41 · For an extended summary of the multilevel plot structure of *The Grandissimes*, consult the biographies of Cable by Philip Butcher, Arlin Turner, and Louis Rubin.

42 · William Bedford Clark, "The Serpent of Lust in the Southern Garden: The Theme of Miscegenation in Cable, Twain, Faulkner, and Warren," Ph.D. diss., Louisiana State University, 1973, pp. 55–56.

43 · Butcher, *George W. Cable*, p. 54.

44 · Newton Arvin, Introduction to Cable, *The Grandissimes*, ed. Arvin, pp. v, vi. Louis D. Rubin, Jr., is preeminent among those who believe that Cable's heart was fatally divided by his reforming and his creative impulses. Rubin writes that the result of this conflict is that *The Grandissimes*, though Cable's best novel, "a work of social observation of Southern society unsurpassed in its time, . . . remains even so a deeply flawed work" ("The Division of the Heart: Cable's *The Grandissimes*," in *Critical Essays on George W. Cable*, ed. Arlin Turner [Boston: G. K. Hall, 1980], p. 208). But there are perhaps other reasons for disjunctions in *The Grandissimes*. For an illuminating discussion of the novel as an imperfect synthesis of two distinct and competing genres, the historical romance and the realistic novel, see Richard Bozman Eaton, "George W. Cable and the Historical Romance" (*Southern Literary Journal* 8 [Fall 1975]: 82–94). Eaton locates Cable's Joseph Frowenfeld within the heroic tradition adumbrated by Walter Scott.

45 · One might quote any of the scholars who have examined the history of Cable's dealings with his publishers. Edmund Wilson, as has been noted, speaks of the "slow strangulation" of Cable (*Patriotic Gore*, p. 579). Arlin Turner is tempted "to speculate on the kind of fiction Cable would have produced if from the time he first

submitted 'Bibi' onward his work had been judged by an editor less fearful of the unpleasant and the touches of horror" (*George W. Cable*, p. 67). Warner Berthoff catalogues Cable's defects as an author and then says that "if his editors and publishers had had their way, these objections would make up our whole account of him" (*The Ferment of Realism*, pp. 85–86).

46 · Turner, *George W. Cable*, p. 95.

47 · Robert Underwood Johnson, quoted ibid.

48 · Johnson, quoted in Ekström, *George Washington Cable*, p. 60.

49 · Irwin Russell and Cable, quoted in Turner, *George W. Cable*, p. 96.

50 · In *Woman's Fiction* Nina Baym deals with the works of Evans and Southworth in some detail.

51 · John C. Ruoff, "Frivolity to Consumption: or, Southern Womanhood in Antebellum Literature," *Civil War History* 18 (September 1972): 227.

52 · G. H. Clements quoted in Ekström, *George Washington Cable*, p. 178.

53 · William Evans, "French-English Literary Dialect in *The Grandissimes*," in *Critical Essays on George W. Cable*, ed. Turner, p. 215.

54 · Quoted in Turner, *George W. Cable*, p. 101.

55 · George Washington Cable, "After-Thoughts of a Story-Teller," *North American Review* 158 (January 1894): 21.

56 · George Washington Cable, "Literature in the Southern States," in *The Negro Question*, pp. 43–44.

57 · Clark, "The Serpent of Lust in the Southern Garden," p. 56.

58 · Emily Toth, "That Outward Existence Which Conforms: Kate Chopin and Literary Convention," Ph.D. diss., Johns Hopkins University, 1975, p. 188.

59 · James R. Frisby, Jr., "New Orleans Writers and the Negro: George Washington Cable, Grace King, Ruth McEnery Stuart, Kate Chopin, and Lafcadio Hearn, 1870–1900," Ph.D. diss., Emory University, 1972, p. 71.

60 · Rubin, *George W. Cable*, p. 91.

61 · The Grandissime ladies' request for Bras-Coupé's story at the *fête de grand-père* occasions the retelling of the story that is fast becoming legend. Palmyre's mistress believes in the righteousness of Bras-Coupé's curse, although it falls on her own new husband: "'Why in the name of—St. Francis,' asked the priest of the overseer, 'didn't the señora use her power over the black scoundrel when he stood and cursed, that day?' 'Why, to tell you the truth, father,' said the overseer, in a discreet whisper, 'I can only suppose she thought Bras-Coupé had half a right to do it'" (*The Grandissimes*, pp. 187–88).

62 · In *Roll, Jordan, Roll: The World the Slaves Made*, Eugene Genovese mentions the practice of making the master's illegitimate, mulatto children the servants of his white offspring: "Some white southerners frankly admitted that personal maids and body servants in the homes of some of the best families were in fact children of the Big House. 'In numbers of cases,' wrote M. T. Judge of Mobile, Alabama, 'the girl picked out for the young lady was her half-sister'" ([New York: Random House, Vintage Books, 1974], pp. 420–21).

63 · Ekström notes that "Cable denied that the notorious Marie Laveau was his model for Palmyre in *The Grandissimes*" (*George Washington Cable*, p. 104n). For an

illuminating discussion of the mysterious life and legend of Marie Laveau, see Jewell Parker Rhodes, "Marie Laveau, Voodoo Queen," *Ms.* 11 (January 1983): 28–31.

64 · George Fitzhugh, quoted in Anne Firor Scott, *The Southern Lady: From Pedestal to Politics, 1830–1930* (Chicago: Univ. of Chicago Press, 1970), p. 17.

65 · Clark, "The Serpent of Lust in the Southern Garden," p. 56.

66 · The reluctance of the media to portray interracial love can be seen in the treatment *Madame Delphine* received when it was proposed for film. Although Benjamin B. Hampton purchased an option on behalf of Great Authors Pictures in 1919, no movie was made. The contract with Cable was renewed but allowed to lapse again in 1921 because the distributors refused to take a picture with such potentially explosive content. The distributors were probably correct in forecasting a negative public response, for the premiere in 1914 of D. W. Griffith's *The Birth of a Nation*, scripted from Thomas Dixon, Jr.'s, *The Clansman* (1905), had inflamed the nation. Community fear of violence kept this successful but pernicious movie from being shown in some cities.

67 · Turner, *George W. Cable*, p. 107.

68 · Henry James, "Preface to 'The Aspern Papers,'" in *The Art of the Novel: Critical Prefaces* (New York: Charles Scribner's Sons, 1934), p. 164.

69 · George Washington Cable, *Madame Delphine*, in *Old Creole Days*, p. 2. Subsequent page references to this story are given parenthetically in the text.

70 · It is instructive to compare Zora Neale Hurston's description of the nascent yearning of Janie in *Their Eyes Were Watching God* (1937) with Cable's description of Olive. Also of mixed race, Janie discovers at age six that her café-au-lait skin differentiates her from her white playmates. Janie's response to this discovery is quite different from that of Cable's women characters. However, Janie's sexual awakening, like Olive's, is evoked in lush natural imagery. Hurston writes:

> [Janie] was stretched on her back beneath the pear tree soaking in the alto chant of the visiting bees, the gold of the sun and the panting breath of the breeze when the inaudible voice of it all came to her. She saw a dust-bearing bee sink into the sanctum of a bloom; the thousand sister-calyxes arch to meet the love embrace and the ecstatic shiver of the tree from root to tiniest branch creaming in every blossom and frothing with delight. So this was a marriage! She had been summoned to behold a revelation. Then Janie felt a pain remorseless sweet that left her limp and languid. ([Urbana: Univ. of Illinois Press, 1978], p. 24)

Three · Grace King: Ingenues on the Color Line

1 · "Monsieur Motte" was first published in the *New Princeton Review*, January 1886. It was reissued as the first part of the novel *Monsieur Motte* (New York: A.C. Armstrong, 1888). "Bonne Maman" was first published in *Harper's*, July 1886. "Madrilène; or, The Festival of the Dead" was first published in *Harper's*, November 1890. "The Little Convent Girl" was first published in *Century*, August 1893. "Bonne Maman" and "Madrilène" were later published in *Tales of a Time and Place* (New

York: Harper & Bros., 1892). "The Little Convent Girl" was later published in *Balcony Stories* (New York: Century, 1893).

2 · Grace King, *Memories of a Southern Woman of Letters* (New York: Macmillan, 1932), p. 60. Long after her angry exchange with Gilder, King's attitude toward Cable changed. By 1915, when she heard Cable speak before the Louisiana Historical Society, King was ready to honor Cable as her fellow New Orleanians were honoring him. Later she said, "I am so glad that at last he got that compliment from New Orleans. He deserved it, not only as a tribute to his genius, but as a compensation for the way we had treated him." Analyzing her youthful outburst against Cable, King said: "I abused him as only a New Orleans person could—not really abuse you know, it was a sense of resentment, of having had our feelings hurt. . . . Of course I understood even then that he was a genius, but he did not understand the Creoles" (quoted in Louise Hubert Guyol, "A Southern Author in Her New Orleans Home," *Louisiana Historical Quarterly* 6 [July 1923]: 365).

3 · David Kirby, *Grace King* (Boston: Twayne, 1980), p. 38. Kirby finds a consistent portrayal in King's fiction of women bonding together in a world "sadly mismanaged by men."

4 · Larzer Ziff, *The American 1890s: Life and Times of a Lost Generation* (New York: Viking Press, 1966), p. 297.

5 · Robert Bush, "Grace King: The Emergence of a Southern Intellectual Woman," *Southern Review* 13 (April 1977): 278. King described the trepidation with which she confronted the task of preparing "Heroines of Novels":

When my name was announced in due course of routine for a paper, I shrank back in consternation from the ordeal and had to be coaxed and persuaded by my friends to stand in the group of the previous brave volunteers. When I saw there was no escape from it, I went home miserable, but at the same time determined to stand the test for which, in truth, I had been waiting secretly. . . . A rather caustic review it must have been, and an arrogant one. I read it at the club meeting in a trembling voice and could hardly believe my ears when I heard expressions of compliment and applause. (King, *Memories*, p. 58)

6 · Bush, "Grace King: The Emergence," p. 278.

7 · Grace King, "Heroines of Novels," New Orleans *Times-Democrat*, Sunday, May 31, 1885, p. 9. Subsequent references to "Heroines," except where context makes the reference unclear, are given parenthetically in the text of the chapter.

8 · King, *Memories*, pp. 153–54.

9 · Both Eliot and Brontë had inveighed against the injustice of women's lot. In *Jane Eyre* Brontë speaks through Jane of the limitations imposed upon women, a theme that would also concern King:

It is in vain to say human beings ought to be satisfied with tranquillity: they must have action; and they will make it if they cannot find it. Millions are condemned to a stiller doom than mine, and millions are in silent revolt against their lot. Nobody knows how many rebellions besides political rebellions ferment in the masses of life which people earth. Women are supposed to be very calm generally: but women feel just as men feel; they need exercise for their faculties and a field for their efforts as much as their brothers do; they suffer from too rigid a restraint, too absolute a stagnation, precisely as men would suffer; and it is narrow-minded in their more privileged fellow-creatures to say that they ought to confine themselves to making puddings and knitting stockings, to playing on the piano and embroidering bags. It is thoughtless to condemn them, or laugh at them, if they seek to do more or learn more than custom has pronounced necessary for their sex. ([New York: W. W. Norton, 1971], p. 96)

10 · Grace King to Charles Dudley Warner, September 17, 1885, quoted in Robert Bush, Introduction to *Grace King of New Orleans: A Selection of Her Writings,* ed. Bush (Baton Rouge: Louisiana State Univ. Press, 1973), p. 14.

11 · Notebook 6 (1886–1901), acc. no. 1282, Grace King Papers, Grace King Collection, Louisiana and Lower Mississippi Valley Collections, LSU Libraries, Louisiana State University, Baton Rouge.

12 · Ibid.

13 · Ann Douglas Wood, "The Literature of Impoverishment: The Women Local Colorists in America, 1865–1914," *Women's Studies* 1 (1972): 31.

14 · Ibid., p. 16.

15 · Quoted in King, *Memories,* p. 60.

16 · Richard M. Weaver, *The Southern Tradition at Bay: A History of Postbellum Thought* (New Rochelle, N. Y.: Arlington House, 1968), p. 321.

17 · Ibid., p. 308.

18 · Grace King, *Balcony Stories* (New York: Century, 1893; rpt. ed., Ridgewood, N. J.: Gregg Press, 1968), p. 2.

19 · Merrill Maguire Skaggs, *The Folk of Southern Fiction* (Athens: The Univ. of Georgia Press, 1972), p. 181.

20 · Bush, "Grace King: The Emergence," p. 282.

21 · Edmund Wilson, *Patriotic Gore: Studies in the Literature of the American Civil War* (New York: Oxford Univ. Press, 1962), p. 576.

22 · King, *Memories,* p. 377.

23 · Grace King, *New Orleans: The Place and the People* (New York: Macmillan, 1904), pp. 347–48.

24 · Ibid., p. 348.

25 · King, *Memories,* p. 274.

26 · King, *New Orleans,* p. 348.

27 · Ibid., p. 350.

28 · Bush, "Grace King: The Emergence," p. 283.

29 · King to Warner, September 17, 1885, quoted in Bush, Introduction to *Grace King of New Orleans,* ed. Bush, p. 14.

30 · In "American Victorianism as a Culture," Daniel Walker Howe reflects on the pervasiveness of racism among even the most enlightened Victorians, noting the inverse relationship between their didactic impulses and their view of the innate depravity of other races: "The Victorians' perception of outsiders tended to be a confused mingling of hostility with didactic paternalism; they looked at someone of another race and saw him, in Kipling's words, 'half devil and half child.' The conflict

between didacticism and racism, between assimilation and rejection of others, turned out to be one of the most tragic contradictions within American Victorian culture" (*American Quarterly* 27 [December 1975]: 528). This contradiction continued to have tragic effects. For if blacks were by nature beyond the reach of moral uplift, whites could more easily justify ignoring their moral claims. Thus reasoned white social hygienists who rationalized neglecting the treatment of blacks who contracted venereal diseases by blaming the victims for their supposed hypersexuality. For a terrifying look at the malign neglect of black syphilis patients, see James H. Jones's *Bad Blood: The Tuskegee Syphilis Experiment* (New York: Free Press, 1981).

31 · Emily Toth explains: "The word *calling* is often used [in this period] to describe woman's role. Man labors, but woman has a *calling:* the word seems intended to suggest an extra spiritual dimension" ("That Outward Existence Which Conforms: Kate Chopin and Literary Convention," Ph.D. diss., Johns Hopkins University, 1975, p. 32). "Little sufferers" were those angelic children the women of the period nursed and lost to illness. The true woman was supposedly ennobled by the deaths of her little sufferers, especially if they, like Little Eva, languished instructively before they died. See Ann Douglas's "Heaven Our Home: Consolation Literature in the Northern United States, 1830–1880" (*American Quarterly* 26 [December 1974]: 496–515) for an illuminating discussion of the role of the blighted or dying child in Northern popular culture of the nineteenth century. The South, of course, was also afflicted by childhood death and lamented the sad fact in story and song. Country music preserves the image of the "little sufferer" to this day.

32 · Grace King, "Madrilène; or, The Festival of the Dead," in *Tales of a Time and Place* (New York: Harper & Bros., 1892; rpt. ed., New York: Garrett Press, 1969), p. 154. Subsequent page references to "Madrilène" are given parenthetically in the text of the chapter. Language borrowed from the cult of Thanatos paints the stylized landscape of death in "Madrilène" in a manner reminiscent of Poe's "The Fall of the House of Usher" (1839). King's Madeleine seems to share the pathogenic isolation of Poe's Madeline Usher. Their names link them to the weeping, repentant Magdalene, the reformed prostitute Jesus healed of demonic possession in Luke 8:2 and 7:36 ff.

33 · King, "Heroines," p. 9.

34 · Grace King, "Bonne Maman," in *Tales of a Time and Place,* pp. 69–70. Subsequent page references to "Bonne Maman" are given parenthetically in the text.

35 · Marie Fletcher, "The Southern Heroine in the Fiction of Representative Southern Women Writers, 1850–1960," Ph.D. diss., Louisiana State University, 1963, p. 126. King was not alone in her attack on this tradition. In *Virginia* Ellen Glasgow says of her heroine that the education she received at Miss Batte's Academy was based upon the theory "that the less a girl knew about life, the better prepared she would be to contend with it" ([Garden City, N. Y.: Doubleday, Page, 1913], p. 22).

36 · Charles Dudley Warner to Grace King, December 22, 1885, quoted in Bush, "Grace King: The Emergence," p. 285.

37 · Bush, "Grace King: The Emergence," pp. 285–86.

38 · Ibid., p. 283.

39 · Grace King, "Monsieur Motte," in *Monsieur Motte* (New York: A. C.

Armstrong, 1888; rpt. ed., Freeport, N.Y.: Books for Libraries Press, 1969), p. 12. Subsequent references to "Monsieur Motte" and to *Monsieur Motte*, its eponymous sequel, are given parenthetically in the text.

40 · In Cable's *The Grandissimes*, Aurora Nancanou cautions her daughter, Clotilde, to remember this first duty of all women. Social critics, such as Andrea Dworkin, have noted the role of pain in procuring beauty and defining women's place. Dworkin writes:

> Pain is an essential part of the grooming process, and that is not accidental. Plucking the eyebrows, shaving under the arms, wearing a girdle, learning to walk in high-heeled shoes, having one's nose fixed, straightening or curling one's hair—these things *hurt*. The pain, of course, teaches an important lesson: no price is too great, no process too repulsive, no operation too painful for the woman who would be beautiful. *The tolerance of pain and the romanticization of that tolerance begins here,* in preadolescence, in socialization, and serves to prepare women for lives of childbearing, self-abnegation, and husband-pleasing. (*Woman Hating* [New York: E. P. Dutton, 1974], p. 115)

41 · King to Warner, September 17, 1885, quoted in Bush, Introduction to *Grace King of New Orleans,* ed. Bush, p. 14.

42 · Robert Bush suggests perceptively that the excruciating irony of Marcélite's climactic cry resembles the irony of Huckleberry Finn's "All right, then, I'll *go* to hell" when he tries and fails to "pray a lie," deciding to risk damnation by helping Jim escape. According to Bush both characters' moments of truth shed a "terrifying critical light . . . on the injustice of caste" (Bush, Introduction to *Grace King of New Orleans,* ed. Bush, p. 4).

43 · In *Illness as Metaphor* (New York: Farrar, Straus and Giroux, 1978), Susan Sontag discusses the vogue of tubercular symptoms in the nineteenth century, when women, apparently for hormonal reasons, succumbed to the disease at a greater rate than men. During a period when many men were putting on flesh to flaunt their power and prosperity, many women yielded to the fashion imperative that dictated emaciation and a tubercular look.

44 · Fletcher, "The Southern Heroine," pp. 91–92.

45 · Anne Goodwyn Jones, *Tomorrow Is Another Day: The Woman Writer in the South, 1859–1936* (Baton Rouge: Louisiana State Univ. Press, 1981), p. 121.

46 · Winthrop D. Jordan, *White over Black: American Attitudes toward the Negro, 1550–1812* (Chapel Hill: Univ. of North Carolina Press, 1968), p. 148.

47 · Grace King, "The Little Convent Girl," in *Balcony Stories,* p. 143. All subsequent references to "The Little Convent Girl" are given parenthetically in the text.

48 · Jones, *Tomorrow Is Another Day,* p. 124.

49 · Toth, "That Outward Existence," p. 265.

50 · In "The Ever Widening Circle: The Diffusion of Feminist Values from the Troy Female Seminary, 1822–1872" (*History of Education Quarterly* 19 [Spring 1979]: 3–25), Anne Firor Scott argues convincingly that the movement toward higher education for women in America inculcated feminist values by changing the self-perceptions of women and the way they lived their lives. However, as Grace King's

"Monsieur Motte" attests, some women were deeply critical of the stunting education afforded by many of the finest girls' schools during this period.

51 · Charlotte Perkins Stetson [Gilman], *Women and Economics* (Boston: Small, Maynard, 1898), p. 70.

52 · For a valuable discussion of the aborted journeys to adulthood of girls in American literature, see Elaine Ginsberg's "The Female Initiation Theme in American Fiction." Ginsberg observes that a "sense of disillusionment, disappointment, and regret is perhaps the most significant characteristic of the female initiate in American literature" (*Studies in American Fiction* 3 [Spring 1975]: 35).

53 · Helen Taylor, "The Case of Grace King," *Southern Review* 18 (October 1982): 701.

54 · Bush, "Grace King: The Emergence," p. 272.

Four · Kate Chopin: From Stereotype to Sexual Realism

1 · "Désirée's Baby" was published in *Vogue,* January 14, 1893. "La Belle Zoraïde" was published in *Vogue,* January 4, 1894. "At the 'Cadian Ball" was published in *Two Tales* (Boston: October 22, 1892). These three stories were later reissued in *Bayou Folk* (Boston: Houghton Mifflin, 1894). "The Storm" was completed on July 19, 1898, but was not published until 1969, when it appeared in *The Complete Works* edited by Per Seyersted. *The Awakening* was published on April 22, 1899, by Herbert S. Stone and Co., Chicago. These dates of publication or composition are given by Per Seyersted, ed., *The Complete Works of Kate Chopin,* 2 vols. (Baton Rouge: Louisiana State Univ. Press, 1969).

2 · Per Seyersted, *Kate Chopin: A Critical Biography* (Baton Rouge: Louisiana State Univ. Press, 1969), p. 114.

3 · Joan Zlotnick, "A Woman's Will: Kate Chopin on Selfhood, Wifehood, and Motherhood," *Markham Review* [1] (October 1968): [17].

4 · For a discussion of the narrative ambiguities in *The Awakening,* see Paula A. Treichler's "The Construction of Ambiguity in *The Awakening:* A Linguistic Analysis," in *Women and Language in Literature and Society,* ed. Sally McConnell-Ginet, Ruth Borker, and Nelly Furnam (New York: Praeger, 1980), pp. 239–57.

5 · Per Seyersted and Emily Toth, eds., *A Kate Chopin Miscellany* (Natchitoches, La.: Northwestern State Univ. Press, 1979), p. 90.

6 · Emily Toth, "That Outward Existence Which Conforms: Kate Chopin and Literary Convention," Ph.D. diss., Johns Hopkins University, 1975, pp. [ii], 120.

7 · In her *Revolt against Chivalry: Jessie Daniel Ames and the Women's Campaign against Lynching* (New York: Columbia Univ. Press, 1979), Jacquelyn Dowd Hall tells the story of Ames and other white women who joined with black women such as Ida B. Wells in the fight against lynching. Kate Chopin was one of many women in America at the turn of the century who recognized the inextricable connection between sexism and racism.

8 · Kate Chopin, "A Horse Story," in *A Kate Chopin Miscellany,* ed. Seyersted and Toth, p. 13. Subsequent references to "A Horse Story" are to this collection and are given parenthetically in the text.

9 · In *Difference and Pathology: Stereotypes of Sexuality, Race, and Madness* (Ithaca, N.Y.: Cornell Univ. Press, 1985), Sander L. Gilman describes the scientific and the artistic purveyance of an image of black female sexuality in the eighteenth and nineteenth centuries. He notes that in the visual arts the presence of a black servant was "a ma[r]ker of the sexualization of the society in which he or she was found" (p. 79). The nude display in polite European society of the "Hottentot Venus" in 1829 was only one piece of evidence and reinforcement of the notion of anomalous and monstrous female sexuality (or, as Gilman notes, what was regarded as "an anomalous sexuality not only in black women but in all women" [p. 89]). In playing on the loose association between black women and white women that was being made on the Continent by science and the visual arts, Chopin challenged the view of Victorian Americans concerning what they still believed to be the "dark" woman's depravity and the "white" woman's purity.

10 · James D. Hart, "Kate Chopin," in *The Oxford Companion to American Literature*, 4th ed. (New York: Oxford Univ. Press, 1965), p. 155.

11 · Susan Cahill, ed., *Women and Fiction: Short Stories by and about Women* (New York: New American Library, 1975), p. 1.

12 · Merrill Maguire Skaggs, *The Folk of Southern Fiction* (Athens: Univ. of Georgia Press, 1972), p. 72. Skaggs credits George Cable with introducing the Cajun as a local-color figure in his *Bonaventure: A Prose Pastoral of Acadian Louisiana* (1888). In Cable's writing we find no hint that the Cajun was racially mixed.

13 · Seyersted, *Kate Chopin*, pp. 123–24.

14 · Kate Chopin, "A Rude Awakening," in *The Complete Works of Kate Chopin*, ed. Seyersted, 1:144. Subsequent references to Chopin's works are to this edition and are given parenthetically in the text.

15 · Henry Mills Alden, quoted in Larzer Ziff, *The American 1890s: Life and Times of a Lost Generation* (New York: Viking Press, 1966), p. 123.

16 · Page Smith, *Daughters of the Promised Land: Women in American History* (Boston: Little, Brown, 1970), p. 234. As Lillian Faderman notes, the discovery of woman's sexuality did not usher in an age of women's liberation in America. With the changing discourse about women's sexuality in particular and human sexuality in general, new controls and sanctions were brought to bear on the sexual identity and expression of every woman (*Surpassing the Love of Men: Romantic Friendship and Love between Women from the Renaissance to the Present* [New York: William Morrow, 1981]).

17 · Emily Toth, "The Cult of Domesticity and 'A Sentimental Soul,'" *Kate Chopin Newsletter* 1 (Fall 1975): 12.

18 · Seyersted, *Kate Chopin*, p. 71.

19 · Gertrude Atherton, *Patience Sparhawk and Her Times* (New York: John Lane, 1897), p. 177.

20 · Henry James, *The Portrait of a Lady* (New York: W. W. Norton, 1975), p. 489.

21 · Kate Chopin, quoted in Seyersted, *Kate Chopin*, p. 68.

22 · Peggy Skaggs, "A Woman's Place: The Search for Identity in Kate Chopin's Female Characters," Ph.D. diss., Texas A&M University, 1972, p. 97.

23 · Toth, "That Outward Existence," p. 219.

24 · Robert D. Arner, "Kate Chopin's Realism: 'At the 'Cadian Ball' and 'The Storm,'" *Markham Review* 2 (February 1970): [22].

25 · Frederick Anderson, Lin Salamo, and Bernard L. Stein, eds., *Mark Twain's Notebooks and Journals,* vol. 2 (Berkeley: Univ. of California Press, 1975), pp. 297, 323.

26 · Simone de Beauvoir, *The Second Sex,* trans. and ed. H. M. Parshley (New York: Vintage Books, 1974), pp. 528–29.

27 · W. M. Reedy, quoted in Seyersted, *Kate Chopin,* p. 177.

28 · Ruth Sullivan and Stewart Smith, "Narrative Stance in Kate Chopin's *The Awakening,*" *Studies in American Fiction* 1 (Spring 1973): 73.

29 · Margaret Culley, "Edna Pontellier: 'A Solitary Soul,'" in Kate Chopin, *The Awakening,* ed. Culley (New York: W. W. Norton, 1976), p. 226.

30 · Adrienne Rich, "Disloyal to Civilization: Feminism, Racism, Gynephobia," in *On Lies, Secrets, and Silence* (New York: W. W. Norton, 1979), p. 299.

31 · In *"The Awakening:* A Political Romance," Lawrence Thornton notes that "Mademoiselle Reisz's music symbolizes the antithetical modes of romance represented by Chopin and Wagner, and her evocation of Tristan and Isolde becomes an important part of *The Awakening*'s imagery of destruction" (*American Literature* 52 [March 1980]: 55).

32 · James H. Justus, "The Unawakening of Edna Pontellier," *Southern Literary Journal* 10 (Spring 1978): 115.

33 · An inventive and exploitative storyteller throughout the novel, Victor, like Robert, tells stories that are, as far as Edna is concerned, a breach of sexual decorum. Chopin's repeated use of the word *droll* to characterize these stories may suggest that they are either racist or sexist or both. They are certainly impolite or scandalous. It is a measure of Edna's growing rejection of convention that she finally listens to one of Victor's stories when she visits Madame Lebrun in the city. Both of the stories he tells in Edna's hearing concern girls of ambiguous race and class he has gotten to know in the city. On the second occasion Edna betrays "some degree of interest or entertainment" (2:942), and Victor is encouraged to proceed before his mother interrupts.

Edna is oblivious to the similarities between the men she knows, but Chopin makes these similarities obvious through suggestive comments about the stories they tell, the cigars they smoke in Edna's presence, and the newspapers they read. The world of male bonding proves too strong for Edna, who rejects the world of women and finds no place among men, who exclude or violate her with their private talk.

34 · Edna is centered in herself to such an extent that she only feels vague malaise when Mademoiselle Reisz tells her of an argument between Victor and Robert over Robert's attentions to Mariequita (2:930). Similarly, she fails to understand the significance of Robert and Alcée's discussion of the "stunning" women of Mexico, though she realizes that Robert "had seemed nearer to her off there in Mexico" (2:987) after listening to Alcée and Robert compare notes following Robert's return.

35 · Otis B. Wheeler, "The Five Awakenings of Edna Pontellier," *Southern Review* 11 (January 1975): 123.

36 · John William De Forest, *Miss Ravenel's Conversion from Secession to Loyalty* (New York: Harper & Bros., 1939), p. 356. In this novel, first published in 1867, De Forest idealized the laboring woman. He wrote: "The mortal pain, the supernatural expectation, the light of that other world which was so near, spiritualized her face and made it unhumanly beautiful" (p. 357).

37 · In a section entitled "Impressions 1894" in *A Kate Chopin Miscellany*, ed. Seyersted and Toth, Chopin described her memory of the birth of her son Jean:

I can remember yet that hot southern day on Magazine street in New Orleans. The noises of the street coming through the open windows; that heaviness with which I dragged myself about; my husband's and mother's solicitude; old Alexandrine the quadroon nurse with her high bandana tignon, her hoop-earrings and placid smile; old Doctor Faget; the smell of chloroform, and then waking at 6 in the evening from out of a stupor to see in my mothers [*sic*] arms a little piece of humanity all dressed in white which they told me was my little son! The sensation with which I touched my lips and my finger tips to his soft flesh only comes once to a mother. It must be the pure animal sensation; nothing spiritual could be so real—so poignant. (p. 93)

Chopin's description of her own experience contrasts markedly with De Forest's description of childbirth and with Edna's reaction to the scene she witnesses.

38 · As Paula Treichler observes, Edna achieves individuality in the course of the novel and becomes identified to the reader as "Edna." By the final chapter, Treichler asserts, Edna has fully achieved her identity; having shed her social mask as mother and as wife, "the real Edna is elsewhere" ("The Construction of Ambiguity," p. 254).

Five · Conclusion

1 · Samuel Langhorne Clemens, *Pudd'nhead Wilson and Those Extraordinary Twins* (New York: W. W. Norton, 1980), p. 9.

2 · In *A Southern Renaissance: The Cultural Awakening of the American South, 1930–1955*, Richard H. King examines those Southern male authors who subjected the Southern social order to intense scrutiny after 1930, noting that the Southern cultural ethos they inherited tended to reflect the vision of the South as "the family writ large" and the belief that "individual and regional identity, self-worth, and status were determined by family relationships. The actual family was destiny; and the region was conceived of as a vast metaphorical family, hierarchically organized and organically linked by (pseudo-) ties of blood" ([New York: Oxford Univ. Press, 1980], p. 27).

3 · Grace King to Charles Dudley Warner, September 17, 1885, quoted in Robert Bush, Introduction to *Grace King of New Orleans: A Selection of Her Writings*, ed. Bush (Baton Rouge: Louisiana State Univ. Press, 1973), p. 14.

4 · George Washington Cable, "The Due Restraints and Liberties of Literature" (delivered at commencement, the University of Louisiana, June 15, 1883, and reprinted as a pamphlet in New Orleans, 1883), in *The Negro Question: A Selection of*

Writings on Civil Rights in the South, ed. Arlin Turner (Garden City, N.Y.: Double-day, 1958), p. 52.

5 · King to Warner, September 17, 1885, quoted in *Grace King of New Orleans,* ed. Bush, p. 14.

6 · Kate Chopin, "The Western Association of Writers," in *The Complete Works of Kate Chopin,* ed. Per Seyersted (Baton Rouge: Louisiana State Univ. Press, 1969), 2:691.

7 · Carl Degler called such dissenters "other Southerners." In many senses these Southerners were otherized or made invisible in a distorted version of the history of Reconstruction. For a treatment of these Southern dissenters, see Degler's *The Other South: Southern Dissenters in the Nineteenth Century* (New York: Harper & Row, 1974).

8 · In *Black Reconstruction: An Essay toward a History of the Part Which Black Folk Played in the Attempt to Reconstruct Democracy in America, 1860–1880* (New York: Harcourt, Brace, 1935), W. E. B. Du Bois began the process of correcting the myth of the Solid South.

9 · In *The Black Image in the White Mind: The Debate on Afro-American Character and Destiny, 1817–1914* (New York: Harper & Row, 1971), George M. Fredrickson calls attention to the fact that the history of blacks in the United States has been predominantly a history constructed to accord with the prejudices of white people.

10 · C. Vann Woodward, *The Strange Career of Jim Crow,* 2d rev. ed. (New York: Oxford Univ. Press, 1966), pp. 93–94.

11 · Charles W. Chesnutt to George Washington Cable, June 5, 1890, quoted in Robert M. Farnsworth, Introduction to *The Marrow of Tradition,* by Charles W. Chesnutt (Ann Arbor: Univ. of Michigan Press, 1969), p. v.

12 · Chesnutt, *The Marrow of Tradition,* pp. 238–39.

13 · "Remarks of Charles Waddell Chesnutt, of Cleveland, in Accepting the Spingarn Medal at Los Angeles, July 3, 1928" (typescript in Charles Waddell Chesnutt Collection, Fisk University Library, Nashville, Tennessee), quoted in William L. Andrews, *The Literary Career of Charles W. Chesnutt* (Baton Rouge: Louisiana State Univ. Press, 1980), p. 219n.

14 · C. Vann Woodward and other historians have established with fair certainty that racial segregation in the North antedated legal segregation in much of the South and that Tocqueville's observation of the intensity of Northern prejudice against blacks had its basis in fact. The recent reissue of Harriet Wilson's *Our Nig* (1859) also demonstrates Northern animosity toward black people in the antebellum period.

15 · W. E. B. Du Bois, "The Talented Tenth," in Booker T. Washington et al., *The Negro Problem* (New York: James Pott, 1903), p. 33. Du Bois wrote: "The Negro race, like all races, is going to be saved by its exceptional men" (ibid.).

16 · Barbara Christian, *Black Women Novelists: The Development of a Tradition, 1892–1976* (Westport, Conn.: Greenwood Press, 1980), p. 45.

17 · Ibid., p. 53.

18 · Nella Larsen, *Quicksand,* in *Quicksand and Passing,* ed. Deborah E. McDowell (New Brunswick, N.J.: Rutgers Univ. Press, 1986), p. 4.

19 · Ibid., p. 87.

· INDEX ·